Angela —

Vatican II, Berkeley and Beyond

First string !

With appreciation .

+ John S. Cummins

Vatican II, Berkeley and Beyond

The First Half-Century of the
Oakland Diocese, 1962–2012

A Bishop's Memoir

John S. Cummins

Design and production: Thomas P. Fenton
Front cover photograph: The campanile and Mt. Tamalpais from Memorial Stadium at sunset, 2006 (Tristan Harward, 2007)
ISBN-13: 978-1507711644
ISBN-10: 1507711646

Contents

Dedication   *vii*

Acknowledgments   *ix*

Foreword   *xi*

Introduction   *xiii*

1   Personal Experience of Vatican II   1
Bringing the Council from Rome to Oakland

2   Cathedral Fondly Remembered   21
Loved for Liturgy and Community

3   Genesis of Two Cathedrals   28
Tale of Two Faithful Women

4   Ecumenism Flourishes in the Diocese   42
Bishop Begin Leads the Way

5   Bishop Begin and the Graduate Theological Union   53
Ecumenical Enterprise for Theology Studies

6   The Hopes of the Graduate Theological Union   74
"This Is the Work of the Holy Spirit"

7   Berkeley and Beyond   85
Part I. University and Church in Dialogue   85
Part II. Dialogue on Nuclear Deterrence   97
Part III. Dialogue on the U.S. Economy   103

8   Restyling Church Authority   108
Dignity of the Human Person Recognized

9   Endorsing Enlightened Dialogue   115
    Essential Prelude to Decision
10 The Laity Empowered   127
    Council Builds on Vigor Already Present
11 Religious Women on the Rise   139
    Sisters Launch Pastoral Initiatives
12 Priesthood Blossoms in New Diocese   151
    Young Priests Given Major Responsibilities
13 Remorse in a Healing Garden   160
    Pledge to Victims of Abuse: "Never Again!"
14 Bishops and Theologians Related   165
    Common Pursuit of Wise Decision-Making
15 Bishops and Scientists in Dialogue   177
    Talks Marked by Respect for Differences
16 Ministry with the Church in Asia   189
    Part I: Vocation and Avocation   189
    Part II: Fraternal Delegate to the Asian Bishops   206
    Part III: Persons and Personalities   229
17 A Blessed Half-Century   250
    Gifts of Magi as Historical Metaphor

    Index   259

Dedication

To Archbishop John R. Quinn of San Francisco and Bishop Pierre DuMaine of San Jose, contemporaries and neighbors in ministry embracing the shorelines of San Francisco Bay—confreres, collaborators, and exemplars of the mind of the Second Vatican Council.

Acknowledgments

My indebtedness reaches to Frank Maurovich for his initial and ongoing editorial help; Father Joseph Chinicci, OFM, of the Franciscan School of Theology with his love for history; Deacon Jeffrey Burns, of the Franciscan School, who instructed me on the difference between a history and a memoir; and Thomas Fenton for his editorial expertise in leading us through the book-production process.

My thanks, too, for the encouragement of Dr. Ron Olowin of St. Mary's College and of Michael J. Buckley, SJ, John Wright, SJ, and Sandra Schneiders, IHM, from the Jesuit School of Theology, for their congenial outline of relations of bishops, theologians, and scientists.

Our gratitude goes to the Paulist Fathers at Newman Hall, who carried on their tradition of hospitality that began when they arrived in Berkeley in 1906 and, with the new chapel on Dwight Way, provided their facilities for liturgy and meetings of the Catholic community related to the university and the Graduate Theological Union, with particular mention of Father Jack Campbell, CSP, in the 1970s.

My gratitude embraces the late Father Edward F. Malone of Maryknoll and his colleagues in Hong Kong and elsewhere who facilitated my role as fraternal delegate to the Federation of Asian Bishops' Conferences. My thanks include my own staff: Sister Felicia Sarati and our vicar general, George E. Crespin, and my longtime friend and associate Anthony Maguire, all of whose participation in my role with the Asian bishops enhanced the mission of witnessing American interest and concern for the Asian churches.

Thanks to Al Pacciorini, Carrie McClish and Sandi Gearhart of *The Catholic Voice* for researching photos; to photographers Jerry Rubino and Sean Sprague for permission to use theirs; also to Kristin Aswell, Christopher Renz, OP, and Clay Edward Dixon (all three affiliated with the GTU) for supplying photos.

Finally, my thanks to the staff of the diocesan offices, whose names may be unmentioned but who by their faithful collaboration and support enabled with generosity and joy our diocese to implement the directives and spirit of Vatican II. Also, special thanks to my successor, Archbishop Allen H. Vigneron, who provided for me circumstances in which I could produce this memoir.

Foreword

This loving memoir captures the promise and excitement of the post–Vatican II era as experienced by a priest and bishop who embraced both the spirit and the letter of the Council. The Diocese of Oakland was founded in 1962, the same year the Second Vatican Council opened. Under its first two bishops, Floyd L. Begin (1962–1977) and John S. Cummins (1977–2003), the Diocese of Oakland took pride in being a Vatican II diocese. Both bishops grasped the Council's mandate that the Church engage the modern world, or, as Begin put it, "build bridges to all men and women." The Church could no longer float blissfully aloof to the real struggles of human beings, especially the poor.

To engage the world, the diocese was willing to try new things, to give enough freedom for initiatives to grow and blossom. This was particularly evident in the splendid liturgy that developed at the Oakland Cathedral and epitomized the Council's call for full and active participation in the liturgy. In addition, as Cummins carefully records, Bishop Begin actively promoted the ecumenical movement and played a pivotal role in Catholic participation in the Graduate Theological Union in Berkeley.

Cummins himself placed the stamp of the Council on the diocese, serving as its first chancellor and its second bishop. Hospitality, openness, and dialogue were hallmarks of the Cummins era. He exemplified the Council's call for a new style of authority, grounded in humility and service, an authority that could listen and learn from a wide variety of sources, especially the people. Cummins actively encouraged dialogue with other faiths, with theologians, with scientists, with professors from the University of California, Berkeley, and with theologians from the Graduate Theological Union, with women, and with many others. Dialogues fearlessly explored the relationship between faith and science, science and ethics, nuclear deterrence, and the issues raised by the U.S. bishops' pastorals on peace and the economy, and much else.

Cummins writes warmly of his long-standing service to the Church in Asia as "fraternal delegate" to the Federation of Asian Bishops' Conferences, which benefited his work with the burgeoning Asian community in the East Bay. He records the rich insights and deep friendships he developed with many in Asia, admiring especially Dominic Tang Yee-Ming, the once-imprisoned Chinese archbishop.

This heartfelt memoir captures the era's promise and excitement. Cummins's deep humanity provides a model of episcopal leadership that genuinely values and privileges the basic goodness and dignity of each human being. As such, his example provides good reason to hope in the future of the Catholic Church.

Jeffrey M. Burns
Director, The Frances G. Harpst Center
for Catholic Thought and Culture at the University of San Diego

Introduction

A Diocese Immersed in Vatican Council II

THESE ESSAYS AROSE FROM A SENSE OF OBLIGATION to our first bishop, Floyd L. Begin, and the essential role he played in the development of the Graduate Theological Union (GTU) in Berkeley. Almost upon his arrival in the new Oakland Diocese, Bishop Begin was invited by the newly formed GTU corporation to engage Catholic participation. Conversations were already underway with the Dominicans, who in 1932 had chosen Oakland to be the site of their formation house in order to be close to the University of California, Berkeley (UC–Berkeley). Further conversation had taken place with the Jesuits from Los Gatos and the Sulpician Fathers in Menlo Park. Preparations for the Second Vatican Council, which began in 1959 during the reign of Pope John XXIII, had stirred the imagination of those engaged in seminary formation and attracted them to an urban setting rather than an isolated locale.

Bishop Begin faced the novelty quite alone. Regularly scheduled dialogues with other bishops would be a decade away. But his inclination to favor ecumenical interchanges and pursue improved dialogue with the flagship UC–Berkeley would soon find support in statements from Vatican II. Another reason of mine for wanting to place the record of

Bishop Begin's in the archives is to correct the impression given to me in statements by two prominent members of the American hierarchy that Bishop Begin "of course was opposed to the Graduate Theological Union."

The time spent in writing that history led to stirrings. Frank Maurovich, who had served as founding editor of our diocesan newspaper, along with Father Joseph Chinnici, OFM, an Oxford historian from the Franciscan School in Berkeley, and the archdiocesan archivist Jeffrey Burns, who was also deacon of the diocese and doctor in history from the University of Notre Dame, recommended further archival essays.

The first of these deals with my participation, together with Bishop Begin, in the second session of Vatican II in the fall of 1963. This one suggestion led to others. As a result no master plan will be evident. Part history and part memoir; neither is complete.

A word about the prominence of Berkeley in the title. The germinal inspiration for this book centered on the ecumenical collaboration of the path-breaking enterprise of the GTU. The ensuing dialogue was blessed by Vatican II, as was Bishop Begin's outreach to the markedly secular institution of the University of California and the eventual circle of dialogue within the church that extended to the churches of Asia. Also in the interest of full disclosure, the Cummins family home has been situated in south Berkeley for ninety-one years.

My hope is that these recollections of a diocese that was established in the same year Vatican II began—and that absorbed the Council's teachings so well—will serve historians in the future as a remembrance by someone from my generation of the blessed times in which we served. Much can be learned from those times about the people of God, styles of authority, responsibility to the world, and the creative initiatives undertaken in the Diocese of Oakland, Berkeley, and beyond. For our generation the years encompassed a good and exciting period well worth remembering.

John S. Cummins
Oakland, California
August 1, 2015

1

Personal Experience of Vatican II

Bringing the Council from Rome to Oakland

In 1959, POPE JOHN XXIII SURPRISED EVERYONE, including Vatican officials, by calling an ecumenical council for the entire church, only the twenty-first such event in the church's 2000–year history. I had no idea then what a decided influence the Council would have on priestly ministry in our generation. After all, we had no experience with such meetings—the First Vatican Council had ended in 1870.

After three years of preparation, the first session of the Second Vatican Council opened in 1962—for me, it occurred after a decade in the priesthood. I was beyond what my insightful confessor in the seminary told me would be the "honeymoon years," when I would come to a decision about my manner of serving—whether it would continue with the early generosity or settle into something comfortable. I presumed he was referring to some kind of "cruising altitude."

As it turned out, Vatican II would have influenced me no matter what, but its effect on me was magnified—completely by accident. In January 1963, scarcely nine months after my job description was changed from dean of boys at Bishop O'Dowd High School to chancellor of the newly founded Diocese of Oakland, Monsignor John P. Connolly, head of the Diocesan Tribunal and pastor of St. Anthony parish, hosted a dinner to which Bishop Floyd Begin, Monsignor Nick Connolly, vicar general, and five other priests, including me, were invited.

Since the two Connollys (not related) had accompanied the bishop to Rome for the first session of Vatican II, the conversation moved naturally to events of the Council. Among other matters, John Connolly brought up the rejection of the first proposed document *On Divine Revelation* and registered a kind of disturbed concern. I volunteered that nine of the ten priests on the faculty of Bishop O'Dowd High School during the spring the year before had attended a course of Wednesday evening sessions in Lent at St. Mary's College in Moraga on the new Scripture studies explained by Sulpician Father Frank Norris of St. Patrick's Seminary. I suggested that the developments in Scripture studies had provided us with more information and understanding than to any generation before us.

From the corner of the room came the very weighted words of the bishop, "You took an oath as chancellor to interpret the Scriptures *sensu stricto*. If you cannot support that oath, you should resign as chancellor." The room fell into what was for me an uncomfortable silence. Our bishop, however, who had a temperament that could change temperature quickly and easily, took a page from Good Pope John and surprised us all by announcing his plans for the year with no prior notice or consultation. Among them, he said he would be sending me for canon law studies, presumably abroad. This was the usual qualification for those working in the chancery and it hinted at a long bureaucratic career to which I was not aspiring.

Nonplussed, Monsignor John Connolly, who was the bishop's closest adviser as well as his Tuesday golf partner, reacted strongly. "You can't do that," he told the bishop frankly. "You will leave me all alone in the office in the fall months." The bishop, a Roman student as was Connolly, seemed intimidated. He paused for a brief moment before he looked at me and, perhaps with some sense of consolation, said, "I will take you to the Council in the fall."

After I returned home, Monsignor Nicholas Connolly, with whom I lived at the time, came to my door and sympathetically asked how I was feeling. The question was presumably prompted by the

Pope John XXIII created the Diocese of Oakland in 1962. Bishop Floyd L. Begin, above, from Cleveland, Ohio, served as its first bishop until 1977. (J. Wright / *The Catholic Voice*)

bishop's reprimand and abrupt curtailment of my graduate studies. I told him not to worry. I was elated by the consolation prize.

Vatican II—An Educational Process

Our mood by 1963 was expectant, unclear but not unsettling. Clerical conversations in every generation looked to improve priestly ministry. The confident openness of Pope John XXIII, the three years that followed the announcement of the Council, and the intense experience of the Council's opening session flavored those discussions. Something was going to be different.

The seminary was the remote preparation. Liturgical change, for example, was not unfamiliar. We had Pope Pius XII's lengthy encyclical *Mediator Dei* (1947), his encouraging encyclical on the liturgy, along with Benedictine studies in Collegeville, Minnesota, the monks of Solesmes, and the annual national liturgical conferences. Our dogma professor, Father Edward Wagner, had familiarized us with the debates on church–state questions in *The American Ecclesiastical Review* between Monsignor

Joseph Fenton, of the Catholic University of America, and Jesuit Father John Courtney Murray, of Woodstock, Maryland. Extracurricular interests had familiarized us with two movements flourishing in our time: one originated in France with Canon Joseph Cardijn and his process of observe, judge, and act for the Young Christian Workers; the other, the Christian Family Movement, had spread widely from its origins in Chicago. When I think back, I realize that Scripture studies, though weak for us at that time, were going to be a very different experience for those who immediately followed us.

Then, in my first priestly appointment at Mission Dolores parish, I found illustrations abounded for the laity beyond the inherited Catholic Action role. A union steward came daily to the 6:30 A.M. Mass. Another, a graduate of the University of San Francisco Law School, who also had hoped to serve the union movement, moved into public service. The director of the Creative Arts Department at San Francisco State University, J. Fenton McKenna, explained that in the 1950s the teaching of Pius XII inspired him to encourage our young people into fields of communication, economics, and the world of art and drama.

My concurrent duties as Newman chaplain at San Francisco State gave me experiences in the fields of science and religion. I recall being on a panel with a chemistry professor—a nonbeliever though he had begun his career under the Jesuits at Santa Clara University, promoting an unhappily popular book by a Paul Blanshard entitled *American Freedom and Catholic Power*. Blanshard's thesis was that the Catholic Church is for dialogue when it is a minority, but demands official status in a country where it is the majority. My simple reply at the time was that the scholarly Dominican archbishop Joseph McNicholas, of Cincinnati, years earlier had declared that the "American arrangement" was theologically acceptable.

At Mission Dolores, I also came into contact with developments in religious life. I was deeply impressed by a young woman who had worked for the Bank of America and then took some years to decide to enter a new community of Oblates of Mary Immaculate (OMI) and begin a ministry in Alaska. Virginia Leary, an international lawyer with family connections in the East Bay, came by to explain the work of the International Auxiliaries, a secular institute to which she belonged. Soon after, Cardinal Leo Joseph Suenens of Belgium, who was to become a forceful leader at the Council, struck a responsive chord among women religious, when he wrote *The Nun in the World,* encouraging Sisters to modernize and take a more active and varied role in the church's mission, a role many of them had already assumed.

With my next appointment, to the faculty of Bishop O'Dowd High School, I was named chaplain at Mills College, an elite women's institution in Oakland. There, I was thrown deeply into ecumenical associations. I became part of a campus team with George Hedley, a Protestant chaplain whose ecumenical breadth had put me off in the early days. But my thinking gradually broadened and later led me to invite Dr. Victor Gold, distinguished professor of Old Testament at the Lutheran Seminary in Berkeley, as a speaker.

Amid all this came the election of the unknown Angelo Roncalli in 1958 as Pope John XXIII. Within the year he had announced the calling of the ecumenical council. That same year he established a Secretariat for Promoting Christian Unity with the soon to be familiar names of Jesuit Cardinal Augustine Bea and Paulist Father Thomas Stransky. As high school faculty, we paid some special attention to the pope's first encyclical, *Mater et Magistra,* on the church's social teaching and its muted reception by the *National Review*'s William F. Buckley Jr. as "Mater, si—Magistra, no!" The pontiff followed with his majestic encyclical *Pacem in Terris* on world affairs, addressed to men and women of good will. The encyclical resulted locally in a public seminar at the University of California, San Francisco, led by then mayor Joseph Alioto.

The stirrings led me to prepare a master's thesis at the UC–Berkeley on the concept of the church from the writings of Erasmus, the sixteenth-century scholar. In those early 1960s, popular readings caught our attention, particularly the works of Dominican theologian Yves Congar, especially his influential book on the dignity and responsible roles of the laity within the church. Other path-breaking, controversial theological books on church and sacraments appeared by Swiss theologian Hans Kung and Dutch Dominican Edward Schillebeeckx, along with a cheerful, thoughtful ecumenical work, *From Diatribe to Dialogue*, by our local Stanford Presbyterian theology professor Robert McAfee Brown. The educational process was to continue.

Prelude to Participation

Many of us had been following the first session of the Council, not just from skimpy official Vatican releases but also from insider reports in *The New Yorker* written under the pseudonym Xavier Rynne (much later revealed to be Rome-based and highly connected Redemptorist Father Francis X. Murphy), telling us that the majority of the bishops favored a change from Latin to vernacular language in liturgy and had surprisingly rejected the first draft of the document *On Divine Revelation*, which one bishop described as "negative and pessimistic," as well as the initial document on the church.

As Jesuit historian John W. O'Malley describes it in his classic work *What Happened at Vatican II,* "The lines had been drawn." The majority of the 2,200 bishops assembled, in dialogue with one another and with the theologians they brought with them, had found their voice. They refused to simply rubber-stamp previously prepared documents. They had been encouraged by the impressive, memorable opening statement of Pope John XXIII:

> In the present order of things divine providence is leading us to a new order of human relations which by men's own efforts and even beyond their very expectations are directed toward the fulfillment of God's superior and inscrutable designs.... In the daily exercise of our pastoral office we sometimes have to listen, much to our regret, to voices of persons who, though burning with zeal...can see nothing but prevarication and ruin.... We feel we must disagree with those prophets of gloom.

Added to Suenens were the names of such cardinals as Julius Dopfner of Munich, Josef Frings of Cologne, Franz Koenig of Vienna, Giacomo Lercaro of Bologna, and our own Albert Meyer of Chicago, who brought freshness to church and Council leadership by their careful, scholarly interventions. Cardinal Koenig had visited UC–Berkeley in that same year with compliments to the academic quality of the institution. Accompanied by Archbishop Joseph McGucken of San Francisco, the Austrian prelate favorably appraised the infant Graduate Theologi-

Bishop Begin, right, participated in all four sessions of the Second Vatican Council, held in St. Peter's Basilica, 1962–1965. (Vatican photo)

cal Union (GTU).

By 1963, interest in the Council by so many of us here at home had grown prodigiously. We loved what was happening. Of course, our joy was dampened by the death in June 1963 of the pontiff, universally known and loved as Good Pope John, after a reign of less than five years. His spirit of openness, joy, and trust in God's providence would be missed.

On the Scene in Rome

On October 31, 1963, I arrived in Rome, a month after the second session had begun. Newly elected Pope Paul VI had seized the energy of John XXIII with an enthusiastic welcome, praising the delving into the mystery of the church and looking forward to a renewal that would promote the solidarity of the whole human family. It was an echo of our Oakland bishop's comment that the aim of the Council was "to build bridges to all men and women." I would learn later with admiration of the role Pope Paul, as Cardinal Montini, played in preparation and direction for the first session of the Council. He also approved a critical change in the daily running of the Council from the cumbersome ten cardinal council presidents to four moderators: Cardinals Agagianian of the Curia, and Dopfner, Lercaro, and Suenens, three leaders of the majority, who possessed conciliatory skills, yet were not afraid to speak their minds on the issues in their own name.

On the day I arrived, Bishop Begin left with Cardinal John Krol on a visit to Germany, taking advantage of the three-day weekend occasioned by the holy day of All Saints. I was gathered in by my classmate Monsignor Warren Holleran, then serving as spiritual director at the North American College. He took me to an evening presentation in St. Peter's Basilica by Cardinal Stefan Wyszynski of Poland, delivered amid the beauty of light and color of that majestic church—and entirely in Latin. An impressive beginning.

Bishop Begin and I resided in a hotel in the Parioli area of the Eternal City, a forty-five-minute walk to the Via Della Conciliazione, where the American press conferences were held. Our daily routine was to serve each other's Masses (concelebration had not yet been implemented), have breakfast, and then board the bus to arrive before 8:30 A.M. at St. Peter's. Bishop Begin somehow, as he had for both monsignors Connolly, acquired the status of *periti*, or expert, for all of us. That

This official Vatican credential (*tessera*) allowed Monsignor John (Giovanni) Cummins, as secretary and advisor to Bishop Begin, to enter the balconies between the pillars in St. Peter's Basilica and observe the second session of Vatican Council II.

provided me a *tessera,* or credential, that permitted entry into the basilica and to what were called tribunals, elevated stations between the pillars of St. Peter's, looking down on the 2,200 bishops. Along with this credential came access to all Council documents, or schemas, as they were called, many of which were admirably and efficiently produced overnight by the Latin Press Office. These were all in Latin and subject to great change, such as, for example, the original proposal on ecumenism, which included Jewish relations and religious liberty (these eventually became separate documents) or the early schema on our Blessed Mother, which was later incorporated into the *Constitution on the Church in the Modern World.*

The daily procedure was to have a topic to which bishops would speak with a ten-minute limit, again in Latin. It would take a three-day notice to acquire the position. Within weeks I could follow some of the oral presentations, particularly by those whose original language was English. Council secretary Pericle Felici, however, made the daily announcements, often interjecting humor that provoked widespread laughter, no part of which I ever caught.

On my arrival in St. Peter's, Monsignor Humberto Medeiros, secretary to Bishop James L. Connolly of Fall River, Massachusetts, waited to introduce me to the Council environment. I told him I already had a date with Monsignor Mark J. Hurley, secretary to Bishop Hugh A. Donohoe of Stockton, Calif., who had once been my principal at Bishop O'Dowd High School and longtime friend. My choice was fortuitous. Mark knew virtually every important personage. At the coffee break in mid-morning, Mark led me on the wide circle through St. Peter's, stopping at the two coffee bars, one off the main floor to the right, the other on the left. At the first one, he introduced me to Father Yves Congar. I had noticed earlier the familiar faces of Cardinals Krol, Dearden, Shehan, and the firm Joseph Ritter of St. Louis, but meeting Congar surpassed them all. I recall him as slender and tall in his Dominican habit. I wished I had had the language to express my appreciation of his works, but at least we had a cup of coffee together. Much more was available in the bar—wine and spirits, including a rather decent scotch—evidence of the non-puritanical European atmosphere far different from the American scene.

Monsignor Cummins, to the right of Pope Paul VI, looks on as the pontiff greets Monsignor Humberto Medeiros, later cardinal archbishop of Boston, during an audience for theologians and other advisors to the bishops during the second session of Vatican II. (Vatican photo)

Circling back to our places, we encountered Father Hans Kung, as strikingly handsome as his pictures, with his red hair, upright posture, and energy. Mark took advantage of the encounter to stir up a readily available strong response on some particular topic, which I do not recall. Immediately, we encountered Scripture scholar Passionist Father Barnabas Ahern, gentle in professing that he was honored in meeting us. Within the next few days I would meet, in turn, Jesuit liturgist Joseph Jungmann, highly regarded theologian Henri de Lubac, ecumenist George Tavard, and, from Canada, Augustinian theologian Gregory Baum.

In the first week after my arrival, Monsignor Jack Egan from Chicago, whom I knew, took me to dinner. We ate early that particular evening because the place on the agenda for religious liberty had been secured. We returned to the Villa Nova House, where Jack Egan lived together with John Courtney Murray, George Higgins, Mark Hurley, Bill Baum from Kansas City, and Joe Baker from St. Louis. As we entered, the conversation stopped. Jack Egan pointed to me and said—I remember it so clearly—"He's all right." The conversation continued on. I realized that the evening had great significance, and I felt privileged to be present.

In the tribunal in which I was situated daily were the two Rahner brothers, both of whom were influential German Jesuit theologians, the better-known Karl and the talented but lesser-known Hugo, his elder. Both were quiet and reserved and not daily attendees. In contrast, I became very friendly with another one of my fellow-tribune occupants, Italian Father Pietro Pavan, a professor at Rome's Lateran University and later to be a cardinal. We were chatting amiably one day, when I noticed Mark Hurley waving rather frantically across the basilica. I signaled to meet him downstairs since I could not translate his motions. He told me that the man I was chatting with was the principal writer of John XXIII's *Pacem in Terris.* When I returned upstairs, I asked the short, gentle priest if he had written the document. He looked at me with a smile that reflected something like compliment, but also whimsy. It turned out he had written it and was to do much more. He had also been involved in the writing of *Mater et Magistra* and would aid principal author Belgian theologian Gérard Philips in writing *Gaudium et Spes,* the *Constitution on the Church in the Modern World,* and he would be a consultant to principal author Jesuit John Courtney Murray in writing *Dignitatis Humanae,* the *Declaration on Religious Freedom.*

A decade later, I would meet Pavan again in Washington, D.C., as part of a panel before the American bishops' meeting on the unfinished business of Vatican II. The Italian theologian along with our own American John Courtney Murray could be cited as outstanding examples of the collaboration and cooperation of the world's best theologians engaged with the bishops in dialogue with one another in the production of doctrinal guidelines for the universal church—a model ever needing imitation.

Vatican II's Critical Issues

The Council, of course, was much more than personages. The issues were vital, and unfortunately, in the month before I arrived, the bishops had held their stimulating discussion on the reworked and well-received schema *Lumen Gentium,* which had been retitled from *The Nature of the*

Church to *The Mystery of the Church*. But plenty of other critical issues remained to be discussed on the Council floor.

Ecumenism was one. My recollection is that the proposed document was seen as a fundamental concern and well received by the Holy Father on down. Our Bishop Begin was appointed chair of an American bishops' ad hoc committee on the subject. I remember the friendliness as well as the conviction of Bishop Charles Helmsing of Kansas City, Missouri. There was great favor toward the Orthodox churches. Cardinal Bea asked that the issue of anti-Semitism be introduced. Others suggested that religious liberty would be a necessary chapter. As mentioned, the latter two issues became separate documents.

Protestant observers entered the conversations, particularly Robert McAfee Brown from Stanford and Albert Outler of Southern Methodist University. Brown was a regular presence in the Bay Area. I would meet Outler again at the University of Pacific Colliver Lectures, alongside Jesuit Father Walter Burghardt, of Woodstock. The Council's final ecumenical statement was strong: "This discord openly contradicts the will of Christ…and inflicts damage on the most holy cause of proclaiming the good news to every creature." The Council made explicit that the ecumenical movement was "fostered by the grace of the Holy Spirit."

The document unleashed extraordinary vitality in the Diocese of Oakland. Father Pat Finnegan of St. Ambrose in Berkeley made the parish a vibrant center. As a priest in my younger days I had heard a remark, "A priest might appear in a Protestant pulpit once; he would not appear there twice." Pat Finnigan in reflecting on a Scripture at the Congregational Church in Berkeley began with the sign of the cross just, in his words, "to make sure where my friends were." The Graduate Theological Union was a prepared locus for dialogue. So too were local parishes and the "Paulist Living Room Conversations." In these later years, while some describe the ecumenical climate as "the doldrums," the early associations allowed friendships and had collaboration at the neighborhood level as a fruitful outcome.

In those early November days, the liturgy document was completed. On November 22, it was voted 2,178 in favor to 19 opposed. The first draft of *Gaudium et Spes*, known as *Schema XIII* and dealing with the church in the modern world, was introduced, a document that carried heavy responsibility for our thoughts as well as for its implementation. There was doubt in many quarters that it would ever be accepted. Lastly, the restoration of the diaconate, opposed by many, seemed destined for what we thought of in those days as missionary lands.

Collegiality—A Lightning Rod

Two other discussions remain in my memory, both highly controverted. One was collegiality, "a lightning rod" in the words of historian John W. O'Malley. The other, the distinctive American contribution, was the Council's *Declaration on Religious Freedom*. Some saw in the collegiality issue an effort to reinsert the pope into the college of bishops. For most others, the aim was to clarify the place of the bishop ordained in his own right as shepherd of a diocese but responsible with the pope for the universal church as well. From this flowed, imperfectly according to some, the scheduled synods of bishops in Rome through the years. The 1971 World Synod of Bishops saw the delineation of *Justice in the World*, a document oft quoted and influential for the direction of the contemporary church:

> Action on behalf of justice and participation in the transformation of the world fully appears to us as a constitutive dimension of preaching of the gospel, or, in other words, of the church's mission for the redemption of the human race and its liberation from every oppressive situation.

From experience, U.S. bishops spoke easily to the formation of episcopal conferences in countries and regions. Their predecessors, after all, had been operating in a communal pattern within the National Catholic Welfare Conference since 1919, the year the NCWC was established. (In 1966 the NCWC was renamed the National Conference of Catholic Bishops.) Cardinal Meyer of Chicago recommended the binding power of such conferences. In particular, Meyer stated that the president of such institutions should not be the oldest cardinal. Cardinal James F. McIntyre of Los Angeles was very opposed to Meyer's proposal, as were Italian Cardinals Ernesto Ruffini and Antonio Bacci—all of them senior citizens.

The concept of national conferences survived and became an instrument for collegial exchanges from one conference to another, such as the bishops in North America meeting regularly with those from Latin America. For years on the West Coast we had met semiannually with the bishops of northern Mexico (the Alta–Baja Californias). Under the leadership of Pope Paul VI, Asian bishops who wished to converse and build relationships with one another formed the Federation of Asian Bishops' Conferences in 1970. I served as American "fraternal delegate" to that organization for twenty-two years. That responsibility played a role in my participation in the Synod of America in 1997 and the Synod of Asia in 1999 (both events held in Rome).

Collegiality also involved the question of a retirement age for bishops (set now at seventy-five). This met with a mixed response. The perennial question of auxiliary bishops and coadjutor bishops surfaced again. In 1963, I remember a press conference at which Bishop Jerry McDevitt (Pittsburgh) discussed the idea of a permanent auxiliary, one who was not assigned his own diocese. Since being a bishop demanded a diocese, McDevitt explained how Rome regularly followed the letter by assigning an auxiliary to a defunct diocese from the early days of the church, or, in his words, to a "region in North Africa that contained four goats."

At one meeting, Redemptorist Father Bernard Haring, a recognized theologian, spoke at length about restoring the theology of "the local church," an expression not familiar to me. What did echo with me were the permissions that we in the local church had to seek from Rome on so many details. One of my first acts as chancellor was to petition the Apostolic Delegate's Office in Washington, D.C., for permission for one of our priests to say Mass aboard a cruise ship. The tax included was three dollars.

Most passionate were discussions about reform of the Roman Curia. Steven Leven, auxiliary bishop of San Antonio, spoke rather bluntly on the issue. Cardinal Josef Frings and Cardinal Alfredo Ottaviani took opposing sides. Pope Paul decided to consign reform of the Curia to the Curia, causing members of the Curia to relax.

A second critical issue was the matter of religious liberty. Once a part of the ecumenical document, it became a focus on its own. Francis Cardinal Spellman, who strongly favored treating this matter, brought

Father John Courtney Murray as his *peritus* for the second session. Murray had called religious liberty "a greatest need." Support for the issue came not only from the United States but also from Europe, with the participation of bishops such as Thomas Holland of Portsmouth, England, the lively and sharp commentator bishop Emile-Joseph De Smedt from Bruges, Belgium, and the blunt-speaking Patriarch Maximos Saigh from Damascus, Syria. (The patriarch always delivered his interventions in French to contrast with the church that was Latin.) Prague's Cardinal Josef Beran's notably eloquent intervention on this issue was greeted with fulsome applause. As late as 1980, Monsignor George Higgins would address the faculties of the University of California/Graduate Theological Union on the responsibility of the U.S. theologians to develop the concept of religious liberty. Speaking at a dinner in Berkeley, Higgins called religious liberty the singular contribution of the American bishops to Vatican II.

Daily Analysis by Experts

The fall of 1963 was a striking learning opportunity for me. In Rome, the tools were the daily press conferences as well as frequent lectures. On my first day at the Council, I learned that a U.S. press conference was scheduled at 3 P.M. at the USO building, a few blocks down from the Piazza San Pietro. Since the eye but not the ear could translate the Latin, I felt I should attend. Archbishop Joseph McGucken (San Francisco)—a familiar and friendly face—was in charge of the sessions. Regular panelists who commented on the Council and responded to reporters' questions were Father Robert Trisco of the Catholic University of America's Department of History; George Higgins, a learned social justice commentator; Jesuit ecumenist Gustave Weigel; and later, Mark Hurley, from San Francisco by way of Stockton. These were joined at times by a sprinkling of experts including Bernard Haring, Godfrey Diekmann, Francis Connell, Francis McCool of the Gregorian, and Paulist Father John Sheerin. Frederick McManus, the canon lawyer who was such a leader in liturgical development and whom I had met in Seattle in 1962 at the National Liturgical Conference, was a frequent guest on the panel.

The afternoon sessions, which ran for no less than an hour, ranged far beyond asking and answering questions to include background information, explanations of terms, and appraisals of directions. At one session, Monsignor Henry Cosgrove of Brooklyn explained the procedures of what was then called the Holy Office. I was sympathetic to him because of the force of the challenging questions he had to field and also because I realized that obligations of confidentiality were preventing him from speaking freely on some issues. I remember as well the strenuous dialogue that ensued. At the close of the session, a reporter asked Father Gustave Weigel whether he wished to be back for Vatican III. He responded quickly, "No, given sufficient time all human efforts turn out badly."

I discovered that, in addition to press conferences, lectures on Council issues were held daily in the city. These were not advertised, however. One learned about them by word of mouth. At the first American press conference I attended, Paulist Father Bob Quinn, from the Paulist Center in Boston and brother of Paulist Joseph Quinn, who at the time was pastor of the Newman Center in Berkeley, asked me, "Are you going to Piet Fransen's lecture at the North American College this afternoon?" I felt like the Samaritan who had "not even heard of the Holy Spirit."

Fransen's talk, in my mind to this day, foreshadowed in a sense the popular book written later by Cardinal Avery Dulles, *Models of the Church*. Fransen presented the church as mission or as sacrament. His conclusion was that the church embraces both. At the hotel that evening, Father Ivan Parenti, an Oakland priest who was studying canon law in Rome, came to dinner with the bishop and me. I was enthusiastic about my afternoon experience. I even encouraged the bishop to attend what I felt was at least a smorgasbord if not a banquet of theological reflection. The bishop caught my excitement and, as he said to me on more than one occasion over the years, "I want you to go all the way with this." That permission was a rich blessing for me.

For the rest of my stay my one regret was that I was relegated to English speakers. Even just one more language would have greatly enlarged my opportunities.

Special Memories of Roman Days

I have some special remembrances from the days in Rome. One was the tragedy of November 22, 1963. The bishop and I were at dinner when a waiter approached to tell us that President John F. Kennedy had been shot in Dallas. The bishop surmised correctly that the president would not survive the attack. We went for a walk after the meal, shaken by the news. An elderly Italian woman passed us and must have identified us as Americans. "Poor Kennedy," she said softly. Both of us were touched by her graciousness.

The days ahead were filled with questions and puzzlement. I was very much in the company of George Higgins those days. One recollection is our moving through town in a taxi in heavy rain one evening. We stopped at the Piazza Colonna, where George picked up a stack of papers. "The White House has to speak," he explained. "Germany and Europe have concluded that this is the result of a conspiracy."

A happy memory was an invitation that we received for an audience with Pope Paul VI. I went with Monsignor Hugh Dolan, a priest from the Galveston-Houston Diocese. For some reason we arrived at the bronze doors of St. Peter's early. We found our way to the hall for the reception. I headed toward the back since I felt that abundant numbers of persons of stature were sure to come. Hugh questioned me, "Didn't your grandmother ever tell you not to be backward about being forward?" We moved and sat in the front row, Hugh on my right, Humberto Medeiros on my left. The pope came down the row. Humberto had a long conversation with him. The pope took my hand. I merely said, "California." He smiled raised his arms and said warmly, "Ah, California." I had been at a large audience with Pope Pius XII in 1956. This experience was even more overwhelming, not just for the privilege of the office but also because of the growing admiration I felt for Pope Paul VI as his writings and sensitive leadership blossomed in the post–Vatican II years.

So many of the personalities I became acquainted with in Rome remained friends and associates in the years after the Council. Monsignor William Baum of Kansas City, who became the ecumenical officer for the American bishops, invited me to join the Roman Catholic–American Baptist dialogue for a number of years. This experience was enriching because of new learnings I acquired and also due to my newfound appreciation for the piety of our dialogue partners. Father Bill Keeler, from Harrisburg, frequently attended ecumenical gatherings that were important for the administration of Bishop Begin. Monsignor Charles Moeller, a prominent Belgian theologian, writer, and literary critic from Louvain, would end up in Berkeley at our request. His positive appraisal of the GTU gave our bishop timely support. (Monsignor Moeller had a position at that time with the Congregation of the Doctrine of the Faith.) Sulpician Father James Laubacher, a peritus of Cardinal Lawrence Shehan of Baltimore, would become president of St. Patrick's Seminary in Menlo Park. Bishop Alonso Escalante, the American Maryknoll missioner who founded Mexico's missionary society, the Guadalupe Missionaries, was among the many guests whom Bishop Begin invited for dinner. Sylvester Treinen, another Rome acquaintance, became a bishop in Idaho. Our lives were much intertwined for many years thereafter.

Amid all the probing and diverse judgments of so many people during those intense weeks in Rome, one impression has stayed with me through the years. It relates, perhaps, to Monsignor John Tracy Ellis's imposing essay on the intellectual life of Catholic universities in the United States. As always in the church, pastoral responsibility urges us to be particularly sensitive to the simple and weaker members of the community, but one day after the American press conference someone noted that we also have a responsibility not to scandalize the bright. That thought has refreshed itself in mind from time to time through the years.

Even the Alitalia charter flight home from Rome remains fixed in my memory. Seated in the window seat to my right was Maryknoller Joseph Regan, a native of Massachusetts who, after being exiled from China, had become bishop in Tagum, a new diocese in Mindanao in the southern Philippines. His diocese and the Diocese of Oakland were both one year old at that time. The population of each of the dioceses was estimated to be over 400,000, but Oakland then had about 160 priests, while the Diocese of Tagum had only five. Coincidently, I met the bishop again when I visited Tagum in 1979. (Bishop Regan had a host of young priests around him, all of whom seemingly rode motorcycles. One of the priests explained to me that they were known as "Regan's Raiders.") The quiet bishop I remembered from the plane ride had become a very public witness against the martial law regime of President Ferdinand Marcos. Additionally, he had trained and organized an extraordinary group of catechists who carried the message of the gospel with a certain bravery. I introduced myself to him as his companion on the flight home after the Council. He candidly replied, "I don't remember you at all."

Just as memorable was standing in the rear of the Alitalia plane for much of the long trip home with George Higgins and Tom Stransky. We reviewed our experiences during the weeks in Rome and shared thoughts about future directions in the church. I recall commenting that some people in the world would remain intensely busy even in an empty room. Tom Stransky and I stayed in touch thanks to a number of ecumenical contacts. I remember one occasion particularly. Returning to San Francisco early after a day off skiing, a group of us went to hear Tom Stransky and Robert McAfee Brown in dialogue at Commerce High School auditorium in downtown San Francisco. (Some of us were still in our ski clothes; others had been thoughtful enough to change back into clerical attire before the event.)

George Higgins would be a frequent dinner companion in Washington, D.C. He played a prominent role through the 1960s and into the 1970s with the farmworkers in California. He stayed with us at the Oakland cathedral three or four times, once to attend a cousin's ordination. He always admired our cathedral liturgy. George later gave us helpful advice during a difficult labor strike that included a major Catholic hospital in the diocese.

Bishop Begin and I came home from the Council through Cleveland, where we spent a number of days in mid-December with the remarkable Begin family. As a California native, I tried to get used to blowing snow. We visited Archbishop Edward Hoban, still active at eighty-six years of age, longtime friend of the apostolic delegate, Archbishop Amleto Cicognani and the maker of American bishops: Floyd Begin, John Krol of Philadelphia, John Dearden of Detroit, Paul Hallinan of Atlanta, Robert Tracey of La Cross, Wisconsin—all came from the Cleveland Diocese.

After I returned home, I wrote an article about the Council for our Catholic paper. I raised questions such as would Vatican II be described as a success? Was change coming too quickly? Was devotion to our

Blessed Mother diminishing? Were there reasons to be suspicious about ecumenism? Was the uniqueness of the Roman Catholic Church assured? My conclusion reflected the belief of Yves Congar that the Council operates *within* the church. Even the Council of Chalcedon was an example of the proper speed of change. My counsel was that the work of the Vatican Council, in Congar's words, was "to aid us, not to disturb us."

It was evident at that time that the Council had unleashed much energy in the church, but there was still much to learn. We could only guess about developments to come in liturgy, the place of Scripture in our prayer life and reflection, the developing role of laity, the need to learn dialogue, the implications of collegiality, and the place of justice in our piety. There was "much wind in our sails," as someone put it well. It was a good and exciting time to be a priest. Would this last?

2

Cathedral Fondly Remembered

Loved for Liturgy and Community

Remembering our beloved St. Francis de Sales Cathedral, I speak of words and of music. Apropos of tonight I draw attention to the letter of St. Peter (II Pet. 1: 13–19), which we read in this Mass, by underlining his words "reminder" and "remember." The words and music, therefore, are in the context of memory, which can be endearing and perhaps sentimental. An English poet has written, "The hands of memory weave the blissful dreams of long ago." But memory can be perilous. According to the novelist Joseph Conrad, "In plucking the fruit of memory, one runs the risk of spoiling its bloom."

Despite the words of warning, St. Peter unhesitatingly plunges into memory because of the value of message. He recalls "the holy mountain," of hearing "the voice come from heaven," himself indeed witness to the unique revelation from "the majestic glory, 'This is my beloved son'.…" He calls it "a prophetic message, altogether reliable, not

A homily Bishop John Cummins delivered in Oakland's Cathedral of Christ the Light on February 8, 2012.

St. Francis de Sales church served as cathedral for the
Diocese of Oakland from 1962 until 1993 when it was
severly damaged in the 1989 Loma Prieta earthquake.
(Artwork by Paul Bailey-Gates)

composed from cleverly devised myths."

Tonight we take advantage of the opportunity for the deliverance
of that message in our time. For within months after the establishment
of the Diocese of Oakland and the naming of St. Francis de Sales as the
cathedral, the Second Vatican Council opened in Rome. The first document produced was that on liturgy. Such prompted Bishop Floyd Begin
with an unambiguous response to engage Robert Rambusch of New
York to renovate the interior of St. Francis de Sales Cathedral.

In 1967, the bishop would appoint to the cathedral a young associate from St. Jarlath's parish, Father Donald Osuna with the instructions,
"Teach the people how to pray." There would be one year of testing and
trying. Then would come the appointment of two more priests of tal-

ent, Fathers Michael Lucid as pastor and James Keeley as associate, along with the gifts and talents of the Holy Names Sisters in the school. Renewal was on its way.

The Second Vatican Council did more than introduce vernacular languages into the prayer of the church. It restored more clearly the two elements of the Mass noted in the fifteenth century by the author of *The Imitation of Christ*: "There is the table of the sacrament, but also the table of the Word." The Vatican Council opened the Scriptures and then enlarged the hearing of biblical passages. It declared that the presence of Christ is not just in the bread and wine, but also in the congregation, in the person of the minister, but especially in the Word proclaimed in the assembly.

Preaching Restored to Prominence

St. Paul understood this well, speaking of the Word of God as "alive," "cutting like a two-edged sword" through joints and sinews. Many in the church would echo an understanding through the years, such as Cardinal Newman speaking of words as "sharp-edged tools." The American poet Emily Dickinson mused on the life and effectiveness of words.

But Carl Sandburg would find a similar theme in a poem read at the funeral Mass of the revered pastor, Monsignor Michael Lucid:

> "Little girl, be careful what you say
> When you make talk with words, words....
> For words are made of syllables
> And syllables, fair child, are made of air
> And air is so thin—air is the breath of God
> Air is finer than fire or mist,
> Finer than water or moonlight,
> Finer than spider webs in the moon....
> And words are strong too
> Stronger than rocks or steel
> And soft too, soft as the music of hummingbird wings,
> So little girl, when you speak greetings...
> Make wishes or prayers,
> Be careful, be careful...."

So came the careful deliverance of the Word at St. Francis de Sales Cathedral. The new ministry of lector was a role taken seriously. Those who would be reading at Sunday Mass appeared at the cathedral rectory every Tuesday evening. The study and preparation resulted in articulate and interpretive proclaiming of the Scriptures. Sometimes it became dramatic, such as the choral rendering of the Passion on Palm Sunday. I remember as well the dialogue between God and Abraham over the fifty or fewer just men in Sodom with a thinly veiled accent of a Jewish mother. The Word of God in the Easter Vigil came with strength in the darkness, joined once by the gathering of red vigil lights on the altar, pointing up the conversation of Abraham and Isaac.

Preaching was characterized by particular importance, recognizing from the Vatican Council the "intimate connection between words and rites…drawing content mainly from scriptural and liturgical resources." What was known as sermon became "homily." Taken seriously was the directive from the Council to preachers: "to share the abundant wealth of the divine Word with the faithful committed to them, especially in the sacred liturgy." And I recall one evening our pastor, Father Osuna, explaining directly to a professor of Scripture the nature of a homily for the Advent season that was to come. My remembrance of that encounter lies some place between surprise and amazement.

The Word and its application were abetted in the summer series in connection with the school. "It's a Classic" was one theme, with Friar Lawrence seen as an omen for Romeo and Juliet, since he was played by a Jesuit. Then came "Faces in the Revolution" with the outcome of the bishop in conflict with Father Osuna's puppy. So, too, came "Ha-ha hallelujah."

Inherent was the Word, not words. Symbols, gestures, poise, and precision did much of the speaking. The measure was always the prayerfulness of the liturgy. The culture and pattern established carried through the Loma Prieta earthquake into the parish hall with the plastic chairs, and on to St. Mary's on 7th Street when the two parishes became a blend.

Music Accompanies the Word

Music, noted once upon a time as "the most moving emotionally of all the arts," accompanied the Word. It was familiar and deep in our heritage with popular hymns and classical compositions. Scripture spoke of harps, pipes, horns, trumpets, flutes, lyres, and tambourines. It omitted what was both desired and controversial, the long-awaited pipe organ. In Scripture, music was joined to joy and remembrance. Song accompanied lamentation and mourning. It was called for at the new moon, but especially it served the praise and the glory of God.

Like most human things, some have found a downside. St. Jerome "feared the pleasures of music as contrary to the Christian ideal." Happily he was countered by Basil and Benedict, who accepted the beauty of music but demanded authentic agreement in voice and in mind.

Allan Bloom, a contemporary author specializing in the classics, has written:

> Students today...know exactly why Plato takes music so seriously. They know it affects life very profoundly.
>
> ...
>
> Music is the medium of the *human soul* in its most ecstatic condition of wonder and terror.
>
> ...
>
> Music...always involves a delicate balance between passion and reason, and even in its highest and most developed forms...that balance is always tipped, if ever so slightly, toward the passionate. Music, as everyone experiences, provides an unquestionable justification and fulfilling pleasure for the activities it accompanies....

Bloom lists those activities as soldiering, loving, and worshipping.

Father Osuna reached into alumni from the particularly talented 1963 class of St. Patrick's Seminary and tapped John McDonnell, his former seminary classmate. Again the directive from the Vatican Council was observed, "that selection of music be not unrelated to people's preparation and sensitivity." There was the familiar "Panis Angelicus" of Gounod. Palestrina found his way into communion meditations. There were the St. Louis Jesuits, E. Donald Osuna, and, I remember once, something of the Beatles.

Music for the congregation, well within people's range and familiarity, invited participation in the common parts of the Mass. Indeed it was ritual, that is, an easy sense of prayer and a comfortable feel for worship. I remember the thrill of the thunderous procession at midnight

Liturgy at St. Francis de Sales Cathedral filled the pews on Christmas Eve, above, and on Sundays in ordinary time as well. (J. A. Rubino photo)

Mass, "O Come, All Ye Faithful." The usual recessional on Easter was resounding, "Jesus Christ Is Ris'n Today," making it easier to believe in the resurrection. The Easter vigil, after the emotional rise from the baptisms, calmly settled in with "Morning Has Broken."

Had not the Vatican Council already used the words, St. Francis de Sales Cathedral would have found the description of "full, conscious and active participation." It would have found the achievement recognized by the Council, namely, "allowing the faith of the people to come forth." But liturgy was not an isolated event. It took place within community. Indeed it was the summit of parish activity, as well as the fountain from which flowed the daily life of the church.

We had many visitors come to the cathedral. Some were rather memorable, such as Virgilio Noe, secretary for the Congregation of Divine Worship in Rome. In a letter after his visit, he wrote, "I recall our visit to Oakland with pleasure, particularly the fine liturgy of Pentecost." He added as well, "and your kind hospitality."

That atmosphere was the fruit of participation in so many ministries. That truly was the encompassing of the local parish people, their families, and guests in a wide range, Berkeley professors, religious, and students of all ages. A veteran priest once stationed at St. Francis de Sales remarked how the parish people were made proud, including the mildly resistant retired pastor Monsignor Richard "Pinky" O'Donnell, and, especially and above all, Bishop Floyd Begin. How could one resist a church building that had become sparsely attended with pews not filled to capacity. This was in a neighborhood in decline, cut by freeways, invaded commercially with a city that in the 1960s was allowing decay west of San Pablo Avenue.

In that atmosphere rose a cathedral attentive to "the treasure of sacred music that must be preserved and fostered." It helped us realize further the words of the Second Vatican Council, "All should hold in very high esteem the liturgical life of the diocese, which centers around the bishop, especially in his cathedral church." So we are in harmony with St. Peter, immersing ourselves thankfully in the endearing, not perilous memory of the St. Francis de Sales that nurtured us, urged, inspired us on our pilgrimage. It remains with the sentiment of Peter, "a lamp shining in a dark place until the day dawns and the morning star rises in your hearts."

3

Genesis of Two Cathedrals

Tale of Two Faithful Women

THE DIOCESE OWES A DEBT OF GRATITUDE TO OUR DOCENTS for their generosity of time and the discipline of trainng for the responsibility of greeting visitors and leading them through our new Cathedral of Christ the Light. The title "docents," derived from the Latin word *docere*, means "to teach." Indeed, docents are not tour guides. Docents are teachers, inspiring visitors with the rich meaning of this holy building. Furthermore, they represent an elemental virtue in the Catholic tradition, which is hospitality.

For many years I served as chaplain at Mills College. One evening we had a speaker, Henry Schubart, an architect who had completed St. Louis Bertrand Church in East Oakland and was developing Holy Name parish in San Francisco. At the time the Archdiocese of San Francisco had entered into discussion and even debate about the replacing of St. Mary's Cathedral, which had been destroyed by fire in September 1962. It was Henry Schubart's judgment that cathedrals should not rival

An expanded and edited version of an address Bishop John Cummins delivered to the docents of Oakland's Cathedral of Christ the Light on August 2, 2008.

the high-rise buildings of the modern city, but should be modest buildings that exude welcome. Patrick Quinn, a professor of architecture at
UC–Berkeley many years ago, but in late years from Rensselaer Poly-
technic in Troy, New York, visited our new Cathedral of Christ the
Light. He felt that our new temple of worship easily qualifies as a welcoming building. To welcome and hospitality, our docents include history.

The worshipping church includes a great sense of poetry about a
church building. St. Peter in his first epistle speaks of a community of
living stones founded upon the apostles, the capstone of which is Jesus
Christ. The sacramentary, a holy book, contains liturgies for the feasts
of the Blessed Virgin Mary, for the apostles, and for the martyrs, but the
dedication of a church merits the first entry. Docents turn a visit to the
cathedral into a religious experience. They also provide encouragement
to many who may not have recognized the boldness of church
architecture through the years.

Three Decisive Events

Three decisive moments stand out in the birth of the Cathedral of Christ
the Light. The first involves the destructive power of the Loma Prieta
earthquake in October 1989, which all of America remembers as dis-
rupting the All Bay Area World Series between our Oakland A's and the
San Francisco Giants, but which we now remember as consequences
that turned us more quickly in an unexpectedly radical direction. The
second happened a year later in our St. Francis de Sales rectory, at dinner
with Gladys Valley. With her husband deceased, the head of their
Wayne and Gladys Valley Foundation in 1990 gave us great encouragement to seriously explore the possibility of a new cathedral. The third
decisive moment came in 1999 when Steve Chandler, president of the
board of the Valley Foundation, came to our chancery office to ask if we
were still interested in fulfilling Mrs. Valley's promise.

The Valley Foundation has been very generous to the diocese
through the years, particularly in the area of education. Each year its
board has given to us a check for $750,000 to aid inner-city schools. The
Performing Arts Center at Holy Names University is the gift of the
Foundation.

When Steve Chandler approached, our response, of course, was positive. I inquired whether there would be an announcement of this decision. Our finance officer, Father Albano Oliveira, had died just two weeks before. We would have been ill equipped to deal with the matter. Chandler agreed. As this was the first substantive resource we had met, I inquired whether we could in discussing this possibility in confidence use a figure perhaps of $15 million. The answer was positive.

Our estimate was based on the recent history we had of new church construction. St. Raymond's Church in San Ramon had been dedicated in September 1977 with a budget of $600,000. Two years later, Christ the King Church in Pleasant Hill went over that budget limitation to $880,000. By the late 1980s, the building of St. Elizabeth Seton in Pleasanton came in with an estimate of $4.1 million. An intuitive projection for the cathedral was $10 to $12 million.

As Steve Chandler left the office that day, he indicated genuine thanks for our making time for him. On the contrary, our gratitude remains to him and to the board and to the Valley family. Without that initiative, we could not have gone ahead. There was no alternative of a parish campaign for rebuilding. Seventeen projects were under way in the diocese at that time.

Historical Perspective

On April 28, 1962, three dioceses were carved out of the Archdiocese of San Francisco. Oakland was one, along with Stockton and Santa Rosa. The Roman document declared St. Francis de Sales Church as Oakland's cathedral. The recommendation, no doubt, came from the officers of the San Francisco Archdiocese. St. Francis de Sales was located in the downtown area of the East Bay city. It was not as isolated as St. Mary's. With a seating capacity of 800, Francis de Sales was the largest church in Oakland's downtown area.

The particular impetus for the church began some eighty years ago. Monsignor Joseph M. Gleason, a pastor in the 1930s, was an erudite gentleman who set up an institute for California history in conjunction with UC–Berkeley. He had a reputation for political and long sermons. His prescient insight projected that Oakland would someday be its own diocese; therefore, he installed a marble episcopal throne on the left side of the sanctuary. The pastor in his accommodation to criticism from the archbishop's office made of the structure a shrine for St.

Francis de Sales, the learned seventeenth-century bishop of Geneva. Bishop Floyd L. Begin, at his inauguration as our first bishop in April 1962, used that ready-made throne.

An incidental fact, well remembered, was that the parish church was built a century ago through the generosity of one woman. Mary Canning, an Irish immigrant, became secretary to the mayor of Oakland, who advised her on real estate investments. Her first gift of $140,000 was followed by another contribution of $40,000. Cornerstone of the new church was laid in 1893. Canning had asked to be anonymous, but Archbishop Patrick W. Riordan of San Francisco on the day of dedication indicated to her that her example was valuable to encourage others to "go and do likewise."

Despite the declining inner-city neighborhood in the last half of the twentieth century and suggestions that the cathedral be transferred from Francis de Sales to Our Lady of Lourdes Church, Bishop Floyd Begin dismissed any idea of moving or building a new cathedral, mindful perhaps of the extensive project that had been going on for those years over a new St. Mary's Cathedral in San Francisco. He engaged the services of Robert Rambusch of New York, a distinguished liturgical artist, to renovate the church. The filigree ceiling was painted over. A new altar was placed in the center of the sanctuary. The altar rail was removed. The five stained glass windows in the apse behind the altar were covered with fine wood paneling. (Incidentally, a pietà purchased in the transition for $200 by a West Oakland artist turned out to be a Bernini of the seventeenth century.) Sadness marked the faces of many of the older people. The pastor for two decades, Monsignor Richard "Pinky" O'Donnell, who grew up in the local parish, found the extensive renovation difficult.

In February 1967, Bishop Begin presided at the rededication of the renovated building with a liturgical theme, "How Awesome Is This Place," prepared by Father Donald Osuna. The mention of Father Osuna brings to mind the bishop's investment, not just in architectural renovation but in the placing of priestly talent at the parish. The bishop appointed a strong administrator in Monsignor Michael Lucid. He added the personable and pastoral genius of Father James Keeley. The Holy Names Sisters likewise generously assigned talent, encouraging the revitalizing of inner-city schools, the need for which had been noted by Father Mel Hary and the Legion of Mary in the early 1960s.

In that era of civil rights unrest and inner-city consciousness, the leadership of the parish settled on three priorities, namely, liturgy, the school, and service to the aging. Father Osuna engaged the services of John McDonnell of Crosby, Heafey, Roach & May law firm. McDonnell had been in the seminary with Father Osuna and had taste as well as competence in music. Worshippers heard music from familiar Latin hymns to occasional popular music.

The common parts of the Mass, such as the Sanctus and the Acclamation, were always familiar to the congregation. The Sunday liturgies were carefully prepared beforehand with the preacher presenting the theme drawn from the assigned Scriptures and the choral leaders blending appropriate music and song with that theme. Lectors gathered each Tuesday evening to be led through the readings for context, meaning, and delivery. The work was disciplined. Special planning would take place well in advance for Holy Week, for Advent, for Lent, and a special summer series. Monday morning would be an opportunity for appraisal, looking to the experience of symbols portrayed without verbal explanation. The measure of the liturgy was its prayerfulness.

The cathedral influenced the entire diocese and beyond. Joy replaced the sadness of older de Sales parishioners, now so proud to see their renovated church filled to capacity every Sunday with visitors from other parishes, from San Francisco and beyond. For twenty years, the leadership remained through Monsignor Michael Lucid, Father Don Osuna, and Father James Keeley. The parish was vibrant with lay participation, with a strong parish council, with task forces on liturgy, social action, and community organization. There was exchange particularly on Reformation Sunday with the First Baptist Church on nearby Telegraph Avenue.

The experience of the cathedral—despite so many years intervening—is remembered to this day. The threads and reputation continued through the temporary journey of the joined St. Mary and St. Francis de Sales parishes, after the earthquake made the de Sales Church unsafe. The momentum for the proposed new cathedral would hardly have been possible without the experience and the remembrance.

The Earthquake

October 18, 1989, marked the Loma Prieta quake. The irony was not lost on us who were in the midst of a second seismic study. In the early 1980s we were faced with an enormous rise in premium and deductible for earthquake insurance. We felt we could not manage the cost. We did, however, budget the same amount for seismic study and retrofit plans. Clem Finney, our diocesan engineer, had both talent and interest in seismic matters. We divided diocesan buildings into three categories of need. St. Francis de Sales was in the first.

The knowledge of this went back to a breakfast I had early on with Father Don Osuna. The red brick school, declared unsafe, had been taken down the year before I came. Osuna was explaining the experience of going to Bishop Begin to say that the school had to be closed. The bishop in response said, "You have to have faith. That is what they told me about the church building." Father Osuna relayed that his reaction was, "You did not need to tell me that!" I, at the moment of breakfast, repeated the very words, "Nor did you have to tell me that."

After the quake, the parish attempted to carry on. The nearby First Baptist Church generously invited us, although the earthquake had knocked out their heating. Father Keeley saw an added ecumenical opportunity, "Let us pray and freeze together." The second attempt took place in the parish hall with the yellow plastic chairs. More than once, I heard the consoling words, "Bishop, do not worry about the building, the church is people." In two months, however, the average Sunday attendance had dropped from an average of 1,900 people to 600 and falling.

February 1990 brought about a particular moment of change. A team of structural engineers, architects, and contractors reported on the two badly damaged churches, Sacred Heart on Fortieth and Martin Luther King Jr. Way and St. Francis de Sales. Four months seemed an extended time. I had presumed that all heavy equipment was engaged at the Cypress Freeway collapse. Reality was situated in the fear of aftershocks within the two buildings.

An unarticulated apprehension on my part foresaw bad news. Invitations, therefore, went to chancery people, to leadership from Sacred Heart parish, and to a wide group active at the cathedral. Explanations

were clear. The estimate for retrofitting costs amounted to $3.4 million
for Sacred Heart and $6.1 million for St. Francis de Sales. In private con-
versation with one of the structural engineers afterwards, I thanked him
for a clear presentation of technological capabilities to restore the damaged buildings. My eventual question arose, "Would you be comfortable
with your family in that building?" In silence, he looked down, raised
both his hands, and with little emotion indicated a negative response.

The unexpected information required time to digest. A public relations professional made us realize that there would be need of full parish leadership consensus and support to move ahead. St. Francis de
Sales people proved very responsible. We ended up at Sacred Heart with
$118,000 on what were considered frivolous cases, overcoming, for ex-
ample, the plea of some that the church should be restored as an histori-
cal landmark. One would have to feel disappointment with the behavior
and tactics of some of the preservation people.

Where Would You Want It?

In May 1990, we held a press conference, with a key part announcing a
cathedral to come. This judgment followed some reflection by the eight
deans of the diocese. Their suggestion of parishes as possible pro-tem
replacements for St. Francis de Sales ranged from St. Cornelius in Richmond and St. Joseph in Berkeley to St. Leander and St. Felicitas in San
Leandro. Later, Father Raymond Sacca, returning from a sabbatical on
liturgy in St. John's, Collegeville, set up a ten-point graph for an acting
cathedral. St. Jarlath and St. Augustine in Oakland came closest, but
neither was judged adequate.

We decided we needed one downtown church that would include
what had been the parishes of St. Francis de Sales, St. Mary's, and probably St. Andrew's–St. Joseph's. Sacred Heart was not considered downtown. St. Patrick's existed in its own pocket. A reporter from Channel 5
questioned afterwards the need of a cathedral. I explained that any notable city in the world, including Jakarta, Indonesia, and Seoul, Korea, had
a cathedral downtown. "Where would you want it?" he asked. "Fourteenth and Broadway," I replied, a remark not as far-fetched as it
seemed. That civic and commercial center of the city indeed offered
possible cathedral sites.

News reports brought an immediate response. John Sabatte of

Berkeley Farms, part of a family of generous benefactors to the diocese, sent a $100,000 check the next day to start a rebuilding fund. A number of the priests spoke positively. Lay leadership from James Vohs, Ed Heafey, John McDonnell, and Ron Courtney were among those who helped give us direction.

City officials proved favorable. City manager Henry Gardner wanted not just the cathedral but the social services from de Sales maintained. Ira Michael Heymann, former chancellor of UC–Berkeley, and Duke Bascom were leading a planning committee for the Oakland City Center. They both encouraged us to rebuild. Chancellor Heymann, a former dean of the UC–Berkeley Law School, demolished church–state objections for the city to help us. Veteran diocesan leaders, including Ross and Lillian Cadenasso, undertook active responsibilities.

James Vohs introduced Glenn Isaacson, who had overseen the development of Oakland's City Center in the early 1990s. After discussion of the possibility of Twenty-First and San Pablo as a site, Isaacson gave his judgment that a cathedral should be in a "prominent" place. "I know you people resist that word. I remember when I went to see Archbishop McGucken after the loss of St. Mary's Cathedral in San Francisco. I told him he had to leave Van Ness Avenue and go to the top of the hill. Isaacson continued, "A cathedral is life giving. There would be no Japantown in San Francisco or St. Mark's Towers as a retirement home, unless the cathedral anchored that corner of Geary and Gough." Ed Blakely, a professor of city planning at the University of California, who likewise reflected on development in downtown Oakland, gave formal, unequivocal encouragement.

The thinking reflected a certain realism. Three large, generous foundations were based in the diocese. One belonged to Walter Gleeson, who had led the reconstruction of Mission San Jose. The Chet and Helen Soda Foundation gave strong support to education and other diocesan works. In approaching the Gleeson Foundation, we found out that Walter's will had not been entirely clear and much of the resources were tied into real estate. The Soda Foundation had contributed in recent months $15 million to the UC–Berkeley. Our hope was that those two institutions would be supportive and, combined with the dependable generosity of the Wayne and Gladys Valley Foundation, would help

Bishop Cummins presents the papal Pro Ecclesia et Pontifice medal to Gladys Valley for her foundation's generosity in the building of Oakland's new cathedral and its ongoing support of local Catholic schools. (*The Catholic Voice*)

us achieve our goal. At least two deeply situated Oakland pastors, Ed Haasl and John Maxwell, while favorable, questioned whether there should not be allowance for people in the city and in the diocese to make their own contribution rather than depend on the foundations.

During those years, we had the leisure to explore many sites. There was no serious discussion of building a cathedral outside of Oakland. First of all, the Vatican chose Oakland as the See City for the diocese. Additionally, Oakland had both reputation and reality for rich ethnic diversity and economic spread. Furthermore, freeways found a meeting place in the city, as did all the BART routes, this latter being a very important consideration. We looked at a site at Franklin and 20th Street; 14th Street and Martin Luther King; 17th Street and Harrison; the Wells

Fargo Building at 14th Street and Broadway, and the southern part of the block associated with the Capwell's (later the Sears) building.

Although opposition rose, indifference probably predominated. The vicar general once asked me if I wanted to be involved in so much controversy for the rest of my life. Controversy that did rise faded. Some felt that we were denying Catholic schools needed support. Barbara Morrill, who instigated the scholarship program for inner-city students, felt the cathedral would not add to the renewal of downtown Oakland, which had an impetus of its own. On the way to my once-ev-ery-five-years *ad limina* visit to Rome in 1993, she and I walked out of St. Vitus Cathedral in Prague, a Gothic masterpiece. Without looking at me, she remarked, "Don't get any ideas."

The question of diocesan priorities has always remained valid. St. John Chrysostom, famous preacher in Antioch and later bishop of Con-stantinople, answered opposition in a fifth-century homily, and, in our own time Dorothy Day replied that even the poor need the experience of beauty. Human need claims the first priority. Buildings and art are, therefore, secondary, but secondary does not mean unimportant.

The ceremonial closing of St. Francis de Sales Church took place in October 1993. My own return weeks later from the *ad limina* visit found not just an empty site, where the cathedral had stood, but a sunken muddy pond following a heavy rain. The sense of loss struck deeply.

"Go For It!"

Wayne and Gladys Valley had been frequent guests at Bishop Begin's house. The tradition continued, even after Wayne's passing. One eve-ning at the end of dinner, I brought up the subject of St. Francis de Sales Cathedral, where Gladys and Wayne had married. "Why don't you reno-vate the present building?" she asked. My response was that it would be a bad business decision, since there was no way to make the building perfectly safe. "I am a business woman," she replied, "one has to make tough decisions." The conversation did not move further.

At a subsequent dinner, I had Jim Vohs as a guest to manage Gladys's extraordinary intelligence and verbal talent. As before, the same questions and the same responses took place. This time, however, she took no more than a short moment for reflection. "That cathedral would be a cultural center, an identity for the City of Oakland." Jim Vohs recalls her emphasizing, "As long as it is built in Oakland." Both John McDonnell and Ed Heafey had familiarized Gladys with the work of Mary Canning in another generation. "Go for it!" was her directive.

On naming the new cathedral, renaming it St. Francis de Sales proved acceptable to half the priests. A new name—respecting diversity in the diocese—rose as an important consideration. Father Don Osuna came up with Lumen Gentium, the document on the church from the Second Vatican Council. He did not win with the Latin expression, but the English adaptation of "Christ the Light" was enthusiastically approved by the cathedral steering committee.

When it came to size, I had thought 1,200 would be sufficient. The suggestion stirred inquiry over the seating capacity of San Francisco, namely, 2,400. The compromise came to 1,800.

With regard to an architect, it seemed logical to select one of our local people who had been so serving of the diocese through the years. The role of Christian Brother Mel Anderson, along with architecture critic Allan Temko of the *San Francisco Chronicle*, ended up with thirteen internationally known architects. Father Brian Joyce, who was in charge of the architectural subcommittee, brought the number down to five who would make presentations that should have been videotaped. The five were expressive of religion, culture, and art that a cathedral brought: Kevin Roche, who had built the Oakland Museum; Lord Norman Foster, who was doing the Hong Kong Airport; Ricardo Legorreta, who had done the cathedral in Managua; Craig Hartman, who, among other projects, did the international terminal at San Francisco Airport; and internationally famous Santiago Calatrava of Paris and Valencia, who was constructing an addition to the art museum in Milwaukee.

I asked one architect why such a moderate city as Oakland had gained such expansive attention. The answer came quickly. No architect expects to have the opportunity to build a cathedral. Furthermore, the engagement includes designing the interior as well as the exterior, and the work lasts for hundreds of years.

The majority of the nine-member committee selected Santiago Calatrava. He opened up a conversation about placing the cathedral at the south end of Lake Merritt on the parking lot of the Oakland Audi-

Oakland's Cathedral of Christ the Light, located on
the western shore of Lake Merritt, was dedicated by
Bishop Allen Vigneron in 2008. (John Blaustein
photo)

torium. The Oakland Museum people were singularly enthusiastic and
saw a thriving downtown center with the auditorium theater as part. Visitors to the cathedral could be enriched by the service of the museum.
Laney College offered their own encouragement. However, the Lake
Merritt development group saw otherwise.

Architect Chosen, Contract Signed

Negotiations with Santiago Calatrava moved slowly, and never reached
a settlement. Conversations thus resumed with the other choice, Craig
Hartman of Skidmore, Owings & Merrill from San Francisco. At this
time, the board of the Wayne and Gladys Valley Foundation, which had
not influenced us in any way regarding name, size, or architect, spoke
out in favor of the site at Harrison and Grand on the northwestern shore
of Lake Merritt. Negotiations were extended and difficult. John McDonnell handled the strenuous dealings for us. A contract for the site was
signed.

The steering committee clearly advocated having both a plaza and a conference center. Later came the notion of a mausoleum. From the beginning, the assumption was that the chancery office with its four buildings would move to be part of the cathedral center. This was a particularly easy sell because of the financial benefit as well as geographical convenience. The seller stipulated as part of the property sale that we establish a cafeteria to serve the local business community, a request not realized.

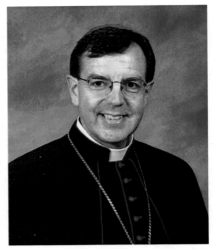

Bishop Vigneron, from Detroit, succeeded Bishop Cummins, who retired in 2003. (*The Catholic Voice*)

Fund-raising moved rather quickly, and we felt encouraged. Property values rose sluggishly early on. The decision was made to sell downtown parish sites as well as the chancery office as part of the funding. The Wayne and Gladys Valley Foundation increased their gift beyond our expectations. Generous diocesan benefactors including Howard and Geraldine Korth and Dan and Katharine Whalen early on pledged encouraging support.

Brother Mel Anderson from the Christian Brothers, who had retired after twenty-eight years as president of St. Mary's College, became available to direct the project. He was followed by John McDonnell, who had a deeply rooted interest in the cathedral as well the experience of participating in the development of Our Lady of the Angels Cathedral in Los Angeles.

By and large our clergy followed the planning favorably, gratified by the Valley Foundation contributions and appreciative of the fact that we did not intend to launch parish fund-raising campaigns. We invited large groups of parishioners for discussions on three different occasions at Holy Names University. Opinions voiced in these meetings in the beginning ranged from support to criticism. Organizing the participants' comments at the conclusion of this process helped us set a clear direction.

In February 2003, Bishop Allen Vigneron arrived as coadjutor. Very shortly thereafter, I had to inform him that plans for a cathedral had already progressed farther than he might find comfortable. We had been forced to make decisions that otherwise might have been postponed until after he arrived. After many thoughtful weeks, he asked me whether the building of a cathedral was important for Oakland. By this time, he had developed a grasp and an articulation of the place of a cathedral in a diocese and its artistic and community value. He then organized fund-raising efforts and, in the process, uncovered both talent and generosity on the part of John Cecconi and others, including Sister Mary Jean Meier of the Mercy Sisters, who was richly experienced in fund-raising for Mercy Center in East Oakland.

To the new bishop fell decisions about liturgical arrangements and art. Bishop Vigneron called on the services of Brother William Woeger, FSC, from Omaha, who had had experience renovating the cathedral in Sacramento. Following his pilgrimage to Lourdes in 2007 the bishop decided to establish a free clinic as part of the cathedral center. This well-received initiative was followed by plans to set up a legal services office for people in need.

We all owe particular thanks to Bishop Vigneron for generously shouldering the heavy responsibility of managing a complex project that was already underway. As we come to the exciting completion of this project and look forward to the dedication of the cathedral, the gratitude of the diocese to him is immeasurable.

Bishop Vigneron presided at the dedication of the landmark edifice of steel, glass, and wood, the Cathedral of Christ the Light, on September 25, 2008.

4

Ecumenism Flourishes in the Diocese

Bishop Begin Leads the Way

I BELIEVE THAT CATHOLIC PARTICIPATION in the Graduate Theological Union (GTU) would have been much diminished had anyone other than Floyd Lawrence Begin been the ordinary of the Diocese of Oakland. In the next chapter, I tell the story of his influence on the presence of Catholicism within that important higher institution of religious learning in Berkeley, but that was not his only significant ecumenical achievement.

From his arrival and installation on April 28, 1962, Bishop Begin's perspective was marked with a bold ecumenical sense. Among the honored guests at St. Francis de Sales Cathedral that day was Presbyterian minister Dr. John Bruere, a neighbor of the bishop from Euclid Avenue and St. Agnes parish in Cleveland, where Bishop Begin had been pastor. Bruere enjoyed a prominent position in the congregation, considering the standard of those days.

On another significant occasion, in September 1962, only five months after his arrival and one month before he boarded a plane for the opening of the Vatican Council on October 11, Bishop Begin, on his own initiative, invited 150 Protestant ministers and their spouses to dinner at Berkeley's Claremont Hotel. Despite the mood of apprehension and the discomfort of many, the evening was congenial, to say the least. The main speaker, Presbyterian theologian Robert McAfee Brown, from Stanford University, contributed well to the easy atmosphere. In words that echoed into the 1990s, Bishop Begin rose at the end to say, "I do not know why I invited you here. I just want to say that I love you."

Ecumenical Pace Quickens

Bishop Begin's ecumenical action was a significant step forward in Pope John XXIII's efforts to improve relations and deepen understanding among Christians—an effort that had been moving slowly. From our days in the seminary we had participated in the Octave of Prayer for Christian Unity, an ecumenical initiative started by Father Paul Wattson and his Friars of the Atonement. We were aware as well of the establishment in Geneva in 1948 of the World Council of Churches. The Vatican sent observers to Geneva with well-understood cautions, but Rome also directed Catholic bishops to prepare their priests for ecumenical participation.

In 1958 the Paulist Fathers sponsored the National Convention of Newman Clubs in Berkeley. (Newman Clubs embodied campus ministry on secular university campuses in those days.) A highlight of that meeting was a panel that included Jesuit Father Gustave Weigel, from Woodstock, Maryland, along with the Reverend Victor Gold, professor of Old Testament at the Pacific Lutheran Theological Seminary in Berkeley. The dialogue was comfortable.

Afterwards, I invited Victor Gold to Mills College, where I was then Newman chaplain. Dr. Gold opened his address to the young women by saying, "I have come a long way in ten years; I do believe that there are some Catholics who are really Christians." The young women hardly reacted. They were not sure that humor was involved.

Dr. Gold's talk was followed by the annual Mills College World Affairs Conference, in which the principal speaker was Dean James Pike, rector of the Cathedral of St. John the Divine in New York City. (Pike later became the bishop of California at San Francisco's Grace Cathedral on Nob Hill.) I remember the greeting Catholic student Mary Stuart gave me as I entered the hall at Mills: "I am glad you are here." She breathed a sigh of relief.

Dean Pike's performance was dazzling, ranging over issues including relations between church and society. Sprinkled into his talk were stories such as one about the boy in Northern Ireland who came home one day looking rather disheveled. "What happened?" his mother inquired. "The Finnegans beat me up," the boy explained. Asked why, he replied, "Because I said, 'To hell with the pope'." "But didn't you know that the Finnegans are Catholics?" "Yes," he said, "but I didn't know the pope was."

Mills College was for me an education in ecumenism. I had been chaplain at San Francisco State University (SFSU) during the four years I was an associate pastor at Mission Dolores. SFSU was much friendlier to religious groups than was the university system represented by the University of California, Berkeley. Mills College was also congenial about religion. Dinners at Mills opened with the singing of the 100th Psalm. The campus had a chapel, actually the old guard house near the ornate MacArthur Boulevard Gate, which had been refurbished as a place of worship. Most significant was the resident chaplain, George Hedley. Hedley was a puckish and respected presence on the campus. In our early days his broad openness put me off, conditioned as I was against indifferentism and false irenicism. Methodist by ordination, Hedley later became an Episcopalian (ordained by San Francisco's Bishop Pike—an event ill received by the Anglo-Catholic element at Mills). Dr. Hedley campaigned and pressed me to offer Mass on campus. In the spring of 1958, I received the necessary permission through Monsignor John Foudy, then superintendent of schools in San Francisco, to celebrate Mass outside of a Catholic Church building. The question put to me was, "Is the situation with the [Protestant] chapel at Mills the same as that at Stanford?" My instinct was to answer no.

I was hesitant to offer Mass in the Protestant chapel. To the chagrin of Dr. Hedley, I offered Mass instead in the student center. Eventually we moved to the chapel for First Friday Mass, then for holy days of obligation. By the time I left Mills after fourteen years and with the opening of a new and modern chapel, we had Mass in the chapel every Sunday. I would take the first week; Father Michael Norkett from St. Cyril's Church would take the second; the third and fourth would be served by young priests studying in Berkeley. In a school with fewer than sixty-five Catholics in the student body, Ash Wednesday was a particularly notable event: 200 to 300 young women would attend our service at the beginning of Lent.

Meanwhile, preparation for Vatican II was underway. In 1959, Pope John XXIII would establish the Secretariat for Promoting Christian Unity, under the strong leadership of Cardinal Augustine Bea, an act affirming the direction Bishop Begin was taking. Further affirmation would come with the appointment of Protestant and Orthodox observers in very respected positions during the Council sessions in St. Peter's.

1963—A Significant Year

The year 1963 held three important events for me. In January, Bishop Begin sent me to Chicago for the first meeting of a National Conference on Religion and Race. In March, it fell to me to bring to the bishop's attention the existence of the recently incorporated GTU, a consortium of religious schools in Berkeley. In October, I was in Rome as his secretary during Vatican II, where he was appointed chair of a newly formed U.S. Bishops' Ad Hoc Committee on Ecumenism.

Less than a year away from my office as dean of boys at Bishop O'Dowd High School, Bishop Begin sent me to the Chicago event, held at the old Edgewater Hotel. One evening the temperature plunged to nineteen degrees below zero. The keynote speaker was Rabbi Abraham Heschel, whose forceful, prophetic voice was unfamiliar to me. Not so was that of Martin Luther King Jr., at the close of whose presentation several hundred of us, arm in arm, sang "We Shall Overcome." Chicago's Monsignor Jack Egan, who was an important force in organizing the event, welcomed me and so began an association, aided by his closeness to Clem and Reggie Finney of our diocese, that would continue until he died.

Cardinal Albert Meyer was a dignified and approachable presence at the conference. The Chicago event was my first encounter with Monsignor George Higgins, who typically jibed and feigned annoyance that "kids were being made monsignors" these days. A long and friendly association would ensue. Prominent Episcopalian layman William Stringfellow, a lawyer and activist, was another important person at the conference who was unknown to me. I became reacquainted with Archbishop Paul Hallinan of Atlanta, an acquaintance from my early days in

Newman work—he was then the national chaplain—and destined to be
an influential and determined leader both in Vatican II and its follow-up.

Issuing from the Chicago meeting was a directive for us to return
home and start local chapters of ecumenical associations dedicated to
serve the cause of human and civil rights. Bishop Begin paid for most of
our budget. The elegant Reverend Robert Hill from Taylor Memorial
Methodist Church in Oakland was among the first to respond generously to the idea of an ecumenical association. We would carry that forward the rest of the decade. Our diocese became an avenue for
collaboration with African American ministers. Rabbi John Zucker of
San Leandro opened us to Jewish leadership.

We were not an aggressive kind of ecumenical group, but we could
speak to local leadership, to the Knowlands, who published *The Oakland
Tribune,* and to Berkeley lawyer Tom Fike and his group, who were working to promote local hiring for the Bay Area Rapid Transit project that
was underway. Some were predicting that Oakland was going to suffer
violence in those turbulent days. That never happened.

More ecumenical activity was to come. In March 1963, on March
17 to be exact, Bishop Begin first heard me speak about the proposal for
graduate theological education in Berkeley. His immediate reaction was,
"That is the work of the Holy Spirit. Dialogue at that level could not be
brought about by mere human ingenuity." It would be four years before
he could bring the matter satisfactorily to the point of decision, but the
decision he made then established with clarity the Catholic presence at
the GTU. In the meantime, he had to deal with bishops locally and nationally, and he had to weather mixed reviews from his own consultors.
He dealt steadily with his own stressful apprehensions as well as with the
leadership in Rome of the Dominicans, Jesuits, and Franciscans and the
Vatican's Congregation of Seminaries. On the local scene his collaborative efforts with GTU dean John Dillenberger, Father Kevin Wall of the
Dominicans, and Father Dick Hill of the Jesuits were exemplary.

I had other occasions to witness the Vatican Council's promotion
of ecumenical relations. Robert McAfee Brown's earlier observation
about going "from diatribe to dialogue" was very much in evidence as
the U.S. bishops established an Ad Hoc Committee on Ecumenism with
Bishop Begin as chair. The committee's agenda was not cautionary. The

thrust of the bishops, as well as of the Protestant and Orthodox observers, was generally directed toward understanding and, hopefully, reconciliation.

After Vatican II

The Council's document on ecumenism proved to be as demanding as it was rich. Whatever efforts, or perhaps fumblings, we had engaged in earlier were clarified and sanctioned, but not without some discomfort. This would have its effect on the diocese. In one case, in planning for my trip to the Council the names of Monsignor Joseph Baker from St. Louis and Monsignor William Baum from Kansas City were offered me as prospective ecumenists. I met them both soon after I arrived in Rome. Bill Baum made a great impression on me. Within a few years after Vatican II, Baum would be brought into the Washington, D.C., headquarters of the bishops to manage ecumenical affairs. He invited me with the enthusiastic support of Bishop Begin to join the dialogue with the American Baptists. We carried on for almost six years in Washington, California, and Green Lake, Wisconsin. I learned something more about prayer and song as well as about the candid uneasiness of Baptists about the rejection of infant baptism and the inheritance of nonclerical leadership.

Along with participating in that dialogue I also inherited a relationship between our St. Francis de Sales Cathedral and the First Baptist Church a block away. Monsignor Michael Lucid observed at the first gathering of the two congregations, "It has taken us 400 years to walk that one block." Rev. Boyce Van Osdel, pastor of First Baptist, preached on one occasion at our cathedral. He opened his remarks by saying, "Today is Reformation Sunday. It is the day when Protestants get together to thank God they are not Roman Catholics."

In 1967, again with the enthusiastic support of Bishop Begin, the Diocese of Oakland offered to host the third meeting of the National Ecumenical Conference in Berkeley's Claremont Hotel. (Earlier meetings had been held in Baltimore and Boston.) Bishop Begin spoke at the final banquet. He remarked to us once that he did not like to prepare his remarks, because he wanted "to speak from the heart." Other speakers might find this approach nerve-wracking, but the bishop's sensitivity that evening was joyous.

Local church leaders who celebrated the 1982 Week of Prayer for Christian Unity at St. Francis de Sales Cathedral included (left to right) Father Thomas Paris of the Greek Orthodox Church; Rev. Dr. Barbara Brown Zikmund, dean of Pacific School of Religion; Rev. J. Alfred Smith of Allen Temple Baptist Church; Bishop Cummins; and Very Rev. C. Julian Bartlett, dean of San Francisco's Grace Episcopal Cathedral. (J. Wright / *The Catholic Voice*)

The GTU, too, carried on the work and the hopes of Vatican II. Dr. Massey Shepherd, as well as President Sherman Johnson of the Church Divinity School of the Pacific, were deeply involved in the Council proceedings. So, too, was Stuart Leroy Anderson from the Pacific School of Religion (PSR), whose noted lack of enthusiasm for both the GTU and the Roman Catholic Church was mollified a bit by his attendance at the Council. At one of the frequently held ecumenical gatherings in PSR's chapel, Protestant historian John Von Rohr registered his chagrin at the order of preference in Rome. Those churches with hierarchy and sacraments were in the front of all processions. Those of his Congregational affiliation were relegated to the back. At another of these many meetings, John Dillenberger announced to the gathering that Vatican II had laid to rest the rationale for Protestantism.

We were not into interreligious dialogue in those days. The GTU attempted to establish its enrollment for interreligious presence and outreach, but the ecumenical dimension gave it cohesion and was key to its identity. From GTU's earliest moments, a Jewish center was put in place with the very capable David Winston, a happy choice, as director. Bishop Floyd Begin should also be noted for his outreach to the Jewish community. The invitation of Rabbi William Stern of Temple Sinai in Oakland to promote Vatican II teaching on Judaism nurtured a mutually satisfying relationship.

Thoraya's Spiritual Journey

I have an interreligious postscript of my own to add. In September 1965, I received a phone call from Thoraya Obaid, a Mills College exchange student from Saudi Arabia, inviting me to meet with her. I had met her briefly the spring before at a reception after the baptism of a very gifted Mills student. At First Friday Mass on campus that same week I inquired about Thoraya of Frances Chew, president of our Newman Club, where I was chaplain. "She is interested in the church," responded Frances, a San Francisco native who eventually became one of Mother Teresa's Sisters in Haiti.

With my curiosity stirred, I called Thoraya and arranged to meet her the following Sunday. My remembrances of that first afternoon remain indelible. Her interest in Christianity came from her father's sending her to a Presbyterian high school in Egypt. Her presence at Mills College followed with a government scholarship to come to the United States with a proviso that she return to her own country. Her almost aside remark placed the situation of women in her own region of the world a half-century behind the West. She had a deep appreciation for her father and his interest in the education of women. An additional aside came when I discovered she had spent a month-long Mills College practicum at Planned Parenthood in Oakland. She said the month had really tripped her interest in religion and culture. So many young people, she lamented, came in with their lives in complete disarray. Then she countered, "But the Holy Spirit lives in them, does he not!"

At another of our meetings I gave her a copy of the recently published and richly appreciated documents from Vatican II. With a boldness that I came to admire she gave me a copy of the Quran and a lengthy History of the Arabs. I was not to be left without my share of responsible dialogue. Within a week she had read the Council documents. She tossed the book on the table with an easy irreverence, and said, "Pretty good." One of her remarks stays in memory: "I thought the church was exclusive." My struggling response indicated that baptism draws us into the community of the church while at the same time laying upon us a responsibility to serve the human family. She did not indicate satisfaction with this explanation. Neither did I.

The year continued with intermittent meetings and conversation. One of the priests at home asked me what was it like to do theology with her. I remarked, it was like being held by the lapels. Her assuredness and boldness were not troubling. It was through those gifts of personality that instead of going home after Mills graduation, Thoraya enrolled in Wayne State University in Detroit in pursuit of a doctorate—multidisciplinary so long ago—in English literature and cultural anthropology. In the early 1970s I had an opportunity to visit Detroit to participate in a gathering of state Catholic conference directors. Together with her roommate, Thoraya took me to a Greek restaurant for a dinner marked by our accustomed dialogue. Afterwards, we corresponded occasionally; then I lost touch.

At breakfast in Oakland one morning in August 2001 I read an article in *The New York Times* headlined "Muslim Christian Dialogue." The person featured had the same family name as Thoraya's. Indeed, it *was* Thoraya, now a UN under-secretary general and executive director of the UN Population Fund. Her confidence and assurance had carried her far. I wrote her. Two months later she responded joyfully and lengthily, beginning with a mea culpa, mea culpafor not answering right away. Instead of returning to Saudi Arabia after her studies in Detroit, she had her government's permission to work with the UN Economic and Social Commission for Western Asia. The organization's headquarters were Iraq, but the war situation caused her to settle first in Lebanon. Later she moved to Iraq and then to Jordan. For more than thirty years she has been connected with UN offices and a variety on nongovernmental organizations. For the last three years she was based in New York. In this role her responsibility involved managing a Social Affairs Office for the Advancement of Women. She would describe this as "the passion of my professional life." Another Mills echo was her bringing into UN development projects the context of each society, taking into consideration cultural values and religious beliefs that shaped the actions of people.

She wrote that she had married and had two daughters. A major focus of the letter, however, was the post-9/11 situation and the apprehension of tensions and conflict that could arise with the Muslim community in the United States. She indicated that besides lecturing and writing she hoped to update her dissertation from Wayne State, which was entitled "The Stereotype of the Moor in English Renaissance Drama," a combined literature/sociology document, how literature reflects the perceptions and beliefs of the societies in which it is written. The same characteristics attributed to the Moor in the sixteenth century appear again in relations to the Arab/Muslim/Palestinian in the twentieth. She reported that the media had done a good job of demonizing Islam, Muslims, and Arabs in a similar fashion. Her hope and patterns were admirable. She wrote, "My message is that of reconciliation and understanding; of hearing what that OTHER has to say, and others are beginning to make the same call—but so far it is a cry in the wilderness." Near the close of her letter, the last piece of the news she shared concerned an invitation from Mills College to deliver the commencement address in May.

My schedule prevented me from attending that Saturday, but Sunday provided the opportunity to drive Thoraya to the airport in San Francisco. We had a two-and-a-half-hour cup of coffee, moving from topic to topic without any sense that a quarter century had passed since our last visit. She was interested in hearing about my responsibilities with the Asian bishops. She explained that she had done work in the Middle East, but her focus was Eastern Africa. She mentioned easily her collaboration with the archbishop of Nairobi, Rafael S. Ndingi. When I said that he had visited us in Oakland when he was the bishop of Nakuru, she said with indications of both surprise and excitement that she was working with three parishes in his diocese.

Thoraya's husband was living in Cairo at that time; the physical separation was a sacrifice for both of them. Her older daughter, a medical doctor, was a graduate of Cambridge with an office in London. Once each year she spent two months serving in South Africa. The younger daughter had just completed a six-year architectural degree in London and was looking for a job in Beirut. Her hope was to build affordable housing in Iraq. I attributed to Thoraya many roles—ambassador for Islam, citizen of the world with a large embrace for the entire human family. An Islamic scholar from the Dominican School in Berkeley reported to me that the Pontifical Council on InterreligiousDialogue many years after 1965 had urged dialogue in four areas—life, spirituality, common work, and theology—to promote understanding between Muslims and Christians. She pointed out that Thoraya and I had experienced particularly the latter two, perhaps the hardest of the four areas.

I look back with gratitude.

5

Bishop Begin and the Graduate Theological Union

Ecumenical Enterprise for Theology Studies

THIS BACK STORY ON CATHOLIC PARTICIPATION in the Graduate Theological Union (GTU) begins on St. Patrick's Day, 1963, at the chancery office of the Diocese of Oakland. About 4 o'clock in the afternoon, Bishop Floyd Begin was wandering through the offices, hands in his pockets, not in a hurry to end the day, unlike the rest of us who were not so well disposed to working on St. Patrick's Day. French Canadian by way of Cleveland, Begin had been with us as our first bishop in Oakland for less than a year. He roamed into my windowless office and sat down.

That evening I was scheduled to be at St. John's Presbyterian Church in Berkeley for an ecumenical dialogue with Reverend Dr. Keith Bridston, a cordial professor at Pacific Lutheran Theological Seminary. The *Berkeley Gazette* had an announcement about the evening with Keith Bridston on the left of the four-column article and John Cummins facing in from the right. I opened the paper for the bishop. He showed little reaction, but I knew he would be encouraging. Bridston was unfamiliar to the bishop, so I read from the *Gazette* that the professor's undergraduate degree was from Yale, his doctorate from the University of Edinburgh, and he had served in Thailand with the Lutheran World Federation. Then I continued on, "John Cummins, St. Augustine's Grammar School...." I laughed, but the bishop was hardly amused by the comparison, reacting with an admonition on the confidence I should have as a Catholic priest.

Perhaps moved by the bishop's encouragement, I took advantage of the moment to bring up what had been on my mind for two months. I started rather gingerly by telling the bishop that I had heard that the Bay Area had theology students in numbers equal to or surpassing the figures for Boston or New York. Without discussing that point, I went on to explain that the seminaries in Berkeley were organizing a graduate center for theology and were desirous of Catholic participation. Truthfully, I was not sure what his reaction might be, but his response was immediate, "That is the work of the Holy Spirit. Dialogue at that high level could not be put together merely by human ingenuity." That remark established the basic position that the bishop would hold for the years ahead.

That brief St. Patrick's Day conversation was my belated follow-up to a January weekend in Lake County. I was there representing Bishop Begin, who had received an invitation from an office of the Carnegie Foundation dealing with international affairs. On the last evening, one of the attendees, Philip Adams, a San Francisco attorney, invited me to meet over a drink. He asked me whether we, in the Diocese of Oakland, would be interested in graduate theological education in Berkeley. Adams identified himself as the chairman of the board of the corporation newly established in 1962 as the GTU. I am sure he explained both structure and goal better than I understood him.

Credits for Religious Studies

I identified the effort with some 1961 conversations about establishing a Department of Religious Studies at the University of California. I had known two of the participants in those discussions rather well. One was Larry Beyersdorf, the student body vice-president at the time; the other was David W. Louisell, Boalt Hall professor of extraordinary reputation. The topic was of interest to me because I was Catholic chaplain at Mills

College in those days, having served the same role with the Newman Club at San Francisco State University some years earlier. Through those associations I had easy and lengthy collaboration with the Paulist priests at Newman Hall in Berkeley, Father Joseph Quinn at that time and Father Kevin Lynch before him, in their outreach to students at UC–Berkeley.

Larry Beyersdorf's remembrance is explanatory. "My own recollection," he said,

> is that interest in getting Cal-Berkeley credits for classes in religion and theology began when some Jesuits from Los Gatos came to Newman Hall around 1961 and taught a semester-long class on biblical history or theology. Credit was offered through Santa Clara or some other Catholic college. Many attending were Berkeley students and wondered why they could not get course credit from the University of California.
>
> I was student body vice-president and sort of functioning as the "Catholic Center Party" in student politics at the time. It fell to me—with a little nudging from the Paulists—to put a resolution before the ASUC Ex Com [Associated Students University of California Executive Committee] asking the university to establish a Department of Religious Studies. It was debated over several meetings. I sought a legal opinion from the general counsel on the subject, and met with [President] Clark Kerr to urge his support.

Beyersdorf reported that Kerr was hesitant, and Chancellor Edward Strong was very opposed, an attitude in contrast to a remark Chancellor Roger Heyns would make to Bishop Begin a few years later, that one could attain a doctorate at Berkeley in any world religion except Christianity. "In the end," the student body leader recalled, "after some serious political arm twisting, the resolution [to establish a Department of Religious Studies] passed and got a surprising amount of media coverage."

The overall atmosphere of those days was congenial. In 1962,

Archbishop Joseph T. McGucken of San Francisco, along with a Catholic student speaker, participated in UC–Berkeley's baccalaureate graduation ceremony. Additionally, in the same year the university hosted the scholarly Franz Cardinal Koenig, archbishop of Vienna. The Austrian prelate was to become chair of the Pontifical Council for Dialogue with Non-believers. In Berkeley, after an introduction by the learned Professor Raymond Sontag of the university's History Department, the cardinal addressed a standing-room audience. Koenig was hosted also by the leadership of the GTU, a project he looked on with favor. His observation was welcome confirmation of Bishop Begin's early intuition.

But I'm getting ahead of the story. Two weeks or so after the Lake County conversation, I accepted an invitation from Philip Adams to lunch at the University Club on Nob Hill in San Francisco. As I recall, there might have been two other board members. The focus of attention, however, was on Dean John Dillenberger, from the faculty of Drew University in New Jersey, but in recent years professor of theology at San Francisco Theological Seminary in San Anselmo, California. His explanation was serious, rather complicated, and at times lightsome. He spoke of respecting the autonomy of the theological schools in Berkeley and San Anselmo but creating, through what he called "the pooling of our poverty," an institution that would provide superior graduate education. Faculty would come from the seminaries with the expectation that they would have sufficient academic credentials to be peers of the university faculty.

My initial response was, "You are not talking about a religious studies department at the university. You are proposing an international theological center." I would describe his reply as "a laconic yes." I returned home that day with the understanding that the proposed GTU was far beyond the 1961 conversations about religious studies. Here the intention was to involve Catholic institutions at the foundational level. That proposition would make Bishop Begin a significant player.

I needed time for reflection. The GTU represented a bold initiative and a radically different pattern of training from our traditional seminaries, removed from the hubbub of urban life and confined in an atmosphere of recollection as formation to serve in ministry. I knew, however, that the Dominicans at St. Albert's had been situated within the City of Oakland since 1932. Their taking advantage of graduate studies in Berkeley at GTU would be no different from their priests attending the University of California. I thought of the experience of classmates of mine who had studied in Rome, living immersed in the heart of that city. I remembered, too, a comment by a pastor with whom my brother, the superintendent of schools in San Francisco, lived. Monsignor Thomas Millet, an urbane and insightful observer of the ecclesiastical scene, remarked that we who studied at St. Patrick's Seminary in Menlo Park, perhaps a mile from Stanford University, could have profited had we been able to take advantage of that prestigious institution's offerings.

For me personally the positive experience I had had taking graduate courses for a degree at UC–Berkeley in the summers and evenings when I was on the faculty of Bishop O'Dowd High School was instructive. I felt very respected in those days when we wore our Roman collars as normal attire. Friendships I made with some admired faculty proved a particular blessing, particularly those with professors David Louisell and Raymond Sontag, whose wise counsel both to me and to the bishop would prove invaluable as we moved ahead.

In a short time I was convinced that Catholic participation would be a profitable ecumenical investment, but I also knew that traditional forms of priestly preparation might be hard to set aside. My worry proved groundless. Our bishop, as it turned out, moved more by religious instinct than intellectual argument, needed no convincing. Recognized by his brother bishops during the second session of the Vatican Council in 1963, Begin had been appointed chair of the U.S. bishops' newly formed Ad Hoc Committee on Ecumenical Affairs.

The Bishop and the Dean

Dean John Dillenberger early in the spring of 1963 met with Bishop Begin. The meeting would mark the beginning of a confident and fruitful relationship. The bishop would remark in a letter to Archbishop Joseph McGucken of San Francisco, "We have in Dean Dillenberger a dependable man." The dean would report to me an observation of Bishop Begin's that if John Dillenberger were to remain in Berkeley forever, anxiety about the project would greatly diminish.

The bishop accepted Dean Dillenberger's invitation to be part of the board of trustees of the GTU. The bishop had me attend those meetings in his stead. I would appear in the minutes variously—sometimes as "for the bishop," once reported as "guest," on another occasion with the initials "SJ." I was faithful in giving the bishop written reports.

The bishop found in that first year that some Catholic priests were already on the GTU faculty. Sulpician Father Frank Norris, of St. Patrick's Seminary, was teaching there, as well as Jesuit Father Daniel O'Hanlon. The bishop did not question their involvement, nor that of Jesuit Father Jack Boyle, who was teaching at Cal Extension.

Dominican Father Kevin Wall, vice-regen of St. Albert's, was an easy associate of the bishop; so too was the position of St. Albert's. The presumption in those early days was that the GTU would involve graduate, not undergraduate, work; therefore, without question priests would be welcome to attend the new institution. On June 10, 1964, a letter from Philip Adams and John Dillenberger invited Kevin Wall to "make application as a participating institution in the GTU." They added: "It would change the status, of course," indicating an assumed responsibility for direction, including faculty roles and financial obligation.

Jesuit Father Harry Corcoran was easy with communications. Somewhat to the bishop's surprise, Dean Corcoran explained that the Alma College faculty had unanimously supported the move from the Los Gatos hills to Berkeley. Alma had already commissioned the Arthur D. Little Corporation to develop a plan, one that is remembered now as professional and ambitious. The Jesuits were intent on moving their entire theologate, not just its graduate section. Jesuit Father Albert Zabala, from the University of San Francisco, raised a strong objection, arguing to the bishop among others that Alma College had to remain part of a Jesuit university; otherwise, he contended, the Jesuits would be diminishing their own institutions. He was not alone in this opinion. Another Jesuit, Father Rocco Caporale, a priest who was a member of the Italian Province who taught alternate semesters in the Department of Sociology at UC–Berkeley, agreed with Zabala. He felt that the very large university in Berkeley would treat a small institution like Alma as a kind of satellite and would take advantage of the offering without mutual benefit. The Jesuit provincial at the time, the gentlemanly Father John F.X. Connolly, and his cabinet showed no enthusiasm for a move to Berkeley.

But the Jesuit die had been cast, pending, of course, Begin's permission.

Decision Time

In August 1964, Bishop Begin was joined on the GTU board of trustees by two Dominicans—Fathers Paul Starrs and Kevin Wall—and two Jesuits—Fathers Harry Corcoran and John Huesman. Professor David Louisell of UC–Berkeley's Boalt Hall was also appointed to the board. As I've already remarked, Louisell was a man of extraordinary stature, one in whom the bishop's confidence was well placed.

Throughout 1964 Bishop Begin kept in touch with all parties, but he paid particular attention to the Dominicans, even attending the St. Albert's graduation ceremony in June. He remained on the GTU board of trustees, while apologizing for the limits on his time, particularly due to his participation in the Vatican Council each fall.

In the late summer, following his conversations with Bishop Begin, Father Wall shared with the bishop a report the Dominican provincial had sent to the master general. In it Father Wall referred to the June 5 graduation ceremony—the first of its kind—"to honor our accreditation by the Western Association of Schools and Colleges" (WASC). The WASC recognition meant that faculty of St. Albert's and the GTU would now be peers.

Describing the historic occasion, Dominican Father Antoninus Wall, Father Kevin's younger brother, described the establishment of the Berkeley Priory and the developing relationship between the GTU and what was now being called the Dominican School of Philosophy and Theology. Father Wall's chronology indicated that Father Agius, as provincial, approved joining the GTU immediately after the request to join came from the leadership of St. Albert's. "Our next concern," Father Antoninus wrote,

> focused on Bishop Begin. John Cummins was Begin's chancellor and, being a Berkeley native with a degree from UC–B, [Cummins] was strongly in support of Catholic participation in the Union. Since St. Albert's College had just received its accreditation from WASC, Kevin took advantage of this to hold the first-ever formal graduation at St. Albert's. He invited Dillenberger to offer the graduation talk, and Bishop

Begin was to hand out the diplomas. The strategy was to bring Dillenberger and Begin together in a pleasant setting and present the bishop with our proposal to join the union. John gave a fine talk. We then invited Begin to close the event with some words of his own. Begin went on and on about John [Dillenberger] and this great development of the GTU. When the ceremony was over, Begin was in an enthusiastic mode and said to Agius and Kevin, "The Catholic Church has to become part of the GTU." When Father Agius and Kevin told him that this was their intention, they had Begin's immediate approval. John Cummins still speaks of the conversations that went on between Bishop Begin and Kevin as exemplifying the ideal relations that should exist between bishop and theologian.

Father Kevin Wall reported to Anicetus Fernandez, OP, master general of the Dominicans,

> The meeting of Father Provincial with Bishop Begin took place on the morning of Friday, June 12. His Excellency stated that he wished St. Albert's College to enter the Graduate Theological Union for the good of the Church as well as the Order. Father Agius conveyed this information to the provincial council meeting on the afternoon of the same day, and the council voted its approval.... On June 25, 1964, the board [of the GTU] met and accepted the application thereby making St. Albert's College a member. By a subsequent action of the same board, I was made a trustee in virtue of my position as acting head of the college. Bishop Begin also accepted an invitation and became a trustee of the board.

Father Wall's report to the master general on September 4 received a response from Dominican headquarters in Rome:

> I appreciate, too, the approval and encouragement offered by His Excellency Bishop Begin and shall no doubt have an

opportunity of expressing this to him personally during the forthcoming session of the Vatican Council.

A handwritten note from Bishop Begin to me at that time reflected his pleasure: "This is moving fast, and I'm interested. Keep it moving. Father Agius is enthusiastic about it, too."

On July 27, 1964, Bishop Begin wrote to Philip Adams, chair of the GTU board, in response to an invitation to attend a press conference on July 30. "Sorry," he wrote, "but I have to turn down your invitation to the press conference.... But I am sure Father Wall will provide adequate representation." He went on,

> It seems clear also to me now, particularly in the face of my being away [at the Vatican Council] during the fall again, that my participation in the Graduate Theological Union will be at best occasional. I shall, therefore, direct Father Wall to represent the diocese in this work and to keep me informed of the progress of the union. I am very interested in this project. I am also very happy to have a role in its development and to share with you and others the promise it holds.

In December of that year, Bishop Begin had to send his regrets in reply to another invitation, this time to a meeting of the executive committee of the GTU board of trustees at the Faculty Club in Berkeley. The bishop had me write to Philip Adams to explain that he would be out of town on January 6, 1965, the date set for the meeting. I wrote,

> Apparently, there is no possibility of change from the previous engagement. [The bishop] was sincerely disappointed, as I understand this has happened twice before. Perhaps he may be a little concerned by this time that his absence will be interpreted in less than a favorable light.

On August 11, 1964, Father Wall wrote to Bishop Begin,

> I am most grateful for the support which you have given the

college in this important venture.... Also I will be most happy to work with the chancellor on the preparation of the statement for the Secretariat for Promoting Christian Unity and the Congregation of Seminaries and Universities. The report which I have written for the master general of the order might perhaps serve as a basis for this.... Again, may I express my gratitude for your kindness toward the college and the Order. We were all deeply pleased with your remarks at the graduation ceremony.

Committee of Bishops—Final Decision

A significant moment in the thought and decision-making of Bishop Floyd Begin in relation to the GTU occurred on February 24, 1967. In December 1966, at the direction of the Congregation of Seminaries and Universities in Rome, as well as the urging of the bishop himself, the San Francisco provincial bishops had established a committee consisting of Archbishop McGucken (San Francisco) and Bishop Leo T. Maher (Santa Rosa), under the leadership of Bishop Begin. The group gathered at Begin's home in Piedmont at four o'clock in the afternoon. Bishop Begin opened the discussion with words that echoed from four years previously, "Obviously, this is the work of the Holy Spirit."

The discussion lasted less than an hour. The presumptions were that the GTU would continue as an institution, that Catholic students would be in attendance, as they were at that moment, and that the bishop could not therefore stand aloof from what would be deemed advisable in relation to Catholic participation. The decision was to establish a theological commission from the bishops of the San Francisco province of bishops "so that precise harmony can be established between the demands of ecclesiastical authority and academic freedom in the area of theological learning." The summary of the meeting indicated that the conclusions had reference only to the graduate program in Berkeley. Whatever any other religious community might do in establishing an undergraduate presence would be the concern of the particular community and the local ordinary.

The brevity of the meeting was not an indication of a casual approach. The previous year (1966) showed signs of Bishop Begin's great investments in reflection and consultation, as is evident in his exchange of letters with Dean John Dillenberger. On March 8, the dean wrote in a lengthy letter,

> Concern with the Jesuits may appear central, but only because of their location. We are quietly encouraging cooperation across the Catholic spectrum.... Obviously the formation of priests must have its own integrity and encouragement. An ecumenical thrust which would violate rather than encourage this would be wrong.

He added, incidentally, that he saw "also a new Catholic opportunity in our culture, from the local community to the academic scene."

The bishop responded with a mix of caution and openness. His approach, he noted, "cannot be haphazard." He went on, "I am totally, completely and explicitly responsible for what is taught under Catholic auspices." In that regard, he continued,

> I believe too that I should set up a diocesan committee of priests, brothers and sisters to interest themselves and give direction to our participation. I need to be intelligently represented, and in depth, if we are to contribute anything.

But the rest of the letter offered encouragement. "I am happy," the bishop wrote,

> to assure you of my cooperation...and eventually to enlist the services of Catholic priests and teachers of national and international reputation.... I would not like to see the faculty limited to the local talent of the Dominicans and Jesuits.... I would hope in the near future to prepare a letter to the Holy See, the Congregation of Seminaries and Universities, to obtain their approval of what we are doing and to obtain their help if possible in the assignment of top-level theologians to be available for our program.

The bishop's use of the pronoun "our" is, I believe, significant.

No fresh thoughts were evident in March 1966. Possibly as early as 1963 the bishop had had the sympathetic ear of Monsignor Walter J. Tappe, vicar general of the Santa Rosa Diocese and former editor of the San Francisco archdiocesan newspaper. Early on, Monsignor Tappe raised issues for investigation, such as the autonomy of the seminary, demands from the congregation in Rome concerned with curriculum, hiring of teachers, and the program of priestly formation. He questioned the relationship of the seminaries to the University of California and the university community, particularly their relationship to the Paulist Holy Spirit parish and the participation in what he called "the intellectual apostolate." He, too, brought up the need of a theological commission to oversee "theological orthodoxy."

In this context Bishop Begin invited Dean Dillenberger to address the April 1966 meeting of the diocesan consultors, a canonically established group of advisers to the bishop, an invitation that was readily and cheerfully accepted. The questions that Dean Dillenberger would address were,

> What sort of participation should we engage in with the GTU [and] what should be proper for St. Patrick's Seminary, St. Albert's and for Alma College. The inquiry about the last of these has centered on the possibility of their moving their institution or a house of studies to Berkeley. Also, what provisions should be made for bringing Catholic scholars of international renown here.

Some in the Diocese of Oakland might remember names such as Monsignors Rohan, Wagner, and Breen. From this conservative-leaning group came a unanimous and favorable attitude toward graduate theological education in Berkeley. The bishop was assuredly encouraged, so much so that he agreed to a proposed meeting that the Berkeley institutions wished to have on May 6, 1966, at St. Albert the Great Priory.

Attendees at this meeting no doubt constituted the broadest and highest level of Bay Area Catholics brought together at one time to discuss the GTU. They included the twelve diocesan consultors and four provincials, namely, John F.X. Connolly, SJ; Hubert Ward, OP; Terence

Cronin, OFM; and William J. Fitzgerald, CSSR. The institutions were represented by Kevin Wall, OP, and Paul Starrs, OP, from St. Albert's; Joseph Farraher, SJ, rector, and Harry Corcoran, SJ, dean, from Alma College; Paul Purta, SS, rector, and William Wood, librarian, from St. Patrick's Seminary. Also attending were Monsignor Pearse P. Donovan, superintendent of schools in the diocese, and Herman Hauck, SJ, director of education for the California province of the Jesuits. Charles Dullea, SJ, president, and Albert Zabala, SJ, chair of theology at the University of San Francisco participated in the meeting, as did Sister Ambrose Devereux, SNJM, from Holy Names College, and Brother T. Michael Quinn, F.S.C., from St. Mary's College in Moraga. From UC–Berkeley came professors David Louisell and Arthur Sherry, along with Father John Ritzius, CSP, pastor at Holy Spirit Newman Hall. Bishop Begin expressed some disappointment that the Archdiocese of San Francisco sent no representative.

The meeting was a panorama of information and diversity. Father Paul Starrs, OP, spoke of "a similar operation under way in Chicago, but Cardinal [John Patrick] Cody is not prepared for a commitment as yet." By way of softening a difficult question he remarked that the primary responsibility "addressed itself to graduate programs. There is, however, a voluntary undergraduate education on a cooperative basis chiefly among the Protestants." Both Paul Starrs and Kevin Wall were on the committee for undergraduate cooperation, but "there has been no attempt," they said, "to pressure Catholics on the undergraduate level. The areas of Catholic–Protestant cooperation and sharing are extremely slight, although Hebrew or something of this nature would be possible." Paul Starrs, almost as an aside, mentioned the relation of the GTU to the university. "The two institutions move together," he noted, "but on an unofficial basis. It is premature to say that the GTU works with the University of California."

Professor David Louisell picked up on that aspect of the conversation. "As Catholic professors," he said, "they are interested in a platform for a hearing of theological considerations in modern life, although there is the corresponding hunger on the part of students for such information." He went on to praise the work of the Newman Center and saw the GTU as an assist to Newman. He envisioned increased university cooperation with GTU and the development of a more organic relationship between the two. While he saw no legal problems in the collaboration between the university and the GTU, he acknowledged the practical problem of overcoming secular prejudices.

Father Harry Corcoran, SJ, with a clearly pent-up enthusiasm, announced that the Jesuit superiors in Rome as of the first of the year in 1966 had approved full membership of Alma College in the GTU. Catholic undergraduate programs were an area of concern that Dean Dillenberger understood clearly. Speaking on behalf of the Jesuits, Father Corcoran explained that Berkeley offered a unique opportunity for formation in an ecumenical atmosphere, but—in accordance with the softening by the Dominican presentations—Protestant faculty would not be involved in the direct formation of Catholic seminarians. In this connection, a quote from a letter from Father Joseph Farraher to Bishop Begin is appropriate: "Protestant professors are men of conscience and honor; they would have the same scruple about disturbing a student's faith that we would have."

Father Paul Purta, SS, president of St. Patrick's in Menlo Park, raised three issues for consideration, namely, bibliography, professional training, and finances. He indicated that St. Patrick's was already involved in the first of these, but that its preoccupation was for good pastors. He quoted Keith Bridston of Pacific Lutheran Theological Seminary, who had said that only 30 percent of GTU students were interested in pastoral ministry. Father Purta saw the presence of the Jesuits and Dominicans as viable for the moment. Later perhaps, Berkeley might have a minor Gregorian University patterned for exceptional students, on a par with Rome's prestigious educational institution.

Monsignor John Connolly, Bishop Begin's vicar general, transitioned to another issue, questioning whether with so few doctoral students the expense would be justified. He also wondered what Rome would say about this development. Herman Hauck, SJ, raised four points for discussion. First, GTU was basically the dialogue of scholars. Second, he spoke of the need to condition seminarians for openness in dialogue. He added the difficulty of staffing Jesuit institutions as well as the value of having Alma in a major Catholic university on the West Coast, implicitly the University of San Francisco (USF). Albert Zabala agreed completely. He said that USF's master's program would provide faculty for the Catholic colleges in the area. Noting that Baptist scholar James McClendon had already been hired, Father Zabala added, "There is opportunity for dialogue on the ecumenical level within the campus itself."

Bishop Begin was not long in putting together his notes on the day. He thought it had already been decided that the church was to be "totally and completely involved," but he felt he could not act on this alone and a theological commission would be needed to keep Catholic participation identifiable. The Congregation of Seminaries, the Secretariat for Promoting Christian Unity in Rome, and the U.S. Catholic Conference of Bishops would all need to be involved. The bishop saw that he needed help from the religious communities because "there is not enough talent in the diocese." He remembered the comments of Father Anicetus Fernandez, OP, that the GTU could be "a showplace for theology" and "a compliment to the Bay Area." He saw the talent that could be developed for Sister Ambrose of Holy Names College and the help that the GTU would be to St. Mary's College and to Newman Hall. "Concerning the undergraduate program, however," he said, "I am still hesitant. Physical contact is not necessary and may be damaging to vocations." He disagreed with Father Paul Purta's limited participation, calling it "a halfway with an elite." As to St. Patrick's Seminary, his notes read: "Physically there is no room for them in Berkeley and not enough money to seriously consider the change." Furthermore, "The Dominicans have something to gain by keeping St. Albert's open in its present location." Despite questions raised by his own people and in the face of USF's hesitation, Bishop Begin concluded on a high note, "Since there is agreement on the present participation and on the sharing of responsibility, I shall prepare a letter for the Congregation of Seminaries and Universities."

Follow-up letters included Jesuit Father John F.X. Connolly's comment that participation in the GTU was "highly desirable with the presence of the bishop on the board of trustees, with the Dominicans, Jesuits, and Sulpicians." Sister Ambrose of Holy Names College wrote encouragingly, "Your Excellency, forgive me if I seem somewhat personal, but I am in admiration of your wisdom and your courage in the

Jesuit Fathers Richard Hill, right, and Michael Buckley flank Very Rev. Pedro Arrupe, leader of the Jesuit Order, on his tour of the Graduate Theological Union and the Jesuit School of Theology in Berkeley. Arrupe looked favorably on Jesuit participation in the GTU's ecumenical consortium of theology schools. (JSTB Archive photo)

stand you have taken. It seems so *right* and cannot but be blessed by Almighty God."

Encouragement from Rome

Discovering a five-page letter some years ago in a file of Bishop Begin's correspondence and conversations with Roman authorities, I was impressed by the bishop's concise and accurate understanding of the GTU. In the same file, however, I found an undated draft with my secretary's initials at the bottom. I recalled that this project began in 1964 at the bishop's direction (and with the collaboration of Father Kevin Wall), but the letter to Rome is dated July 13, 1966. With no explanation given for the time gap, the letter states, "There is developing in this diocese a project that I think is of great importance."

Two weeks earlier, on July 1, Bishop Begin had edited my earlier draft of the letter; he made ten corrections or additions. One addition was especially significant. The bishop saw opportunities for laity to acquire theological degrees. He also felt that a GTU degree would give a priest higher standing over a degree from a Catholic institution and make him acceptable in any school. Bishop Begin drew on the encouragement he sensed from the Vatican Council that we ought to engage in dialogue with secular institutions. The bishop indicated that after Roger Heyns, chancellor at UC–Berkeley, had told him, "Departments of theology at state and secular universities were inevitable." Lastly, the bishop directed that his closing paragraph "should be a little more direct." He wrote:

> We not only seek the blessing of this Congregation; we seek its approval of our action and its permission to continue this cooperation with the GTU. Furthermore, we ask for any directives or suggestions they might make to perfect the program.

The master general of the Dominicans had visited Berkeley early on and approved the GTU proposal. In the spring of 1965, Dean John Dillenberger visited Europe and Rome in particular. At the GTU trustees meeting on May 12, he reported on his ten appointments overseas. The meeting minutes reported on one appointment that was clearly significant:

> Talking with Cardinal Bea privately, Dr. Dillenberger said that Cardinal Bea told him that the Church in the United States was in such a position that it should involve itself more with the secular and state institutions in the country.

In April 1966, Jesuit Father General Pedro Arrupe visited Berkeley. He respectfully reserved comments on his appraisal of the GTU until he received word from Bishop Begin. A September letter Father Arrupe had written to the California provincial, Father John F.X. Connolly, shared with the bishop, spoke of Bishop Begin's willingness to approve the establishment of a Jesuit house in the Berkeley area for graduate students. His opposition to moving all of Alma College was not "irrevocable." Father Arrupe accepted that position. He wrote,

The intense interest which the faculty and theologians of

Alma have manifested in the relocation of the theologate, the importance of this house of studies in the formation of our men, and the planning and studies already devoted to the question unite in meriting a final decision of singular prudence.

Cardinal Gabriel-Marie Garrone, prefect of the Congregation of Seminaries and Universities, was also seeking specifics from Bishop Begin. The cardinal wrote to the bishop while on a visit to San Francisco, expressing his regret about not meeting him personally. (Bishop Begin was then at a meeting of the National Conference of Catholic Bishops [NCCB] in Washington, D.C.). The cardinal indicated that the Congregation had not passed the request of the Jesuits at Alma to move their theologate to Berkeley, but it was not yet in a position to say yes or no to it. The lack of a direct answer was not to be interpreted as opposition because the Congregation was not opposed "in principle." The cardinal listed the advantages of the proposed move, one of them being "cultural offerings of unusual high quality." Noting "the great problems of sites, locations and operating expenses," the cardinal said he was leaving the decision to the bishops of the province.

In 1967, Monsignor Charles Moeller, a distinguished Belgian theologian and member of the Congregation of the Doctrine of the Faith, came to Berkeley through the courtesy of Bishop Begin. Monsignor Moeller, professor of literature from Louvain and a leading figure among the theologians at the Vatican Council, offered the bishop encouraging observations about the GTU project.

The bishops of the province decided in December 1966 to appoint Archbishop Joseph McGucken and Bishop Leo Maher to a committee to aid Bishop Begin. I was living in the bishop's house at that time, while awaiting an appointment for residence in a local parish. On February 2, 1967, the bishop asked me to make time that evening for a discussion in preparation for the February 24 meeting. We began in his room at 7:20 P.M.—he at his desk and I on the other side—and finished at ten minutes to 11. We covered as many questions as we could in that time. At breakfast the next morning, the bishop confessed that he had not slept well. The enormity of this enterprise was clearly weighing on him.

The February 24th meeting of the three bishops took place at Bishop Begin's home. It remains clear in my memory. Bishop Begin sat behind his desk, with Archbishop McGucken and Bishop Maher seated facing him. I was on the side looking in the same direction as Bishop Begin. I recall his first comment about the Holy Spirit as a strong Pentecostal wind blowing through the room. The questions and concerns the bishops raised were expected. Bishop Begin was ready with his answers concerning the matter of formation, the problem of Protestant professors of theology and Scripture teaching Catholic seminarians, the assurance of sound ecumenical relations, the hazards of Berkeley in those days, the possible participation of seminarians in demonstrations or protests on political issues, this last a concern that Bishop Begin, San Francisco's Bishop William McDonald (as president of the Catholic University in America), and Jesuit Father Joseph Farraher had all dealt with years before.

The discussion proceeded without argument; it was cordial, agreeable, and decisive. As we picked up some refreshments before dinner, I told Archbishop McGucken that I admired his calmness in the face of his archdiocese losing an important theological faculty. With no hint of mere resignation or gradual acceptance, he stated, "One cannot withstand the tides of history." I excused myself to go downstairs to a remote telephone to call and tell Dean Dillenberger that the meeting went well.

The Franciscans made an appointment with the bishop in the spring, asking to move their school of theology from Santa Barbara to Berkeley as a member institution of the GTU. The bishop sent a letter of permission, while neglecting to furnish a similar document of approval for the Jesuit move, as an inquiry from Father Dick Hill, SJ, noted. I remember bringing up the topic with the bishop in the morning, while he was preparing for a day at St. Patrick's Seminary with his seminarians. He remarked to me that the Jesuits could stand to be patient for a few more days. He was open to some conversation. I gave him the letter I had prepared; he signed it immediately. Back in my office, I looked at the brief four-line letter approving Alma College's move to Berkeley.

This episode made me wonder about the impatience of our young people over how long it takes us to get something done. But my overriding appreciation was for the care, the direction, and the responsibility that the bishop, the religious superiors, the theological faculties, and Cardinal Garrone had shown in the previous years. They came to the GTU invitation with no existing model to draw on but in an atmosphere in which an ecumenical opportunity beckoned and the energies released by the Second Vatican Council were making their contrasting impacts felt.

After the permissions were given, the bishop took a step that I regard as commendable. He wrote to the religious superiors inquiring of their formation plans in this new environment. The plans were well prepared for him, but I thought his expression of solicitude was deserving of a pastoral leader.

Dinner with the Dominicans

One other event deserves to be recorded. The Christmas dinner for the Catholic participants in the GTU occurred at the Dominican House in 1968. I accompanied the bishop. On the way, we went to St. Albert the Great Priory for a tonsure ceremony for a young Dominican. We talked during our ride to Berkeley, but the bishop that evening was, to say the least, out of sorts. Arriving early for the dinner, I encouraged him to walk around the block to see the new house that the Franciscans had acquired. The walk did nothing to change his mood. He confessed that the GTU project had been an unusually heavy burden. Moreover, he had never received a reply to a letter he had written to Archbishop McGucken telling him about the evening's event.

As we returned to the brick house, a Mercedes drove up with Archbishop McGucken and his chancellor chauffeur Monsignor Cornelius Burns. The bishop's mood changed dramatically. He and the archbishop almost bounded up the steps and then sat together in an animated discussion in an alcove area that had been set up for private conversations. Dean Dillenberger came in with his wife, Jane, a capable and amiable art historian of whom Monsignor John Tracy Ellis spoke admiringly as "Lady Jane Dillenberger" and of whom Bishop Begin was fond. She moved into the privacy of the alcove. By the time dinner was called, she had a place at the main table.

The evening's program was brief. Dominican Father Kevin Wall, the host, had risen from a sick bed and the flush of his face reflected the poor state of his health. He invited Dean Dillenberger to speak. The dean's words were brief but eloquent, timely, and pointed: "There is the odd here, there is the bizarre here, that is not us." Next introduced was Bishop Begin, but he told Father Kevin Wall to introduce the archbishop first. With slightly veiled reluctance, Father Wall acceded. Archbishop McGucken began speaking, even as he rose from his chair, of the Holy Spirit leading the church, inspiring theological development, and bringing about change "at his own pace." His statement was good and positive.

Bishop Begin arose next. I was sitting in the corner of the room, with Bernie Loomer from the Baptist Seminary, and I recall looking down at the table, not knowing what mood the bishop was going to reveal in his unscripted comments. The bishop stood up and rocked his chair forward, as he was accustomed to doing, with his hands rolling on top of the wicker back. "I am here as a Roman Catholic," he declared. "You are here as Presbyterian, and you, as Episcopalian. Unless each of us comes immersed deeply in his own tradition, we are not going to serve this institution." Later in his remarks he said, "We are not doing just the will of Christ, we are dealing with the prophecy of Christ that they shall be one." In his conclusion, he spoke forthrightly: "I do not suspect the goodwill of anybody in this room. I trust that that attitude will be reciprocated to me."

On our drive home that evening I was effusive in my praise. "That is just what a bishop should do," I said. "The diocese is not taking any risk. The risk is taken by the religious communities. You thoroughly encouraged them tonight." I also added, "If this were the Super Bowl, they would have carried you out on their shoulders."

When we arrived back at the bishop's residence in Piedmont, he was obviously gratified. He invited me in to continue our conversation. When it was time to go home, I remember him saying, "You have been with this from the beginning; now go all the way." I felt that these words could more fittingly be said of him and his contribution to the development of the Catholic presence in the Graduate Theological Union.

6

The Hopes of the
Graduate Theological Union

"This Is the Work of the Holy Spirit"

T HE INVITATION TO RECALL SOME OF THE EARLY DAYS of the Graduate Theological Union [GTU] made me quickly realize we celebrate this institution's golden jubilee in 2012. John XXIII, who was pope during the founding years of the GTU, once declared that an anniversary is not just an opportunity, but an obligation. One trouble with life, he indicated, is the simple fact that it is "daily." As we move along, we pick up dust off the roads and slip perhaps into routine. Anniversaries provide us opportunity to burnish again the treasures in our lives. I therefore sense some license to anticipate the fifty years' remembrance, and I beg your indulgence as I view those years from the perspective of an aide to a key player in the Catholic Church's involvement in this grand enterprise.

The incorporation of the six schools in Berkeley and San Anselmo

---

An address Bishop John Cummins delivered at the Graduate Theological Union, Fall Convocation, September 17, 2008.

for doctoral programs and for library resources took place in 1962. My personal perspective enters here, because in 1962 the same Pope John XXIII gave East Bay Catholics the first bishop of the newly created Diocese of Oakland. The Holy Father appointed Floyd Lawrence Begin, a native of Cleveland. Within a year of his arrival, he reacted to the prospect of graduate theology in Berkeley as, "That is the work of the Holy Spirit. Dialogue at such a high level could not have been produced by mere human ingenuity."

We must, I believe, start by paying tribute to that era from whose soil grew the Graduate Theological Union. A prospectus from this institution in the early years quoted Karl Barth, "At the start of this century there was no question of my reading a book by a contemporary Catholic." Later, in the 1970s, Professor Martin Marty in his comprehensive work on the history of Protestantism would state, "Not until mid-century was it possible for most of Protestantism to take a second look at the means for overcoming problems of disunity." His scope was broad, but he had particular reference to the creation in 1948 of the World Council of Churches.

The mid-century saw a valuable heritage coming from a confluence of favorable events: the 1910 Edinburgh Missionary Conference, decrying competition in the spreading of the gospel; the 1925 Stockholm meeting of Life and Work, seeking to bring Christian principles into social life; and the 1927 meeting in Lausanne of Faith and Order, initiating doctrinal conversations. The subsequent creation of the World Council of Churches received support from most Protestant communities as well as from the Anglican and Orthodox churches, but did not resonate so well with evangelicals or third world churches.

The Vatican's Holy Office reacted with traditional hesitancy over concerns for orthodoxy and indifferentism, but urged bishops to promote ecumenism and to appoint suitable priests for study and participation in the movement. In 1960, Pope John XXIII established a Vatican Secretariat for Promoting Christian Unity and appointed Augustine Bea, a venerable German Jesuit and biblical scholar, who shared the pope's own heart for the unity of Christians.

By 1962, I think it is safe to say that all of us had both understanding and experience of ecumenism, much of it promoted by the popular

January Week of Prayer for Christian Unity. During those years, I was chaplain at Mills College in Oakland, and I invited Dr. Victor Gold of the Pacific Lutheran Theological Seminary to speak to a Mills gathering. He opened by saying, "I have come a long way in ten years. I do believe that there are Roman Catholics who are Christians."

Beginnings in 1959

Returning to GTU's history, 1959 was reported as

> the beginnings of discussions among several San Francisco Bay Area schools, leading to an exchange of scholars and sharing of library resources. By 1962, the experiences had proved so promising that a common doctoral program was agreed upon and incorporated under the laws of the state of California as the Graduate Theological Union.

Also in 1962, the Second Vatican Council opened in Rome. Pope John XXIII, who asked the church to observe "the signs of the times" as indicators of change, invited sixty observers from Protestant, Anglican, and Orthodox communities. Four of these came from Berkeley: the amiable and erudite Dr. Massey Shepherd, professor of liturgics at the Church Divinity School of the Pacific; Dr. Sherman Johnson, president of that institution; Dr. Stuart Leroy Anderson, president of the Pacific School of Religion; and historian John Von Rohr. Another distinguished Bay Area theologian and renowned ecumenist, Dr. Robert McAfee Brown, professor of religious studies at Stanford University, represented the World Alliance of Presbyterian and Reformed Churches at Vatican II. During Council sessions in St. Peter's Basilica, they occupied a prominent position close to the four presiders' table and privy to papers, discussion, and conversations. That Council in its third session produced a document on ecumenism with Protestant, Anglican, and Orthodox participation, declaring with echoes of our own new bishop, "There increases from day to day a movement fostered by the grace of the Holy Spirit."

In such an atmosphere two personalities came together in the spring of 1963: John Dillenberger, dean of the Graduate Theological Union, and Floyd Begin, bishop of Oakland. Dr. Dillenberger with his

Dominican Kevin P. Wall, left, prior of the Dominican Institute in Berkeley, receives congratulations from GTU Dean John Dillenberger and Bishop Begin for the Dominican School of Philosophy and Theology being the first Catholic school to officially join the GTU. (Dominican Archive photo)

gifts of imagination, diplomacy, and clarity was congenial to the bishop. With vision and personality, the dean explained persuasively that the older isolation of seminaries was neither defensible nor desirable. A freestanding seminary could not gather adequate library resources by itself. Scholarly areas of collaboration were immediately possible. The flexibility and adaptability that the dean presented to the bishop were gracious in considering the role of St. Albert's, which was the Dominican school, Alma College of the Jesuits, St. Patrick's Seminary of the San Francisco Archdiocese, and mentioning also a planned center for Judaic studies and prospective Orthodox and Buddhist centers. "All of these institutions," Dillenberger explained, "cannot be related in equal proportions or in one pattern." With regard to maintaining identity, the dean was clear, stating, "An ecumenical thrust that would violate rather than encourage would be wrong."

The bishop found Dillenberger reassuring. He spoke of him to the archbishop of San Francisco as "a dependable man." He noted to another, the dean's integrity. The bishop accepted an invitation to be on the board of trustees. Within a year, he was encouraging the Dominicans at St. Albert's "to enter for the good of the Church as well as for the Order."

A Providential Appointment

I have to say an important word about Bishop Begin with regard to this institution. His appointment was providential. Why? Because he was distinguished from other California bishops at the time with his developed devotion to ecumenism. At the 1962 investiture of Bishop Begin in Oakland, for example, an uncommon sight for many of us was the welcome and prominent position in the sanctuary of the Rev. John Bruyere, a Presbyterian minister friend of his from Cleveland. Also in September of that year, four months after his arrival and a month before the convening of the Vatican Council, without expressed support from his priests and to the dismay of some, Begin invited 150 Protestant ministers and spouses to dinner at the Claremont Hotel. Robert McAfee Brown was keynote speaker. The bishop in his remarks stated, "I do not know why I invited you here except to tell you that I love you," words remembered into the 1990s.

I would be remiss, however, if I intimated that the bishop, despite his early prophetic recognition of the Holy Spirit's presence, had no qualms. As the earlier GTU discussions took three years, it took four years before Bishop Begin could clearly and firmly see Catholic participation. He indicated in correspondence once that at times he had great enthusiasm for the project, while at other times he wished that it would go away. Some of the questions facing him were easy, such as the sharing of library resources, the attendance of graduate student priests, or faculty participation from Catholic institutions. Also, the opportunity for international scholars coming was attractive to our bishop.

But the idea of young undergraduate seminarians in Berkeley was unsettling. That young men still in their formative years could be taught by Protestant professors or might engage in Berkeley's ever-ready public protests were concerns raised. As a matter of fact, these were not serious worries for the bishop, but he did pore over what the word autonomy meant and what were possible financial liabilities. He also pursued whether the requirements on priestly formation both from the U.S.

Bishops' Conference (NCCB) and, more importantly, from the Roman Congregation of Seminaries and Universities would be adequately met. In the end, however, enthusiasm prevailed.

In response to the draft of a letter he asked me to prepare for Rome, he told me,

> The closing paragraph should be a little more direct. We not only seek the blessing of this Congregation, we seek its approval of our action and its permission to continue this cooperation with the GTU. Furthermore, we ask for any directives or suggestions Rome might make to perfect the program.

Perhaps, the settling moment for Bishop Begin consisted in securing the approval of a committee of bishops of the San Francisco Province, including Archbishop Joseph McGucken of San Francisco and Bishop Leo Maher from Santa Rosa. Begin opened their meeting in February 1967 with his utter consistency, "Obviously this is the work of the Holy Spirit." The bishops recognized the soundness of the Graduate Theological Union, the reality of the continuing and welcomed presence of Catholic students, and the need of a theological commission so that, in Begin's words, "precise harmony can be established, between the demands of ecclesiastical authority and academic freedom in the area of theological learning." Lastly, the committee decided that the presence of Catholic undergraduates was the concern and the responsibility of the particular religious community in conversation with the bishop of Oakland.

I can pay appropriate tribute to the precious mutual relationships and trust that have existed between this institution and the diocese. The original aim was a seminary and the training of priests, but it has moved to continuing education, sabbaticals, the formation of catechists, and, which our bishop saw early on, the preparation of lay theologians, both women and men. Faculty and students have served our parishes and have been counsel for bishops and diocesan officials. Resources here have encouraged and promoted dialogue, for example, a decade of conversation that followed the American bishops' pastoral letter on nuclear arms. Our institutions have returned the favor, providing opportunities for pastoral experience and shared responsibility.

Today we remember achievements. Once there were only twenty-three enrolled in the GTU. A plan for bibliographical resources that early received such easy acceptance became The Flora Lamson Hewlett Library, a monument of commitment on the part of the individual institutions to the Union. This was an early focus. As far back as 1964, Dr. Dillenberger remarked, "Our library resources are in step with the great theological centers of Yale, Harvard, Columbia, and Chicago. The Union is now the largest single purchaser of theological books in the country." A Sealantic grant of three-quarters of a million dollars led to the accomplishment that is the library.

Grace of Geography

Intimately connected to the GTU's history and achievement is what I would call the extraordinary grace of geography. A cliché comes to mind about three necessities for success in real estate or in commercial enterprises. The first of these is "location," and then that word is repeated twice more. We transfer that to location in the San Francisco Bay Area, location on the western edge of the United States, and location in Berkeley.

First of all, the spread of Bay Area theological schools, representing a breadth of diversity, has been blessed with sufficient closeness for conversation. The schools began discussions in 1959. In the words of an official document, "The ecumenical movement itself forms part of the program and objectives of a unique institution known as the Graduate Theological Union." Another blessing of the institutions was their clear identity. The word autonomy had sacredness about it. Dr. Dillenberger explained that it existed without sacrificing the integrity of any group. In faithfulness to academic purposes, he also said, "The Union does not attempt to accommodate religious differences." Claude Welch, so important in the early days, expressed the same kind of sentiment.

One is a member of the GTU without apology. I remember hearing Bishop Begin, speaking at an inclusive Christmas dinner at the Dominican School of Philosophy and Theology, open his remarks by stating, "I am here as a Roman Catholic; you are here as Presbyterian; you are here as Episcopalian. Unless each of us comes immersed deeply in his own tradition, we are not going to serve this institution." The bishop was not enfolding a new exhortation. He was reflecting the climate created in which each person's religious conviction and perspective would, of course, be broadened, but also strengthened rather than diminished.

A second blessing was the location on the West Coast. Early GTU documentation stated,

> Joint use of facilities has been not only an administrative economy for the benefit of each institution but also an opportunity for interfaith contact on a continuing basis. As a seat of learning, the Union will also be a gathering of communication with the Orient.

As we noted, from the beginning there was hope for a center for Buddhist studies. Despite this early vision, however, and a long history of Christian mission activity in Asia, alertness to the world across the Pacific was much more potential than actual as it was elsewhere. Indeed, in Rome twelve years ago at a gathering of Asian bishops, the French cardinal overseeing the Council on Justice and Peace said with some dismay, "Asia is very far from Rome." I responded that Asia was also a long way from California.

The GTU anticipated the growing appreciation of Asian demographics, economics, and religions through its deliberate appointment of faculty members from Asia and its efforts to assure the presence of students from Asia. Recent conversations and visits with Asian theological centers guarantee the strengthening of relationships and enriching of the growing interreligious dialogue.

There is the blessing of the Bay Area—the blessing of the edge of the Pacific Rim. Third, there is the blessing of Berkeley. The Pacific School of Religion is as old as the College of California that once existed in downtown Oakland at 14th and Franklin Streets. The presence of member schools of the Union and the willingness of later members to move to Berkeley speak of the importance of the association with the University of California. The schools established themselves here purposely to take advantage of educational opportunities. In our time, Cardinal Garrone, director of the Congregation of Seminaries and Universities in Rome, the Vatican office that had authority to approve or disapprove Catholic participation in Berkeley, would note even from his distance "the unusual cultural offerings" available.

Recognized by the University

The GTU rejoiced in the recognition that the University of California gave. Dean Dillenberger acknowledged at a trustees meeting,

> The recognition of the Union by the University of California, strongly secular in its reputation, is therefore a major breakthrough for religion and theology as an educational discipline.... This relationship is plainly a recognition before the world of the significance of religion in our society—a recognition which has too often been lacking.

These sentiments were in harmony with a December 1962 article from the *California Law Review*, written in conjunction with an effort in 1961 to establish a Department of Religious Studies at the University of California. The authors were the eminent Boalt Hall faculty member David W. Louisell along with Professor John H. Jackson. The authors quoted Thomas Jefferson, "The want of instruction in the various creeds of religious faith existing among our citizens presents therefore a chasm in a general institution of the useful sciences."

Dr. Louisell concluded,

> The problem of the place of theology in the university has to be faced. The dialogue of our intellectual community is not complete without the participation of theology. We cannot afford to leave its voice indefinitely muted or to hear it at most only tangentially and indirectly. Ideally this discipline overtly and forthrightly should resume its historic university role.

Four years later, at a gathering at St. Albert's College, Dr. Louisell would state that

> Catholic professors [and I am sure he would include others]
> were interested in a platform for a hearing of the theological
> considerations in modern life, and there is the correspond-
> ing hunger on the part of students for such information.

The collaboration of the University with the Union through the years, the cooperation regarding library resources, the joint programs, the presence of university professors on doctoral committees, all represent happy outcomes that were aims from the beginning.

But the early vision was more encompassing: "The GTU has a role in society and in the course of history which may rightly be termed crucial. The unity among theological scholars is far from being a matter of greater educational pleasantness." The unfinished business of the founders may surprise us. "The theme of the Graduate Theological Union goes beyond the ecumenical movement and beyond interfaith programs to strike a much more profound chord in the life of the human family." We may sense through the years from faculty, from the centers aligned to the Union, and alumni the achievement of that broad perspective.

Looking back, one could judge the years as slow moving. Yes, but those making decisions had no existing models to draw from in an atmosphere in which the ecumenical opportunity beckoned and the energies released from the mainly Protestant ecumenical movement, on the one hand, and the impetus of the Second Vatican Council, on the other, were making contrasting impacts felt. However, the ensuing and time-consuming consultations and conversations contributed much to the stability and success of the anniversary we shall soon be celebrating.

English Dominican Father Bede Jarrett, a renowned preacher in the last century, has a homily appropriate for our approaching jubilee. "We are travelers," he said.

> Life is not really a growing up but a journey.... You have
> been driven by the relentless hand of God. You do not real-
> ize that you are being driven along, and you try to settle
> down. This means infinite pain and great dissatisfaction.

You are a traveler, you must not settle down.... It is for the guidance of our attitude to life that we should always remember that we are only pilgrims. The secret of a happy and holy life lies in remembering that.

Amen.

7

Berkeley and Beyond

Part I: University and Church in Dialogue

HIGHER EDUCATION IN THE CALIFORNIA EAST BAY AREA counties of Alameda and Contra Costa, which comprise the Diocese of Oakland, embraces a large industry. By one count seventeen institutions fit this designation: three Catholic colleges, the quality liberal arts college that is Mills College, six community colleges, California State University in Hayward (later CSU of the East Bay), among them. By size and reputation, however, Berkeley claims the flagship University of California. Raymond J. Sontag, a towering figure of faith, scholarship, and wisdom, a professor of history at the university who keynoted the welcome banquet for our first bishop of Oakland, Floyd L. Begin, observed early on, "Bishop Begin has a ramshackle diocese that differs from Peoria, Illinois (the professor's native state), with the existence of the University of California, Berkeley."

In 1962, in his first year as bishop of the new diocese, Bishop Begin followed the accustomed pattern of pastoral care by appointing chaplains to the various institutions. Few proved fruitful. Father Paul Schmidt, an exception, made himself a frequent visitor at Diablo Valley College in central Contra Costa County. Later, with residency in East

Oakland, he became a familiar figure at Mills College, while serving as director of religious education. Bishop Begin with foresight, along with friendship during President Ellis McCune's extended tenure at California State University (East Bay), built a center for service to the Catholic community and to the university itself.

As to the University of California, Berkeley, the bishop brought to completion the Paulist Fathers funding drive that had started the decade before his arrival. The drive was to support the transfer of the 1906 Newman Hall (the Catholic Center) across campus from the northeast corner of the university to its newly built center on the south side, on College Avenue and Dwight Way. (The move was for the sake of the university's College of Engineering.) Along with the building transfer, he worked with the Paulist Fathers to remove Newman Hall from the jurisdiction and placid oversight of St. Joseph the Worker parish in Berkeley and give it its own parish status.

Above all, Bishop Begin evinced no dismay at the tensions and transitions of the decade of 1960s' Berkeley, with its marches, protests, and the resignation of the admired president, Clark Kerr. Our bishop was among the first to make contact with the new chancellor, Roger Heyns, former vice-president for academic affairs at the University of Michigan. At a dinner in the bishop's house, with a number of his chancery people present, he asked the chancellor "How can we be of help?" The evening was the beginning of a lasting friendship.

Relations Began over a Century Ago

The new friendship was reminiscent of far earlier days such as in 1907 when Archbishop Patrick Riordan of San Francisco announced the establishment of the Newman Center at UC–Berkeley. UC president Benjamin Ide Wheeler characterized the archbishop's decision as a "step taken in wisdom and with righteous regard" for the Catholic students "who are coming to the university in increasing numbers." Since his institution, he told Riordan, was unable to provide religious worship services and the local parishes were fully preoccupied with their regular routines, he welcomed this specialized mission because of its aims, namely, to "undertake the somewhat distinctive task created by the presence of university students." Other signs of cordial relations remain; one is the picture of Monsignor Charles Ramm, rector of St. Mary's Ca-

At a Newman Hall reception, Monsignor Cummins welcomes Monsignor John Tracy Ellis, left, considered the dean of U.S. Catholic historians, and friend and colleague Professor Raymond J. Sontag of UC–Berkeley, expert on modern European history and influential Catholic layman. (J. Wright / *The Catholic Voice*)

thedral in San Francisco, leading the parade of alumni on Charter Day in the late 1940s.

In 1962, Professor Sontag introduced Cardinal Franz Koenig of Vienna to faculty and students gathered at the university. This eminent prelate, who would become a leader of the Second Vatican Council, gave assurance to Bishop Floyd Begin in praising the fledgling Graduate Theological Union (GTU) and its surprising accommodation by eight departments of the university. Two decades later, Ira Michael Heymann, from the Law School and later to become chancellor, fruitlessly urged Chancellor Albert Bowker to invite Pope John Paul II for Charter Day, following in the line of so many other human rights promoters, such as Pierre Trudeau of Canada and Archbishop Desmond Tutu of South Africa.

The stirring of interest in the church marked the entire decade of the 1960s. News coverage of Vatican II—beginning with Pope John XXIII's call in 1959—was notable. Berkeley added to the ferment by the development of the GTU, marked by the participation of four ecumenical observers from GTU institutions in the Council sessions in Rome. The ecumenism of Bishop Floyd Begin contributed to this development, as did as the Catholic scholars engaged by the new GTU conglomerate adjacent to the university. These included Jesuit Father Dan O'Hanlon, with his ecumenical outreach; Sulpician Frank Norris from St. Patrick's Seminary, with his insights into the church as people of God; and Dominican Father Kevin Wall from St. Albert's Priory, who was in constant dialogue with developments in Berkeley.

Professor Raymond Sontag followed up his inauguration lecture for Bishop Begin's welcome, wherein he spoke of "racial issues that have brought down empires." He pushed me more than once as diocesan chancellor to take action in the civil rights movement. One evening at the old Newman Hall, he sat next to Bishop Begin at dinner. As an auxiliary bishop in Cleveland, Bishop Begin had made *The New York Times* by challenging the Knights of Columbus for not having a larger African American membership. He boldly opposed the 1964 initiative against the Rumford Act, which advocated fair housing as California state policy. Yet the bishop was slow to move further, perhaps because of the widespread upset that marked Berkeley in those days. The bishop's surprising off-the-cuff statement that Pope John XXIII was an unpredictable man caused Professor Sontag to remark to me, "He can go from full speed forward to full speed reverse without stripping any gears." Professor Sontag prevailed upon the bishop to open up the work of the Catholic Interracial Council, a product of a famous New York Jesuit John LaFarge, to deal with the issue of race.

Monthly Luncheons with the "Irish Mafia"

Catholic professors at the university maintained an exemplary interest in the developments of Vatican II. An initiative by Steve Diliberto of the math department and Karl Pister from the College of Engineering started monthly lunches at the university's Faculty Club. The decade of Vatican II had a parallel in the reform of American higher education in those years. Adopting the name "The Irish Mafia," Diliberto, Pister, and their fellow scholars integrated into their personal and professional lives the teachings of Vatican II not just on the church as the people of God but on the value, autonomy, and call to service of what the Council called the human sciences.

Law professor John T. Noonan Jr. (later a federal judge) and his wife, Mary Lee, chat with Bishop Cummins during the diocese's annual dinner at Newman Hall of Catholic professors from the University of California, the Graduate Theological Union, and the East Bay's three Catholic colleges. (J. Wright / *The Catholic Voice*)

The Council document *Gaudium et Spes,* with its emphasis on Christian responsibility for culture, economic life, war and peace, family, and even contemporary atheism, was welcomed by many of the faculty, one of whom some years before had asked me my thoughts on the proper role and responsibility of a Catholic professor at the university.

Lunch speakers came from their own group as well as from outside. Speakers included Cardinal Leo Joseph Suenens, who delivered the Earl Lectures during his days in Berkeley; Judge John T. Noonan, who was a member of the Papal Commission on Marriage and Family; and local priests such Frank Maurovich, editor of our diocesan paper, *The Catholic Voice*, and Father Jim Keeley, who was then serving at St. Joseph the Worker in Berkeley.

On one occasion Frank Maurovich and I shared the day with a surprise visitor, Etienne Gilson, the French medieval philosopher who had added sparkle to our school days. Surprised that this venerable figure was still alive, we found him energetic and very entertaining. Conversation ranged over contemporary higher education, the Vatican Council, and even church politics. On this last point one of the lunch group commented that Professor Gilson's familiarity with hierarchy made him an expert on church politics. "No," he replied, "I've never met a bishop."

Then he quickly added, "Oh, yes, there was one. I was visiting in Lourdes, and this one [prelate] approached me across the plaza to offer greetings. But he thought I was Maritain!" (Jacques Maritain was another French philosopher of the same era.)

Professors Take Initiative

On July 1, 1977, the day after I was installed as the second bishop of Oakland, I learned of another initiative of the UC–Berkeley professors. Archbishop Jean Jadot, the Vatican's apostolic delegate to the United States, had honored us with his presence at the installation ceremony. The following day he had six items of concern and direction to discuss with me. The fourth item concerned the need to attend to the faculty at Berkeley. The archbishop explained that months earlier two Law School professors at Berkeley, John T. Noonan and John E. Coons, had written and asked to have lunch with him when he was in the Bay Area. The archbishop agreed and arranged to meet them on his next visit. Instead of two, twenty-four faculty members attended the luncheon. Over lunch they complained to the archbishop that the diocese was not paying them enough attention. The archbishop told me that I would be invited to a reception with them in October.

The October event took place as planned, with a late-afternoon Mass followed by a reception. A young Paulist priest arranged the Mass at a coffee table in the upstairs lounge of the Newman Center. I felt at the time that the raucous influence of Berkeley's Telegraph Avenue must have dimmed his appreciation of the seriousness of the occasion and of the stature of the assembled faculty members. Yet, of the more than twenty-four faculty in attendance, no one objected, at least publicly, to the relative informality of the liturgy.

The reception ended with my giving a kind of state of the union message about the diocese. The question-and-answer period that followed went rather slowly. I remember only one specific item, a professor's inquiry about the role for them at the Newman Center. I replied that it was not going to be very much, a stance conditioned by my experience at the Newman Center at the University of California, Davis, in which dissidents from local parishes crowded into the center on Sundays and other occasions and dislodged undergraduates. That was not the case at Berkeley under the leadership of Father Jack Campbell.

While the priest host was bringing the conversation to a conclusion, I asked for time for my own questions. I inquired about the connection between the Catholic faculty at Cal and the Catholic institutions at the GTU. To my surprise the answer proved startlingly empty. Seemingly, during my six years away—I worked in Sacramento from 1971 to 1977, representing the bishops of California as executive director of the California Catholic Conference—the ecumenical dimensions of the GTU had not progressed. Neither had the relationships of the three Catholic institutions—Dominican, Franciscan, and Jesuit—become noticeably closer. This latter was understandable because Catholic participation had grown from an occasional speaker and just a few students in the early years to close to half the entire GTU student body. Furthermore, I noted some distance growing between the chancery and the institutions. Years earlier, when I was chancellor, I witnessed the conflictual relationship between the archdiocesan office and the University of San Francisco, and I did not want to see that repeated. What most surprised me that October evening was the lack of familiarity among the Catholic personnel. Somehow I had anticipated more interpersonal contact beyond serving on doctoral committees and the occasional visits of a few professors to participate in liturgy and evening prayer on "Holy Hill." After the dinner, Fred Collignon, three years out of Harvard and UC professor of urban policy, gave me evidence that my intuitions were on the mark when he said, "I could use theological input in my field, but where can I get it here?"

It did not take us long to decide that we needed to take further steps, and we had no difficulty agreeing what they should be. The Paulists were quick to offer hospitality for an evening dinner in fall 1978. A core of Catholic faculty were known to us, but reaching out to others was problematic. We depended mainly on word of mouth. I thought we had to go beyond the Berkeley community and invite representatives from our three Catholic colleges, Holy Names, Saint Mary's, and Most Holy Rosary College of the Dominican Sisters of Mission San Jose. A smattering of chancery people would also be good. We decided to use place names for the dinner, seating people together according to their presumed common interests. I welcomed the almost eighty guests, and Father Jack Campbell followed with an outline of the Newman Center's programs and needs. During his discussion of the GTU, JSTB president Dick Hill evoked laughter with his comment, "As you go up Euclid Avenue, the Dominicans are surprisingly on the left and the Jesuits equally surprising on the right."

The evening was a stunning success. Many were surprised to discover that faculty members they had served with in the academic senate and other administrative groups were fellow Catholics. The mutual joy of meeting people with such common interests was evident in the group's lingering late into the evening. As he left, Father Hilary Martin, OP, said quietly to me, "We got your point."

The point was not yet altogether clear to me, however. Later I realized that some in this group had been of assistance to me and to the California bishops during my years in Sacramento. I was thus hoping that their counsel would continue and, especially, that the resources of UC–Berkeley would be made available to our National Conference of Bishops in Washington, D.C. In any case, there was no question that we would repeat the dinner the following year.

Fruitful Developments

Archbishop Jadot's interest in Berkeley prompted me to keep him informed about the follow-up of his concern and the annual gathering that had been found a happy formula for welcome and communication. He responded to my communication by offering to attend the dinner himself the following year. By this time we had agreed on the importance of the social aspect of the evening. We therefore placed his presentation at the opening of the evening before the mood and conversation became more relaxed.

The archbishop's carefully prepared dinner speech in 1979 outlined his perceptions of Catholic academic and intellectual responsibility. Some of the strident comments about Rome and academic freedom that surfaced during the question period after his speech left me feeling uneasy. But the archbishop carried himself well. The dinner itself was a gracious affair. Master of ceremonies Professor William Slottman of UC–Berkeley's History Department amusingly praised the archbishop for honoring Berkeley with his presence. "We can understand your going to Chicago or Cambridge," he said, "but coming to such a flaky place like Berkeley!" He added, though, that other famous people had visited

Berkeley, particularly the philosopher Etienne Gilson, "who was several hundred years old at the time."

In 1980, Monsignor George Higgins of the social action arm of the National Bishops' Conference was invited to address the dinner group. I recall his challenge to the theological institutions on the matter of academic freedom. In his thirty-three years of service to the bishops, he said, he had never been interfered with in any of his writing or his lecturing. He also mildly chided U.S. theologians for failing to research the significant American contribution to the Second Vatican Council, namely, the document on religious liberty.

Service was the topic of concern at the dinner in 1981. Sister Rose Marie Hennessy, OP, was asked to join a panel of speakers, moderated by Father John Coleman from the Jesuit School of Theology, to discuss how UC–Berkeley could aid diocesan institutions. As superintendent of schools in the Diocese of Oakland, Sister Hennessy remarked that the diocese was not looking for research. Rather it needed information and insights that had already been gained. In his response to Sister Hennessy's talk, Dr. Karl Pister, at the time head of UC–Berkeley's College of Engineering, later to be chancellor of University of California, Santa Cruz, expressed his hope that the work of his office would become the focus of conversations rather than the protests that had gained such notoriety in those years. Father Joseph Chinnici from the Franciscan School spoke easily of how the Catholic institution of higher education was determined not to isolate itself, but to integrate into the Catholic community.

The dinner gathering had now become a much-welcomed annual event. In response to our request for reviews and recommendations, one Berkeley professor observed, "There is no free lunch. Despite the sociability of the evening, one has to pay by listening to less than exciting presentations." Whether the result of our training or some other conditioning, I and my colleagues take criticisms to heart much more quickly than we do praise for our efforts.

Bishops Ask, Berkeley Responds

Accompanying our review of the program for the 1982 dinner came a stroke of providence. A year earlier, the U.S. bishops had taken up a suggestion by Auxiliary Bishop Frank Murphy of Baltimore to study the

question of nuclear arms, a
prominent national concern
at the time with terms like "sa-
ber rattling" and "limited nuclear strikes" in the air. A first
draft of the bishops' document was available by the time
of our 1982 dinner. In the inclusive spirit of those days,
the U.S. bishops had invited
responses. The hope of align-
ing the resources of the Catholic community of Berkeley
(i.e., the university and the
GTU) on nuclear issues with
the work of the bishops suddenly became a reality. And
this collaboration gave rise to
more than one diocesan enterprise for the next decade
and more.

Scripture scholar Sandra Schneiders, IHM,
from JSTB, offered biblical underpinning for
the U.S. bishops' peace pastoral. (IHM Archive photo)

The Catholic community in the United States knew well that the
bishops were studying the morality of nuclear armament. The report
presented at our 1982 dinner, therefore, spoke to many whose interest
had already been aroused. Twenty-three of the university faculty volunteered to offer written responses to the draft; these were forwarded to
the office in Washington. Seventeen of the written responses were favorable to the bishops' document. They ranged from enthusiasm to
moderate acceptance. Six were negative, some categorically and others
reservedly. Notably, all of the negative views came from individuals who
had lived or taught in Central or Eastern Europe.

The discussion of the bishops' peace project had become part of
table conversations in Oakland's Catholic community.

Berkeley spawned its own developments. *The Catholic Voice* ran a
series of articles. Jesuit Father Dan O'Hanlon wrote on Asian traditions
of harmony and nonviolence. Geoffrey Chew, chair of the university's

Physics Department, spoke of the transcendent message of love. With admirable humility, Czeslaw Milosz, the Nobel Prize–winning poet, declined an invitation to contribute.

Within months after our annual dinner, Denise Chew, wife of Professor Geoffrey Chew, invited me to stop in Paris on my way to Rome for an *ad limina* visit in order to discuss the draft with the assistant rector of the Catholic Institute of Paris. The three of us met for lunch in an outdoor restaurant. In a mix of English and French, I recall especially the word "*dissymétrie*," suggesting that the French church was not in sync with the U.S. bishops on this issue.

In the course of writing the bishops' document, Father J. Bryan Hehir (on the committee's staff) called on Sister Sandra Schneiders of Berkeley to present New Testament themes relevant to the document. On short notice, she prepared a thirty-page paper and sent it to me for approval. My one recommendation was to delete page nineteen since I thought its tone was condescending. On her return from what indeed turned out to be a gratifying visit to the committee, she told me, "Bishop Jim Malone told me to put page nineteen back in."

In May 1983, after an unusually wide consultation, the U.S. Catholic Conference (NCCB) formally approved their peace pastoral, entitled *The Challenge of Peace: God's Promise and Our Response.* The committee under the direction of then archbishop Joseph Bernardin from Chicago, moderate by reputation, joined with bishops of divergent views, such as John O'Connor, then bishop of Scranton, Pennsylvania, a former Navy chaplain for twenty-seven years, and Auxiliary Bishop Thomas Gumbleton of Detroit, an outspoken peace advocate, properly associated with Pax Christi.

Debate throughout the year had been strenuous. The final document spoke of the immorality of the arms race and declared that the policy of nuclear deterrence was acceptable only as a "provisional" ethic; that the just war theory begins with a "presumption against war"; and that the nonviolence movement and the just war theory both spring from the same consistent Catholic Social Teaching.

Without being strident, the document was strong. So much so that I remember a lunch during an administrative board meeting at the National Conference of Bishops in March 1983 when most of us at the table doubted that the body of bishops would be able to come up with a two-thirds vote in support of the document. The actual vote in May—238 in favor, 9 against—emerged because of the respectful dialogue and civil discourse that had taken place during the previous two years. This cooperative spirit helped create a document that marked a watershed in the history of the U.S. Catholic Church.

Part II: Dialogue on Nuclear Deterrence

A STARTLING COINCIDENCE TOOK PLACE IN OUR DIOCESE in the same week the bishops voted to publish their peace document (May 1983). I had been scheduled to offer Mass at St. Charles Borromeo parish in Livermore to welcome twenty-three neophytes who had been been baptized at the Easter vigil after completing the Rite of Christian Initiation of Adults (RCIA). It so happened that sixteen of the neophytes were employees of Lawrence Livermore National Laboratory, whose research function was to ensure the safety, security, and reliability of the U.S. nuclear deterrent and reduce threats to national and global security. The UC–Berkeley President's Office had responsibility for oversight of the lab's work. Besides the gospel of the day and the focus on the newly baptized, it was also Mothers' Day. Obviously, too heavy a weight to be carried by one homily, and I easily resisted the temptation to focus on the peace pastoral.

After Mass, however, a group of the Livermore scientists, along with pastor Father James Keeley and Presbyterian minister Reverend William Nebo, gathered in the rectory to discuss the bishops' peace document. A strong consensus among them agreed that the document was seminal and merited thoughtful pursuit.

The meeting with the Livermore group took place at the end of a process that had begun for me two years previously when Father Royale Vadakin, the talented ecumenical officer of the Archdiocese of Los Angeles, invited me to join a panel discussion on disarmament at All Souls Episcopal Church in Pasadena. The pastor at All Souls, the Reverend George Regas, had the reputation of being a thoughtful activist.

The dialogue proved enriching. Additionally I learned much from my preparation. I was surprised to discover that as far back as Leo XIII (1878–1903) modern warfare was judged to be so destructive as to be morally unacceptable. Even Pope Benedict XV (1914–1922), more of a name than a figure in history, loomed as a towering figure in the efforts he undertook to prevent World War I and to open up a broad consensus for the making of peace. I was surprised, indeed embarrassed, by how much I had to learn.

During discussion of the U.S. bishops' letter on
peace, Bishop Cummins engages physicist Owen
Chamberlain, who helped develop both the atom
bomb in the 1940s and the Nuclear Freeze Movement in the 1980s.

I brought home from southern California a determination that
with Lawrence Livermore National Laboratory in the diocese we had a
responsibility to promote the experience of Pasadena. The laboratory
had long been a site for demonstrations, especially on Good Friday. I
felt, however, that we needed to take a step beyond protests. I wanted
the diocese to initiate an academic dialogue, and I thought that the university and the GTU would be a good site for an academic day or weekend on the history of and contemporary church teaching on the matter
of armament. I brought together Dr. Tom Hayes, from the Donner
Laboratory in Berkeley, and Jesuit Fathers Drew Christiansen and Bill
Spohn. Our initial conversations were fruitful, and we added to the
committee.

After the initial May meeting, I was invited again, along with Father Joe Carroll, to lunch at St. Charles Borromeo with Father Keeley
and Reverend Nebo. Two scientists from the laboratory insisted that
they and their colleagues had to be part of the developing dialogue.

They argued that their laboratory's connection with the university gave them the right to participate.

Decade of Discourse

The group's work was not easy. Some felt that identifying the project only with the university would cause some to be biased against the outcome of our deliberations. We could not arrive at a consensus as to what our specific contribution might be. Whatever we decided, it was clear that the project included changing people's attitudes, and this work—to which the diocese was suited—would take a generation. The arrival of the bishops' peace pastoral in 1983 quickly gave us focus.

Providentially, the services of Father Raymond Decker, from San Francisco, a fellow seminarian in my time and a GTU alumnus, became available to us through the generosity of San Francisco's Archbishop John R. Quinn. Under his capable direction we planned the decade of discourse that followed. Father Decker visited with the president of the GTU, the chancellor in Berkeley, and the director of the Lawrence Livermore National Laboratory.

We aimed to involve fewer than one hundred participants. Responses from each institution were positive and amazingly interdisciplinary. We had to face tensions between some university faculty and Livermore Laboratory over whether or not the university should be aligned with the laboratory.

Concerned that the group might become polarized, Father Decker sought from the Franciscan Foundation in San Francisco a grant to hire facilitators. The friars graciously gave us $1,100.

We chose San Damiano, the Franciscan retreat house in Danville, as a site for the 1984 discussion. I welcomed the group, telling them that the expectation was for civil discourse. I explained that the participants were no more divided than were the U.S. bishops at the beginning of their project. Edward Doherty, who had U.S. State Department experience and more recently had been on the bishops' staff during the development of the document, was our presenter.

In a discussion group report near the close of the day, Nobel Laureate Owen Chamberlain, who had deep concerns about the nuclear weapon that he had helped develop, expressed a word of thanks, especially to the diocese. "We are sister institutions, but have built walls against each other," he said, referring to the university and the laboratory. "We thank the diocese for bringing us together."

The extraordinary consensus we reached at the end of the day arose from broad acceptance of the bishops' pastoral letter, which everyone agreed was seminal. Nuclear proliferation was clearly an urgent concern, and material on this issue was sufficient enough for us for another decade. We all wanted our gathering to continue. (The symposia that followed did not replace the annual Newman Hall dinner, which carried on as usual.)

Follow-up Symposia

In 1985, St. Mary's College in Moraga hosted a follow-up symposium with Sidney Drell, from the Stanford Center for International Security and Arms Control, and Father Bryan Hehir, staff person for the writing of the bishops' document. (Father Hehir's research and writing focused on ethics and foreign policy and the role of religion in world politics.) The earlier recommendation for more group discussion was voted out of the schedule.

Two symposia were organized in 1986. In February, the presenters were Roy R. Woodruff, associate director at the Livermore Laboratory, and Father Drew Christiansen, from the Jesuit School of Theology in Berkeley. The main speakers in October were Paul Brown and William Zagotta, both from Livermore. Enriching contributions came from Michael Nagler, a professor of classics and peace studies from UC–Berkeley, and Burns Weston, a trained international lawyer and regent from the University of Iowa.

The level of intensity varied from year to year, but the number of participants stayed very much the same, ranging from seventy-five to ninety-five. Spearheading the continuing dialogue were Livermore Laboratory's Bill Zagotta and Jim Hannon, both parishioners of the local St. Charles Borromeo Church. We spent one memorable day stimulated by the overarching perspective of Dr. Robert Bellah, religious sociologist from UC–Berkeley, and, again, Father Bryan Hehir. A sidebar thought that remains with me since those times is the first of three principles from the Peace of Augsburg in 1555: *"cujus regio, ejus religio"* (whose realm, his religion), an influence to our day on church–state relations.

A gratifying part of the decade was the discovery of local talent.

Michael May, formerly the director of the Livermore Laboratory, exhibited a profound grasp of ethics and public policy. Bernie Adenay, a Baptist from New College, drew from his doctoral thesis in philosophy from UC–Berkeley related to natural law. Karen Lebacz, from the Pacific School of Religion brought her own moralist perspectives, along with a colleague, Harlan Stelmach.

A particularly memorable day was November 28, 1989. Someone from the group had discovered that Arseny Berézin, a science professor from a university in St. Petersburg, was on a sabbatical leave at Stanford University, with his children enrolled at St. Nicholas School in Los Altos. On short notice Professor Berézin joined a group of us at the Franciscan San Damiano Retreat House in our diocese. (I'll always remember how devoutly the professor said his grace before meals.) Our morning session was devoted to an assessment of political, economic, medical, and educational patterns in the Soviet Union. A critical sidebar noted Moscow's unwinnable war in Afghanistan. He then moved to a discussion of the free market that gave rise to fluctuating prices as well as the development of the black market. Land was not restored to the peasants and food production was low because farmers had no incentive to gather in a potentially rich harvest. In his comments on education the professor acknowledged some good universities in the Soviet Union, but noted weaknesses in so many other Soviet schools. He mentioned *glasnost* and recommended that President George H.W. Bush might encourage farm cooperatives for some benefit.

Professor Berézin had high hopes for Prime Minister Mikhail Gorbachev, "the first educated leader of the country" beyond the limited background of Joseph Stalin and Nikita Khrushchev. Gorbachev's philosopher wife, Raisa Gorbacheva, also received high marks from the professor. Lastly, the professor discussed the return to religious practice in the Soviet Union in the 1980s, stimulated in good part by the failure to find utopia in earlier generations. He saw hope in the ecumenical outreach by the patriarch of Moscow and Leningrad's Orthodox archbishop, who were then participating in an ecumenical assembly in Basel, Switzerland, along with Cardinal Carlo Martini of Milan. With no apology, Professor Berézin stressed the importance of faith in Russian identity and argued that religion was more deeply embedded in their cultural fabric than in ours.

Three years later, a group of us on a Baltic cruise visited Professor Berézin in St. Petersburg. We enjoyed his hospitality and benefited as well from an explanation of the work he was doing, transferring military research into civilian practice. As we left him that afternoon, he pulled me aside and said that his work was under some investigation by the government. If anything happened to him, he asked if I could help arrange that his youngest son, who was twelve years old, might somehow be brought to the United States to be educated by the Jesuits.

Thinking back to our conversations in Berkeley in those years, I see that they replicated those of the U.S. bishops themselves, an exchange of ideas marked by respectful dialogue among those with divergent viewpoints and by constant movement toward consensus. The steadiness of attendance showed that the participants found the discussions of interest and of value.

The conversations were never publicized and no media were present. Relations between UC–Berkeley and Livermore were still uneasy and we all felt that publicity about our discussions would call attention to the tensions and might damage what we were trying to accomplish. A greater reason, however, was the resistance of scientists to journalistic interpretation. I had experienced this instinct among so many U.S. bishops, but I was surprised to find it in professional academics as well. The obvious advantage of the privacy was that participants could speak their minds without concern about entering the public arena for argument or criticism.

A number of years after we had let the Livermore dialogues languish, I met Professor Owen Chamberlain on a path in Tilden Park in the Berkeley Hills. I mentioned that perhaps we should have continued the meetings. His response was immediate but calm. He felt that the discussions were held at a most appropriate moment, with participants free to express divergent viewpoints and to speak constructively. This, he said, served our conflicted time.

As I walked away, I wondered if any diocese in the world, besides our own, had been blessed by a discussion among four-score scholars, scientists, and theologians for a decade on such a critical problem facing our world.

Part III: Dialogue on the U.S. Economy

On THE HEELS OF THE HIGHLY REGARDED PEACE PASTORAL, a number of bishops across the theological spectrum had suggested a similar pastoral letter on the U.S. economy. The project sought to appraise the free market in the light of Catholic Social Teaching, an aim that would have caused more divisions than the peace pastoral itself.

As with the peace pastoral, the preparation of the letter on the economy was well publicized in the media by the National Conference of Bishops. This stirred the university and the Catholic institutions at the GTU to organize an evening at the university's Pauley Pavilion, with John Kenneth Galbraith and Milton Friedman as the main speakers. A large tapestry on the façade announced the work of the bishops on the economy. Fathers Lyn Farwell from the Jesuit school and Father Kenan Osborne from the Franciscans welcomed the audience to an evening that, except for a demonstration against Friedman, which I felt was gross, moved along well.

Not long after this event, the possibility of a West Coast hearing began to be discussed between our diocese and the U.S. Catholic Conference (USCC). This led to the scheduling of hearings at the university, with Father Raymond Decker responsible for the arrangements. The USCC was familiar with the university's contribution, and Father Decker's in particular. In light of the famed secular reputation of the university, I recall with amusement the sign taped to the front door of Boalt Hall, "Catholic Bishops' Meeting—Second Floor."

The hearing went on for two days under the direction of Archbishop Rembert Weakland of Milwaukee and Bishop William Weigand of Sacramento. Presentations were made by and large by Bay Area locals. The spectrum was broad. Kenneth Arrow, Nobel laureate from Stanford University, stood out among the early speakers. Also speaking were Professor Gérard Debreu, French economist and professor at UC–Berkeley, who won the 1983 Nobel Prize in economics, César Chávez of the United Farm Workers, and environmentalist and author Frances Moore Lappé.

The Franciscan School provided hospitality on the first evening.

Bruce Russett, who had taken a leave from his post as Yale professor of political science to lead staff of the bishops' letter was complimentary both to the program and to the obvious collaborative pattern that marked the relations of the schools with one another and with the university and diocese. I was gratified.

Soon after, I received a surprise invitation to speak at the university's highly regarded Haas Business School. With much anxiety about addressing such an august group, I decided to explain the process of the bishops' letter for the twenty-five or thirty attendees. The phrase "Catholic Social Teaching" drew some attention. One of the faculty came up right after my talk and said with some chagrin that he had never heard of the subject. Other very informed Catholics present that evening were able to help with an explanation. The only hostility I experienced during an otherwise congenial gathering was a self-identifying Catholic professor who complained that the bishops were entering the field of economics at a time when we had such a poor record of fair policies in relation to women in the church. I accepted the criticism, but pointed out, not without some defensiveness, that UC–Berkeley, which had a public policy of equal opportunity for women and men, had only 3 percent of its departments headed by women. A woman executive from AT&T, seated in the front row, pumped her elbow in Tiger Woods fashion in support of my comment.

A markedly significant contribution from Berkeley to the economic pastoral came from the Scriptural talent of Jesuit John R. Donahue. The university's Dr. Robert Bellah would later assess the value of the bishops' pastoral according to its Scriptural basis and orientation, which clearly had a Vatican II flavor.

I must note that after more than a quarter century, students in economics at St. Mary's College in Moraga still hold the bishops' pastoral in high regard.

Our Berkeley dinners, which had become an established diocesan tradition, continued to welcome the occasional outside guest. Through the hospitality of Michael Hout, from the university's Sociology Department, and his wife, Flo, priest-sociologist Father Andrew Greeley was an honored guest in 2003. Father Greeley had known and collaborated with my brother when he was superintendent of schools in the Archdio-

cese of San Francisco. Known for his often critical and even acerbic observations, Father Greeley was nevertheless complimentary regarding
our scholarly gathering.

Annual Dinners Continue

The dinner organizers reached out to a number of UC–Berkeley professors, including William J. Bousma, history professor and a scholar
marked by an admirable professionalism. Professor Sontag had directed
me to Professor Bousma when I had inquired about summer school at
the university years earlier. I recall this Harvard graduate looking at me
over his glasses as he read my seminary transcript and remarking, "I
envy you your classical education." Unfortunately I lost touch with him
after I finished my Berkeley studies. Surprisingly, he had kept track of
me during my years in Sacramento. When he mentioned this one evening at a Boalt Hall dinner, I was chagrined that I had neglected to invite
him to my installation as bishop of Oakland. A devout member of the
Dutch Reformed Church, Professor Bousma had served on doctoral
committees of the GTU. In the years since his attendance at the Boalt
Hall dinner, I have enjoyed a continuing relationship with the professor
and his wife, Beverly.

I had heard of Dr. Robert Scalapino, the director of the Asian
Studies Department at the university. Presuming his Catholicity, I recommended inviting him to our dinner in 1981. When I began my association with the Federation of Asian Bishops' Conferences in 1982, Dr.
Scalapino's office, particularly through his secretary, Susan Saxby, provided me with important background materials related to the assembly
of Asian bishops, which I attended every four years thereafter.

Through the efforts of Jack Coons, from the university's Law
School, our circle embraced his colleague Ira Michael Heymann, who
became UC–Berkeley's sixth chancellor. Years later after his retirement,
Professor Heymann chaired a committee on the renovation of the City
Center in Oakland and proved to be a strong champion for our develop-
ment of the Cathedral of Christ the Light.

Through the Berkeley connection, Heymann's successor as chancellor, Chang-Lin Tien, the university's China-born professor of me-
chanical engineering, appointed me to his Community Advisory
Committee. At one of the committee gatherings, the chancellor an-

nounced with great enthusiasm that Pope John Paul II had asked me about the university during my *ad limina* visit to the Vatican.

Another prominent participant in the annual faculty dinners was Dr. Charles Townes, with his wife, Frances. In my second year in Oakland he called to talk with me about an invitation that he and twenty to thirty other Nobel laureates had received to attend a ten-day convocation in Rome on contemporary problems facing Western nations. At first I was at a loss to know how I could help. After he explained that the invitation had come over the signature of Cardinal Franz Koenig of Vienna, I strongly encouraged him to attend. After he returned from Rome, Dr. Townes invited me and Father Joe Carroll from our office to lunch at the Faculty Club. He shared pictures and documentation with us, as well as a sense of satisfaction. He remarked on the hospitality of the Vatican and the thorough planning of the days for the twenty international participants. As he described the group's prioritizing of the ten urgent questions of the contemporary era, I recall how surprised I was that urban violence globally was among the major concerns.

Within months, the Pontifical Academy of Science at the Vatican inquired about the worthiness of the same Charles Townes to be invited into its membership. I responded without reservations that this devout member of the First Congregational Church in Berkeley would indeed be suitable. Charles and Frances have been faithful in attending the annual meetings and could be depended on to make complete reports. Dr. Townes strongly supported—and helped develop—our nuclear issues dialogues during the decade after the U.S. bishops' peace pastoral was released.

A digression related to the Townes's visit to Rome: in 1980, the year that Pope John Paul II made his visit to Asia and to the Philippines, Bishop Felixberto Camacho Flores of Guam, invited the West Coast bishops to be present for the pope's visit. (Guam at that time was in the province of the Archdiocese of San Francisco.) Following a celebration of the pope's arrival at the cathedral in Agaña, the visiting bishops were invited to dinner. I had met the pope in Guadalajara, Mexico, two years earlier, but in contrast to that brief encounter this was an intimate gathering of thirteen. At dinner, I sat two seats down from the pope on the right side. Diagonally across on my right was a bishop who was accompanying the pontiff. Concerned that the bishop might be on the edge of the conversation, I asked who he was. He explained he was Archbishop Martin, in charge of Vatican protocol. I told him with enthusiasm about the welcome that Dr. Townes had received during the visit of the Nobel laureates. Leaning forward, the pope interrupted and said, "You have many Nobel Prize people in Berkeley." He added—somewhat as a question: "They are mostly

Bishop Cummins congratulates Father Walter Burghardt on the renowned Jesuit theologian, writer, and preacher's reception of an honorary doctorate from the Jesuit School of Theology in Berkeley in 1987. In the following chapter, Cummins traces Burghardt's enlightening history of authority in the church as it has evolved to its current understanding. (JSTB photo)

in science." I admitted that scientists had indeed been honored, but I explained that other departments in the university had won Nobel Prizes as well. Unfortunately, I neglected to mention Czelaw Milosz, a fellow Polish poet and prose writer who was then professor of Slavic Languages and Literature at Berkeley and had that very year been awarded the Nobel Prize for literature.

A Backward Look

The fruitfulness of the initiative law professor Jack Coons and Judge John T. Noonan took no doubt exceeded their expectations. Of course this came at a moment when the signs of the times were favorably aligned, namely, the scholarship and openness of the U.S. Bishops' Conference as well as the ecumenical and evangelistic spirit of Bishop Begin and the responsiveness of his diocese.

8

Restyling Church Authority

Dignity of the Human Person Recognized

IN JANUARY 1971 I HEARD JESUIT FATHER WALTER J. BURGHARDT of Woodstock, Maryland, speak at the Colliver Lectures at the University of the Pacific, along with Dr. Albert Outler, an articulate Protestant observer at the Second Vatican Council from Southern Methodist University. I am very indebted to Father Burghardt for his understanding of the style of authority in the post–Vatican II generation.

My own insight into this issue had been enhanced by Jesuit Father John Courtney Murray in an article in *America* in 1966. From the time of Vatican II Father Murray's vision had swept through the church's teaching on the people of God, collegiality, responsibility of all the baptized, the communion-creating Spirit in the church, the recognition of the value of human sciences and disciplines, and the consequent need for consultative bodies, particularly at the diocesan and pastoral levels.

The direction we had to take in this area was not clear at that time, though some things came with ease. On authority, for example, Pope Paul VI's thoughts echoed in our minds: authority should promote freedom as much as possible and restrict only as much as necessary. And we should respect the law without being enslaved to it. Lastly, dialogue before decision was obligatory, so that those affected by a policy would have a word to say about its formation. This last resonated best for me, but I, along with the rest of us in authority, had to discern the context of these emerging issues, the presence of the Spirit, and the careful listening that was going to be required.

In his 1971 talk, Father Burghardt sketched a history of authority in the church that was easily grasped. Discussion of this issue does not have a long history, he explained; it goes back only a century to Pope Leo XIII. The Jesuit scholar quoted from two encyclicals. One was *Immortale Dei* (1885), in which the pope's words *fuit aliquando tempus* ("once upon a time") described a Golden Age of authority in church and society. Then came the Reformation and the French Revolution. Pope Leo XIII read the signs of the times as a revolt against the authority of the church and against the authority of God. He spoke of the vertical relationship between those who ruled and those who were ruled. There was only an inchoative reference to personal and civil rights and the responsibility of the participant citizen. The second encyclical, *Satis Cognitum* (1896), centered on the role of authority in the church. Father Burghardt explained that the pope's focus in this encyclical was on the Petrine office and the responsibility of the faithful in obedience to doctrinal and jurisdictional authority.

Clear in both of these encyclicals was the classical conception of the freedom–authority relationship that was our heritage. And this heritage had much to recommend it: a vivid awareness of God, the charism that accompanies authority, and obedience as the sharing in the humanness of Christ. The elements of Christian truth that exist in that vision, Father Burghardt said, should not be mocked by anti-historian caricatures. These were *religious* elements; they produced holy people; they were good.

In our times, however, this is not good enough. This understanding of authority was true, but it did not contain the whole truth. People today do not believe that sheer submission to a superior's will and mere execution of his or her orders satisfy the demands of personal dignity. This approach does not call into play the freedom of the person at its deepest point, where freedom appears as love. Nor does it value the responsibility of each person to participate fully in community and contribute actively to community.

Dignity of the Human Person

Father Burghardt praises Vatican II for being keenly sensitive to a new awareness. He recognizes two signs of the times as crucial. The first was the growing consciousness of the dignity of the human person, so championed by Pope John Paul II. Pertinent here are the sentences that open the Council's *Declaration on Religious Freedom*:

> A sense of the dignity of the human person has been impressing itself more and more deeply on the consciousness of contemporary man [*sic*]. And the demand is increasingly made that men and women should act on their own judgment, enjoying and making use of responsible freedom, not driven by coercion but motivated by a sense of duty. (Walter M. Abbott, SJ, *The Documents of Vatican II,* p. 675)

The second sign was the growing consciousness of community in the human family. The contemporary mind can find today's emphasis on independence and self-subsistence dissatisfying. To be fully a person, to be fully human, one must be *with* others and *for* others. It is in community that human dignity is realized, Father Burghardt wrote, as this biblical insight makes clear: "...a vision that harmonizes splendidly with the Christian understanding of the Trinity where the persons are constituted by their relationship one to another." Discerning the truth of this vision, however, took years of religious and secular experience.

In the mid-twentieth century, Vatican II's bishops analyzed dignity-in-community on four levels. First, was the people of God, whose condition is basically equality, dignity, and freedom because all are possessed by the one same Holy Spirit (I Cor. 12:7). Second, the church is a communion united to the Father and its members with one another through Christ and the Holy Spirit, realized here in time but destined to endure hereafter beyond time as the communion of saints. Third, communion and its love were bound to service and to witness in its mission of love. Fourth, the church was a visible society in which authority, while necessary, has a very special quality: ministering to the community for the sake of communion and for the sake of the church's missionary function.

Three Elements of Authority

Authority in this communion has three elements, each of them pointing to service. The first is a unitive role. Authority gathers and unites as God the Father brings the human family together. Reflecting Paul VI's 1964 encyclical *Ecclesiam Suam,* Father Burghardt taught that God is in the dialogue of salvation with the membership of the church. From this comes initiative, or the current word "charism." The community is to be discharged through dialogue.

Second, authority has a decisive and directive role to play in ensuring that the path to positive faith will be preserved, but dialogue is presumed as well. Cardinal Suenens calls this "co-responsibility."

The third function of authority is corrective: an accidental function necessary for a sinful people, a function of service to the unity of the community. Obedience still has a place serving the growth of community. On occasion this obedience will clearly appear to be self-sacrifice, an expression of one's self-awareness that we are all called to be in the image of Jesus Christ.

I agree with Father Burghardt that the vision of authority bequeathed us in Vatican II is "profoundly insightful, basically biblical, splendidly Christian."

Vatican II moved words into issues of practicum—supporting initiative, the freedom to bring concerns to people in authority, to share competence in what is called "human sciences." The Council was particularly clear in recommending the institution of consultative bodies at the parish level and then at the diocesan level—the Diocesan Pastoral Council—with clergy, religious, and lay representation. Finance councils would become obligatory with the revision of the Code of Canon Law, and the national conferences of bishops also issued from Vatican II.

I found Father Burghardt's homely directives helpful. Again, echoing Paul VI and the document on religious liberty, authority must allow as much freedom as possible and only as much restriction as is necessary. Our Oakland diocese offers multiple illustrations of diocesan organizations and groups working in this spirit: the St. Vincent de Paul Society's dining room, Oakland Community Organizations, educational initiatives such as the Next Step Learning Center for development and remedial adult education, the La Salle Educational Opportunity for marginal students, the Inter-Friendship House Association, which welcomes Chinese scholars in Berkeley, A Friendly Place, for homeless women, and St. Mary's Parish Center, which cares for the neediest of elderly and the families. Room remains for the testing of the spirits, as St. Paul said, but our fundamental posture must be openness to particular charisms.

The second rule—respect for law without enslavement to law—is more perilous. A high school faculty colleague of mine once remarked that one can discern liberal from conservative tendencies by what rules people break. Respect for law is necessary, but appeal to law may sometimes override human concerns. Liturgy, for example, was a particular area of concern in this regard. Bishop Begin implemented every directive in the post–Vatican II years, but he was equally demanding that nothing should go beyond what had been officially promulgated. The wisdom of the church is apparent in its demand that liturgical decrees be followed. Not even the local bishop can dispense with this requirement. Ritual requires that participants should know what to expect from liturgical rites so that they can enter into them in a comfortable and familiar manner.

Pope John Paul II issued his *Instruction concerning Worship of the Eucharist (Inaestimabile Donum)* in 1980, some three years after I was named the second bishop of the Oakland Diocese. The document's forty-four directives outlined the Vatican's expectations regarding the Eucharist. In a series of meetings with our deanery priests, I noted that we were not conforming in two respects. We were then in the early stages of the distribution of communion under both forms. My judgment was that at the cathedral and in certain other parishes trained extraordinary ministers would handle the number of communicants and the logistics of distribution better than visiting priests and deacons, who would be performing this ministry in an unfamiliar setting. The priests agreed.

The second area of nonconformism involved the role of women as acolytes in a dozen or more of our eighty-five parishes, an issue about which our priests voiced strong and conflicting opinions. I was hesitant to impose the canonical rule. In my observations, pastors were not deliberately flaunting the directive by allowing women and girls a greater role in the liturgy. I suggested a compromise: allow seventh and eighth grade girls to continue as altar servers wherever they were then functioning, but do not introduce the practice where it did not exist. We settled the issue on those terms, although some priests agreed only reluctantly. Afterwards, a grandmother phoned to say that it did not seem right that one of her grandchildren was permitted to serve in one parish while the neighboring parish did not allow this. Despite the clarity of our consensus, one of our priests decided to introduce the practice. In light of the 1980 document, this disappointed me.

Dialogue before Decision

A congenial rule for Father Burghardt was "dialogue before decision," meaning that those affected by the judgment deserved to participate in its formation. Vatican II had shown that dialogue was an avenue to greater wisdom in decision-making as well as in fostering of communal harmony. Council documents were explicit about parish councils. Bishop Floyd Begin twice set deadlines for every parish to form a parish council, but only half did so over the next ten years. In that same decade, seventy of our eighty-five parishes had embraced the Rite of Christian Initiation of Adults (RCIA), long before the practice was required. I once asked Father Oliver Lynch, one of our veteran priests and a Franciscan pastor of extraordinary gifts, why the RCIA was so well received in contrast to parish councils. He wisely responded, "RCIA does not tell the pastor how to run the parish."

Much of the resistance to instituting parish councils disappeared with the publication of the revision of canon law in 1983. Some difficulties accompanied council functioning. I called one "selective responsibility," some people taking care of their particular interests but taking no responsibility for other concerns. In some cases, for instance, no conversation took place before a person was dropped from his/her church position or the person's job responsibilities were radically changed. "People will get over it," a close coworker of mine said, but I disagreed strongly. The aftershocks of a lack of respectful conversation would last very long.

A particularly bright experience with consultation involved our Diocesan Pastoral Council. Vatican II had set this in place and urged its creation. Our Council of Priests decided to move with it. I myself felt that it was premature, that we needed a larger base of parish councils to succeed. Under the leadership of Father Brian Joyce and with the collaboration of the pastors, two weekend gatherings brought together some four hundred people from our eighty-five parishes. Our deliberations, which were richer than we had expected, resulted in a council structure and the formulation of five goals for the diocese for the next decade.

Three of these goals were expected, namely, those concerning lay leadership development, education, and youth. Two were a surprise. One was evangelization, a concern of ours, but not one we had moved on. The other was the high priority given to social justice. Ordinary conversations around the diocese had never shown these to be priorities. The follow-up on social justice was particularly enriching because the issue moved into the realm of mainline Catholic practice rather than being a concern only of activists. This change was evident in the St. Vincent de Paul Society's prisoner rehabilitation work, in education ministries in our inner-city schools, and in the support and advocacy by our Catholic hospitals for universal healthcare. Such was an unexpected assurance that Catholic Social Teaching was embedded in the minds and religious practice of our people.

In his closing remarks on authority, Father Burghardt urged us to be open to new solutions. "Unparalleled crises call for unparalleled solutions," he said. "The answer, 'This is the way we've always done it,' proves only one thing: 'This is the way we've always done it'." We clergy had to have a contemporary understanding of authority. But so, too, did religious and laity as they took on more and more responsibility in diocesan and parish leadership. In this regard, the Council, the popes, and our National Conference of Bishops had served us all well. As we learned new ways, authority-as-service would undoubtedly be an underlying condition for the work of the New Evangelization.

9

Endorsing Enlightened Dialogue

Essential Prelude to Decision

For THE PAST HALF-CENTURY, the familiar word "dialogue" has en-joyed particular attention within the Catholic Church. Much of this is legacy from the Second Vatican Council (1962–1965), where dialogue had been described as "prominent and symptomatic," as the church at-tempted to deal with its internal life and to converse with other Christian brothers and sisters and with society. Appreciation for the term had grown the decade before, even to the point of one caustic observer call-ing it seemingly "cultish and faddish."

In the eyes of many, however, there has been a diminishing of that revered practice of heartfelt dialogue with consequent loss to the life and mission of the church. Many deplore the recent lack of respectful dialogue in the public arena. Many of us also feel that this element of our heritage should be accessible within the people of faith and a wel-comed obligation. In the university, of course, structured and disci-plined dialogue is the expected pattern of instruction and for us, here at St. Mary's College, is embedded in the tradition of the La Salle Christian

---

Bishop John Cummins delivered this address at St. Mary's College, March 28, 2008.

Brothers who founded this liberal arts school.

Today may be an opportunity to refresh the heritage of papal and conciliar instruction on the responsibility of dialogue, an activity and experience very human, but for us also markedly religious.

In hopes of achieving such reflection, I delve into three Roman documents. The first is the most recent. It is *Ex Corde Ecclesiae* of Pope John Paul II on Catholic higher education, issued in 1990. The second is *Gaudium et Spes*, the authoritative pastoral constitution *On the Church in the Modern World* from the Second Vatican Council. Thirdly, an accompanying document from the same period is the first encyclical letter of Paul VI, *Ecclesiam Suam*, about the church, yes, but largely an insightful and thorough study of the nature of contemporary dialogue.

Ex Corde Ecclesiae
John Paul II, August 15, 1990

The document reads,

> In ways appropriate to the different academic disciplines, all Catholic teachers are to be faithful to, and all other teachers are to respect, Catholic doctrines and morals in their research and teaching. In particular, Catholic theologians are aware that they fulfill a mandate received from the church....

In case there is any obscurity in those words the application of this document for the United States, issued ten years later, read, "Catholics who teach the theological disciplines in a Catholic university are required to have a mandatum granted by competent ecclesiastical authority." That competent authority is the local bishop.

Ex Corde Ecclesiae was not a surprise. Three years earlier, in September of 1987, Pope John Paul II in Los Angeles instructed the U.S. bishops to "involve themselves in their theological faculties." The revision of the Code of Canon Law in 1983 had stated "those who teach the theological disciplines in any institution of higher studies whatsoever must have a mandate from the competent ecclesiastical authority" (canon 812). The early suggestion of that canon stimulated discussion and consultation—and disagreement—with Roman authorities on the part of Bishop James Malone, president of the U.S. Bishops' Conference, and representatives of the American Association of Catholic Colleges and Universities.

After the pope's announcement in Los Angeles, I engaged the three presidents of our Catholic colleges in the diocese and the three from the Berkeley seminaries to anticipate what would be coming. I was certain it would come. With the arrival of *Ex Corde Ecclesiae* at the moment when my resignation as bishop was within sight, I wanted the issue of the relationship of college and diocese to be resolved before a new bishop arrived. Brother Craig Franz, the president of St. Mary's College, invited me to lunch and then arranged a meeting with three of the faculty from religious studies. The conversation focused where it was expected: on academic freedom and autonomy. In time, we moved away from norms and rules to talk about the weighty presentation in the opening part of the document, which dealt with the nature of a Catholic university in our time.

The conversation not only changed but became animated. Questions about the nature of a Catholic college and university and Catholic identity had long been familiar. As far back as 1963, the International Federation of Catholic Universities roused itself from the moribund organization that it once was to establish a secretariat in Paris and sponsor a gathering at a Notre Dame facility in Wisconsin in the town of Land O' Lakes. The main issue was the balance of the autonomy of an institution, while respecting the role of the magisterium and church authority. Conversations continued in Tokyo, then in Kinshasa in the Republic of Congo, and by 1972 in Rome at the invitation of Cardinal Gabriel-Marie Garrone of the Congregation of Seminaries and Universities.

In January 1976, in line with what had gone before, Notre Dame University, with Father Theodore Hesburgh, CSC, as host, sponsored a symposium whose title was "Evangelization in the American Context." At its focus was the identity of the contemporary Catholic university. There were men and women major superiors, thirty-two administrators, including Christian Brothers Daniel Burke from La Salle, Philadelphia, and Patrick McGarry from Manhattan College in New York. There were forty-nine scholars and specialists of prominence such as Dr. John T. Noonan, professor of law at the University of California, Berkeley, Father David Tracy from the Divinity School of the University of Chicago, and Sister Agnes Cunningham from St. Mary of the Lake Seminary, Mundelein. Fifteen bishops were present, including three who would go on to become cardinals.

We might note as well the books written in the decades following: *The Idea of a Catholic University,* by George Dennis O'Brien, who visited here at St. Mary's two years ago; the book with the intriguing title, *The Catholic University as Promise and Project,* by Father Michael J. Buckley, SJ, from Boston College; and the works of Father John Piderit, SJ, and Dr. Melanie Morey, who were with us last October.

With the document *Ex Corde Ecclesiae,* I see the bishops and church authority as somewhat latecomers to the conversation described by Monika Hellwig, of the Association of Catholic Colleges and Universities, as the development of a new phase in identity for Catholic higher education.

Ex Corde Ecclesiae sets itself as a statement of appreciation. There is warmth in the expression "From the heart of the church," the document's title. There is praise in such descriptions as "an incomparable center of creativity and dissemination of knowledge for the good of humanity" and "their irreplaceable task." Through teaching and research, Catholic universities combine "excellence in humanistic and cultural development with specialized professional training and challenge students to continue the search for truth in their lives." They advance human dignity and cultural heritage.

Aligned with the Lasallian heritage, Pope John Paul II expresses his "deep conviction that the Catholic university is without doubt one of the best instruments that the church offers to our age, which is searching for certainty and wisdom."

Pointedly for our reflection today is that the Catholic college and university are immersed in human society and become "the primary and privileged place for a fruitful dialogue between the Gospel and culture...called on to become an ever more effective instrument of cultural progress for the individual as well as for society." The document adds, "In the world of today, characterized by such rapid developments in science and technology, the task of the Catholic university is assuming even greater importance and urgency." Significantly, the pope remarks that the institution is open to all human experience and ready to learn from any culture.

Gaudium et Spes
Pastoral Constitution on the Church in the Modern World
Vatican Council II, December 7, 1965

A description of responsibility for the Catholic university from *Ex Corde Ecclesiae* falls neatly under the instruction of the Vatican Council a quarter century previous. The opening words of the pastoral constitution were in place from the very beginning of the Council discussion:

> The joy and hope, the grief and anguish of the men and women of our times, especially those who are poor or are afflicted in any way, are the joy and hope, the grief and affliction of the followers of Christ as well. Nothing that is genuinely human fails to find an echo in their hearts.

The important point made in the document is that the church is servant to the world. An illustration of this at the very time that this document was reaching its final form was the appearance of Paul VI at the UN in New York. In the words of the Jesuit historian John W. O'Malley,

> This dramatic occasion once again showed Paul VI at his very best. The trip had immense symbolic value. The pope addressed a completely secular institution. He did so not to proselytize for the Catholic Church but to promote the well-being of the human family.

The part of *Ex Corde Ecclesiae* that rings with this Council document has to do with the section on development of culture (53–62). This subject received extended debate at the Council. Strongly in favor were a range of cardinals from Leo Joseph Suenens of Belgium to Francis Spellman of New York, aligned with such theologians as Yves Congar, Jean Danielou, Henri de Lubac, and Marie-Dominique Chenu. A leading force of the Council, Cardinal Joseph Frings from Cologne, whose theologian was Father Joseph Ratzinger, raised critical questions.

Pope Paul VI, author of *Ecclesiam Suam*, congratulates Bishop Begin on the Oakland prelate's report on the vitality of the new diocese. (Vatican photo)

His critique was an accent on the theology of the incarnation to the diminution of the theology of the cross. One has described this as the limited hopefulness of Augustine as compared to the comparative optimism of Aquinas. Karl Rahner was in this camp along with the then archbishop Karol Wojtyla.

The document in its final form stated "that one can come to an authentic and full humanity only through culture, that is, with the cultivation of natural goods and values." It made the point that the encounter with new cultures and the increased exchange between various groups and nations challenge the human family not to destroy ancestral wisdom and the heritage of tradition. Resolution was urgent to harmonize a culture resulting from economic, scientific, and technological progress with an education nourished by classical studies adapted to various traditions. It made the point that the church stimulates and advances human culture and illustrated that even by the effect of liturgy.

The document noted that the church's communion with cultural modes fostered her own enrichment as well as theirs. With clarity it recognized the legitimate autonomy of human culture, especially of the sciences. It noted the importance of literature and the arts to the life of the church. It reiterated the words from the earlier Vatican Council I of the two modes of knowledge with the phrase, "faith and reason," terms in my experience familiar in the atmosphere of St. Mary's College. It urged those who teach in colleges and universities through sharing of resources and points of view to collaborate with those well versed in other sciences. That document after its long and strenuous treatment won the overwhelming approval of bishops of the council, 2,309 to 75.

On October 20, 1965, Cardinal Fernando Cento, who had strong academic credentials, introduced the draft to the waiting gathering. A crucial point of his presentation was that the preferred mode of operation of the church in relationship to the world is *dialogue*.

Ecclesiam Suam
Pope Paul VI, August 6, 1964

Pope Paul VI describes his letter as "a reverent consideration of the subject of Holy Church." Two-thirds of the encyclical—surprisingly for the time—relate to dialogue. I found myself disposed to like and to embrace this instruction because of two experiences.

One was the invitation shortly after the Council closed to join the national dialogue group with the American Baptist Church. It was formal and structured. The Baptist contingent consisted of pastors, two theologians, and one competent, personable historian from Union Theological Seminary in New York. For six years, we pursued common understanding, coming to terms with vocabulary. I learned to admire their sense of prayer and Scripture. After forty years, I still recall a homily from a Chicago minister on Matthew 25. We all gained sympathy for each other's issues, indeed problems that arise from Baptist practice, such as the profession of no formal clerical leadership nor infant baptism. My customary responsibility was to report to the congregation at the American Baptist Church, two blocks from our Oakland cathedral. Over the years, my proficiency drew me the warm introduction, "John, the Baptist."

The second was the experience of the national bishops' document on nuclear arms, *The Challenge of Peace*, issued in 1983. It had been introduced three years before by two bishops, widely separated in the theological spectrum. Cardinal Joseph Bernardin was chosen as the chair of the committee that included, on the one hand, Bishop John O'Connor, at the time auxiliary bishop to the military chaplains' office of the U.S. Armed Forces and later cardinal of New York, and on the other, Bishop Thomas Gumbleton of Pax Christi and Detroit. Because of the political climate of the time, the document received attention at almost every level in dioceses and parishes. Invited to respond, University of California professors provided twenty-three assessments of the first draft, seventeen of which went from favorable to enthusiastic, six, from hesitancy to disagreement. In May 1983, the bishops' overwhelming vote in favor of the final version took many by surprise.

Here, in the Oakland Diocese, there was much restiveness over the issue largely because Lawrence Livermore National Laboratory was so involved in weapons design. Initiative came from a variety of sources, a parish in Livermore, professors from the Berkeley seminaries, and the universities. A first meeting of this group that included representatives from the Lawrence Laboratory took place at San Damiano Retreat Center. The rules were set down sharply and monitored by professional facilitators. The demand was civil discourse, not argumentation, the very quality of exchange that enabled a diverse U.S. bishops' group to produce a vote of 238 to 9 approving their document. The second meeting of our dialogue group took place at St. Mary's College without facilitators, a condition that lasted for another decade of that continuing dialogue.

So much from my experience made this encyclical congenial. Pope Paul began his reflection by indicating that the church had to meet and get to know and love the world. He made this a matter that was desired by the church, but with conviction, he noted, it was vital to the world. Remaining true to the faith was not enough for him. Gifts were to be shared. He declared, "To this internal drive of charity which seeks expression in the external gift of charity we will apply the word dialogue" (65). The word "dialogue" would appear seventy-seven times.

In line with other references from today, the pope noted that culture is where the church lives, ever in the Scriptural understanding of "in the world, but not of it." One is to keep distinct from the world, but, the pope emphasized, we are not distant from it, not indifferent to it, not afraid of it, and not contemptuous of it (65). Our task is to serve society, to deal with its serious problems of solidarity and peace and the rapid developments in science, technology, and social life and currents of philosophical and political thought. Without adapting our thinking to the customs and actions of the secular world—the "relativism" spoken of by Benedict XVI—we need a type of spirituality nourished by the reading of Scriptures and the fathers and doctors, readings graced by contemplation.

The pluralism of our societies recommends dialogue as a method of the apostolate. Paul VI notes the inherited style of popes Leo XIII, Pius XI, and Pius XII, entering into the stream of modern thought, and particularly in his predecessor's encyclical, *Pacem in Terris*, in which Good Pope John appealed to all men and women of goodwill. No other course is open to us. The church must enter into dialogue with the world in which she lives, and the pope says with confidence, "The church has something to say" (65).

For an undergirding by theology, the pope places the origin of dialogue in the mind of God himself. Revelation can be looked on as dialogue. It is through the incarnation and the gospel that God wishes to be known. For us that dialogue finds its expression in prayer. Furthermore, as God took initiative in the dialogue, we too must ask for dialogue (70).

The encyclical gives evidence of much thought and perhaps some of the traditional agonizing moments that we associate with the very sensitive Paul VI. Dialogue for him is something special. It is not proclamation nor, in the worst sense of the word, "preaching," nor is it ingratiating conversation. It does not conflict with the church's responsibility at times to protest and crusade against evils. The practice can be difficult if not impossible with those who utterly reject our invitation or are unwilling to accept it or those who practice a "calculated misuse of words." In these cases silence is the proper posture.

But dialogue has its place. To engage in it is to become a sign of consideration and respect. One listens to what others have to say and seeks to discover elements of truth in their presentations. Dialogue has particular qualities. It requires clarity before all else and intelligibility. It depends on the ability to conduct it with dignity, honesty, and prudence, confident in the power of words and of goodwill so that "truth is wedded to charity and understanding to love" (82). Dialogue thrives on friendship and most especially on service.

Drawing his conclusions, Paul VI sees circles of participants, starting with the human family. He proceeds then to those who worship one God, then to the Christian world. He saves admonition for those of the household of the faith, urging them to nourish and preserve harmony and peace in the church and reminding his flock that obedience based on faith is still operative (114). Additionally, one does not come to the dialogue with bitter criticism or arrogance since that vitiates dialogue, turning it into argument, disagreement, and dissension.

Our Holy Father modeled his instruction first in his meeting with Patriarch Athenagoras, to whom on his election he had written a letter in his own hand, and later during his visit to the UN. Pope Paul VI and Patriarch Athenagoras met in Jerusalem in 1964, the first such encounter between an Orthodox patriarch and a pope since 1054. Paul VI followed up the visit of the archbishop of Canterbury with John XXIII with a welcome to Michael Ramsey in 1966 and setting up the Anglican–Roman Catholic dialogue. He established secretariats for non- Christian religions in 1964 and for unbelievers in 1965.

My best experience with the virtues of dialogue described by the pope began in 1995, when I was named to the American bishops' Committee on Science and Human Values. Established in the 1980s, the committee's purpose was "to monitor development in science and technology that have moral and religious implications for society and church and to provide bishops with resources both philosophically and theologically evaluating such developments." The instrument offered was annual conferences for those responsible for the teaching of the faith and those whose worldview was formed by modern science. The establishment coincided with the comments of Pope John Paul II at the University of Fribourg in 1984: "Such a dialogue should try to clarify problems and questions and to discover a possible convergence of the various truths involved."

A Threefold Dialogue

By way of conclusion, from my own experience what one does instinctively is fortified by someone else's careful analysis. Pope Paul's giving it such attention deserves notice. Dialogue is worthy of focus, but for some it is not easily learned or prized. For many years, I was the "fraternal delegate" (a kind of liaison) of the American bishops to the Federation of Asian Bishops' Conferences. It is an organization approaching forty years of existence containing episcopal conferences from twenty different Asian cultures. Years ago, the bishops decided that their Asian mode of operation would be threefold:

- dialogue with the cultures in which they live,
- dialogue with religions with which they are associated, and, especially,
- dialogue with the poor.

At one of their meetings twenty years ago, Father Catalino Arevalo, a young Jesuit theologian from the Philippines, opened the first session with his appreciation of threefold dialogue, not without a touch of passion. He was followed by Cardinal Jozef Tomko, from the Congregation on the Evangelization of Peoples, equally convinced of the necessity of proclamation: "At the time of Jesus there were world religions; nevertheless, he came." The archbishop of Delhi sitting next to me whispered, "I think there is a war here we know nothing about."

The Catholic college in a special way can deal with the world outside because it has opportunity for motivation. From *Ex Corde Ecclesiae*, however, comes an additional comment: "The Catholic university must become more attentive to the cultures of the world of today...*and to those various cultural traditions existing within the church*" (emphasis added). I would say the obvious by adding the cultures *within* the college.

At the same time, I would quote from the document the practical constraints. John Paul II notes that the integration of knowledge stands high among responsibilities of a Catholic university. He calls this

a process, one which will always remain incomplete; moreover the explosion of knowledge in recent decades, together with the rigid compartmentalization of knowledge within individual academic disciplines, makes the task increasingly difficult.

My impression is that interdisciplinary conversation is much desired in higher education. During our dialogues on nuclear arms in the diocese, for example, the interdisciplinary issue was mentioned commendably a number of times.

Timothy Radcliffe, former master general of the Dominicans, once remarked that the church can channel dialogue to contain both cohesion and progress. I refer again to Monika Hellwig's contention that the understanding of the Catholic university has entered a new phase and is not looking backward. Along with the International Federation of Catholic Universities, St. Mary's participates in that search while the very terrain is shifting beneath our feet.

Dialogue, reverently treated by the Second Vatican Council and emphasized by Paul VI, plays an important role in Hellwig's "new phase."

10

The Laity Empowered

Council Builds on Vigor Already Present

THE VOICE OFTEN HEARD across the breadth of theological position-ing on laity in the church belongs to the nineteenth-century English churchman Blessed John Henry Cardinal Newman. His extensive writ-ing on the subject illumined the church of his day and, in the words of Pope Paul VI and Pope Benedict XVI, heavily influenced the bishops of the Second Vatican Council. Whether viewed as a recovery or a new de-velopment, Vatican II enhanced opportunities for laity to participate in the church—not just as witnesses but also as advisers and those with ministerial and even administrative responsibilities. This teaching had found fertile field in the life and health of the church in the Diocese of Oakland, long before it became a diocese in 1962.

The early history of the giant benefactors stands out. Mary Can-ning, secretary to the mayor of Oakland, funded the entire building of St. Francis de Sales Cathedral in 1886. The McGee and Curtis families provided for the development of St. Joseph the Worker in Berkeley. Un-usual Irish immigrants, they settled for farming rather than urban life in the nineteenth century. The Botelho family, owners of what is now the downtown of Walnut Creek, donated the property for St. Mary's. Faxon

Atherton, a Hayward land owner and philanthropist, gave the commanding hill property of All Saints. Local entrepreneur George W. McNear made possible Port Costa's St. Patrick Church in 1884.

Other benefactors provided leadership—in particular, those who provided vocations for service in the church, such as St. Elizabeth's parish with its German Franciscans and the revered names of Weishaar and Bucher. The Duggans from St. Augustine's in Oakland nurtured one Sister of the Holy Names and three priests for the Archdiocese of San Francisco. Sacred Heart parish in Oakland, at the division of the archdiocese in 1962, had nineteen active alumni from its school serving as archdiocesan clergy and unnumbered vocations to religious congregations of women and men.

One fruitful heritage of the Oakland Diocese was the strength of parish life, including faithful Mass attendance. Holy Name Societies were present in all, many of them sponsoring father-son breakfasts regularly during the year. The Legion of Mary, established by Frank Duff in Dublin in 1922, renowned in China and other mission territories, was in the East Bay within the decade and flourished. Support for Catholic education was high as well as volunteer aid in the diocese's two Catholic hospitals.

St. Vincent de Paul Society, particularly with the efforts of Michael Hester and Cyril Gilfether, and later Ed Moran and Olga Morris, received national recognition. The Catholic Ladies Aid Society, a locally organized body, served those in need along with two other groups of California origin, the Young Men's Institute and the Young Ladies' Institute. The venerable Knights of Columbus and the Catholic Daughters of the Americas rounded out the pattern.

Catholic representation in the civic community was notable. John F. Slavich, graduate of St. Francis de Sales school and long a City Council member, became mayor of Oakland in 1941. A story has been told about his attending the 12:15 P.M. Mass at his home parish in the days when only a few brave souls endured the Eucharistic fast from midnight to receive Holy Communion. The erudite pastor Monsignor Joseph Gleason, as he often did, was analyzing the public square when the mayor in the front row stage-whispered, "Monsignor, it's a quarter to two." (The Mass had begun one hour and thirty minutes earlier.)

Felix Chialvo, of the Italian Catholic Federation, and Frank You-ell, from the Chapel of the Oaks mortuary, remained on the City Council for years. So did Bob Osborne, whose public arguing with the Catholic mayor John Houlihan was not a religious model. The mayor was in place to welcome Bishop Floyd Begin at the banquet of installation and gave a quasi-homily from the reading of the day from the First Letter of John on "water and blood." John Gray, who with his wife, Norma, were mainstays of the choir at St. Joseph's in Berkeley, served for nine years on Berkeley's Planning Commission.

Influential Catholic Alumni

Alumnae from Holy Names College and alumni from the well-positioned Christian Brothers institution, St. Mary's College in Moraga, strengthened parish life. So, too, did outstanding Catholics from other institutions of higher learning in the diocese, such as illustrious law professors David Louisell and Arthur Sherry from UC–Berkeley's Boalt Hall along with the towering figure of Professor Raymond Sontag from the university's History Department. James Hegarty, a legendary figure from St. Mary's College, was reverently appreciated by parishioners as well as generations of students.

Other noted Catholic citizens gained public prominence, despite the reputed Masonic culture of the City of Oakland, among them eminent historian and city librarian Peter T. Conmy, who also served as scribe for the Native Sons of the Golden West as well as the Knights of Columbus; the Honorable Wiley Manuel, justice of the California Supreme Court; and Steve Still, editor of *The Oakland Tribune*. Despite a glass ceiling for feminine journalists, Mary Ellen Leary became Scripps Howard political editor for the West Coast and longtime contributor to the *Economist*. Her editorial enterprise made her the first reporter, man or woman, to interview a prisoner on San Quentin's death row. She was born into a large and professional Catholic family in Salt Lake City. Her father was eminent dean of the Law School at the University of Utah, an extraordinary position for a Catholic in the community of Brigham Young.

Our local Council of Catholic Women (NCCW) boasted of Margaret Mealey of St. Jarlath's parish, alumna of Holy Names, who went on to Washington, D.C., as DCCW national president and became coun-

Margaret Mealey, far left, alumna from Oakland's Holy Names University and longtime executive for the National Council of Catholic Women in Washington, D.C., has a privileged position as President John F. Kennedy honored former first lady Eleanor Roosevelt. (HNU photo)

sel to three presidents and Pope John Paul II. Kay Horsell likewise had a national reputation along with Marie Boedekker, sister-in- law of the saintly Father Alfred, OFM, of St. Anthony's Dining Room in the Tenderloin district of San Francisco.

Two groups that would be seedbeds for more lay involvement to come were represented by the Serra Clubs of the East Bay and by the particular nationality groups that prepared us for the spread of diversity that would mark the diocese. Ethnic identities in the East Bay were long established. Luigi Providenza, with his wife, Lady Augusta, founded the Italian Catholic Federation. Portuguese societies known by their acronyms IDES and the SPRSI flourished, especially in southern Alameda County. Strong Catholic leadership arose in the Black community, particularly with the Knights and Ladies of St. Peter Claver. Some names became prominent, such as Isabelle Kellum and Rose Casanave from St. Columba parish, Morris Soublet, later to be deacon, and George Scotlan, whose wife and family would be important figures in the new diocese. An alumni group from Xavier University in New Orleans produced quality leadership in Dr. Clarence Avery and his family. From these, Bishop Floyd Begin, following the recommendation of UC–Berkeley professor Raymond Sontag, formed with Thom McGowan the Catholic Interracial Council (CIC), a program founded by Jesuit Father John LaFarge in New York in the 1950s that would flower in the era of civil rights development. The CIC nurtured student membership, such as C. Herbert Clemens from UC–Berkeley, and introduced Father Bill O'Donnell into a social action career at home and abroad.

The Serra Club of Oakland was designed to promote vocations to priesthood and to religious life, but it also promoted lay leadership among its members. Without an East Bay presence that would be illumined later by a bishop and cathedral, this gathering of business and professional men, Bill Slakey, Art Melka, Bill Dennis, Ralph Montali, and John Morris, all consciously Catholic, would be both witness and spokespersons to the community. There were, of course, prominent pastors such as Robert Sampson at Sacred Heart and the dean, Monsignor Thomas Scahill at St. Jarlath's, Monsignor Nicholas Connolly from St. Leo's, along with Father Charles Hackel, a noteworthy leader of Catholic Charities. But prominent visibility in daily life belonged to the members of Serra.

Serving in the Public Arena

Others served in the public arena. Rose and Dan Lucey were known far beyond the East Bay as promoters of the Christian Family Movement and their drive to establish a national academy of peace to have the same status as our three military academies. A good number found a vocation in the development and maintenance of labor unions, many of whom were products of a University of San Francisco program, supported strongly by Bishop Hugh A. Donohoe, namely, the Association of Catholic Trade Unionists. An outreach in the early 1960s came through the ecumenical East Bay Conference of Religion and Race, aligned with Tom Fike, a Berkeley attorney who led a group promoting jobs for local people in the proposed development of the Bay Area Rapid Transit system.

Those named above and so many unnamed were believers who could also articulate their faith. I remember an incident from my first

Bishop Begin presents the 1967 Thomas More Award
to Arthur Melka for the layman's outstanding service
to the Diocese of Oakland. (J. Wright / *The Catholic
Voice*)

year teaching at Bishop O'Dowd High School. Noting the success my
brother had had in teaching speech and drama at Marin Catholic High
School, our principal, Father (later Bishop) Mark Hurley, gave me the
responsibility for that extracurricular activity. One of the students, a ju-
nior at the time, set her direction on being an actress in the American
theater.

With serious reservations about the moral environment in which
she would become involved, I turned for consultation to the director of
the Drama Department at San Francisco State University, J. Fenton
McKenna, who was a good friend and a sponsor of the school's
Newman Club when I was chaplain there. He had two questions, "Does
she have talent?" and "Does she have good character?" I said she mea-
sured up on both counts since she made the state finals in Santa Barbara
for dramatic reading and came from a good family. "Then you have to
encourage her," my counselor advised. He followed with a reminder
about Pope Pius XII's directive encouraging talented Catholics to enter
into the worlds of communication, art, drama, law, and economy. "We
will lose some," he grimly commented. "But the risk must be taken. That
is the meaning of the Eucharist in our lives. We carry the banner into the
world. It gets tattered and damaged, but we bring it back, lay it on the altar, and take it up renewed." That year was 1958. I believe his commen-

tary eloquently represented a contemporary understanding of prayer and service to church and community.

After the Council

The Vatican Council would build on the vigor of established Catholic life. For some it would be an articulated understanding. For others it would be intuitive. In any case, the basic thrusts of the Council would take root. From *Lumen Gentium*, the people would easily grasp the notion of "the people of God," a term that described the gift that was membership in the church as well as the added responsibility of the baptized for the life and the health of that church. Underneath lay the call to holiness of life to which our people aspired.

Sacrosanctum Concilium provided full conscious understanding and participation in the liturgy, the kind that would lead as well into the governance of the diocese, particularly through consultation but also through collaboration. We gained wisdom by partnering and listening.

Bishop Floyd Begin arrived in Oakland in April 1962; Vatican II opened in October. Though the tradition was to have priests in charge of all diocesan departments, the bishop appointed a lay director of cemeteries. He then had a layman trained in building to oversee diocesan construction, and he gave a young layman responsibility over the CYO. He also established a finance council with lay experts and appointed a well-connected voice in the community to manage an office of public relations.

Within a decade of the bishop's arrival, the National Conference of Catholic Bishops produced a document entitled "Called and Gifted" in which the expression "lay ecclesial ministers" was used for the first time. (The proper application of this new term has been much debated.) At the same time, at the request of our local Council of Priests, the diocese published a pastoral letter on the role of women. The preparatory committee, co-chaired by Father Bill Macchi and diocesan newspaper columnist Nora Petersen, brought together a mixed group that approached the issue from both ends of the theological spectrum. The genius of Margaret Mealey, recently retired from the national office of the National Council of Catholic Women, facilitated the discussions. The letter that went out under my signature as bishop urged the appointment of women to liturgical and pastoral positions and called for equal representation in consultative bodies that were being formed. The document set a flavor.

The two documents, one national and the other local, plus our own diocesan experiences soon gave substance to the roles of laypeople both in variety and numbers. About that time, Cath McGhee was at a point of decision in her life. She was then serving on the parish staff in Moraga, but wanted to know whether there was a future for laypeople in such positions. I could only state that talent like hers would survive because diocesan and parish staffs would have to grow based on the Council's directions. In fact, this had already happened. Lay journalist Dan Morris had succeeded Father Richard Mangini as editor of *The Catholic Voice*; Rita Belleci was appointed to the Office of Family Life; and Carmen Vinella joined the Office of Worship. Laypeople assumed additional responsibilities in diocesan insurance and, eventually, in finance.

At one Monday meeting of department heads, we realized that more laypeople were in charge of diocesan responsibilities at that time than priests. Soon, women outnumbered men in diocesan positions. This shift raised no serious concerns; it was merely accepted, perhaps even expected. In the minds of some, however, the alacrity of it all was a source of amusement.

Laity Assume Higher Roles

Parish staffs were also growing at this time, with lay principals and teachers in the parochial schools as well as directors of religious education and youth and music ministers. Laypeople took over the role of business managers, allowing priests to focus on their sacramental and pastoral responsibilities.

Another area of greater lay involvement in the diocese involved "pastoral associates," a wide-ranging designation that needed some definition, not to mention training. It was not long before Sister Marie Wiedner took over the administration of St. Charles Borromeo in Livermore, while the pastor went on a three-month sabbatical. That made news. Then a pastoral associate was officially appointed to administer the parish with a young priest in place. At St. Monica's parish in Moraga the Pastoral Leadership Placement Board (now including laypeople) approved the appointment of Cath McGhee as pastoral administrator, with Father Declan Deane as associate. Deacon George Peters was appointed to manage St. Alphonsus Liguori parish; Holy Names Sister Marian Wright, returning from mission work in Peru, took over the administration of St. Andrew's/St. Joseph's on San Pablo Avenue; and Steve Mullin was asked to be parish administrator at All Saints in Hayward. These appointments were well received, but there was no attempt to establish a general policy regarding laity in the diocese. We were just trying to utilize the broadest talent available. The traditional position of the priest as both sacramental and administrative person was the norm, but opportunities for special arrangements were appreciated and worth taking advantage of.

Our greater understanding of the role of laity came at a time when the diocese was also becoming diversified ethnically. Father George Crespin, as vicar general, and Sister Felicia Sarati, as director of ethnic centers, provided needed support in our efforts to serve our ethnic communities. Institutions had already been established for this purpose in the diocese, but in some cases we lacked clergy and religious from the cultures being served. Latino leadership emerged in our central offices as well as in the Cursillo movement and numerous Latino societies. George Scotlan and Morris Soublet, along with Will Harvey from St. Patrick's and Thom McGowan, developed the Black Catholic Lay Caucus. Filipino numbers increased greatly as did their lay leadership. The Chinese vicariate established in Bishop Begin's time took on new leadership with Danny Wong and Agnes Koo and the creation of four liturgical centers. A Chinese house of hospitality carried on in Berkeley after its priest-founder returned to Macao. Father Don MacKinnon, CSSR, and Sister Michaela O'Connor, SHF, served the Khmuu people of Laos and nurtured layman Kan Souriha, whose leadership went beyond the diocese. Koreans in the diocese set up their own centers. Cambodians, newly arrived, had a layman, Francis Samostra, who worked with the diocese along with his friend Bishop Yves Ramousse of Cambodia, who delighted us by his visits and encouragement. The Tongan community, with Tenisha Finau, made contact with the whole Bay Area as did the Haitian people, again with lay initiative.

Each year a different parish in the diocese hosted the Chatauqua (Native American word meaning "gathering of the tribes") that brought together all ethnic groups in the diocese for a Marian procession, liturgy,

Bishop Cummins honors members of the Strategic Planning Group for their four years of work in establishing pastoral priorities for the Diocese of Oakland. (J. Wright / *The Catholic Voice*)

and cultural celebration. The annual event was organized by Sister Felicia and the heads of the various ethnic centers.

Monica Clark, editor of *The Catholic Voice* for more than twenty years, initiated the publication of *El Heraldo Católico* to reach the ever-growing population of Spanish-speaking Catholics. Under her guidance, the paper became a joint project with the Diocese of Sacramento and the Archdiocese of San Francisco.

Diocesan Pastoral Council

At the urging of the Council of Priests and with the leadership of Father Brian Joyce plans were laid for a Diocesan Pastoral Council dominated by the laity. A weekend gathering of four hundred parish representatives at Holy Names College set up a structure for the Council and set five goals for the diocese. I was told as bishop to reserve four appointments to balance the elected group. The concern, of course, was women's representation, though in eight areas of the diocese women had already been selected. Elected chairs were Gesine Laufenberg from St. Monica's followed in a later term by Zelda Humphrey of Corpus Christi. The vice-chair was Priscilla Scotlan of the large Scotlan family from Sacred

Heart. The bishop's appointments went to Asian men.

Accompanying organizational developments were new and inter-
esting thrusts in spiritual formation. Many found the Cursillo and Marriage Encounter movements of value. Interest grew in pursuing inherited
spiritualities: Franciscan, Dominican, Jesuit, Carmelite. Laity joined with
priests and religious in forming Jesu Caritas groups. Some found Liturgy
of the Hours attractive, as the Vatican Council had opened a way for
genuine liturgical spirituality. The search was for a gratifying balance of
contemplative aspirations with organization and action.

A subtle change occurred in the attitude of parishioners who were
beginning to see their participation in parish life as indeed a ministry related to their baptism and confirmation. This showed itself in people
like Patricia Oakeshott, who served as cook for a quarter century in our
cathedral house as well as providing service at times to the Franciscans
and Jesuits in Berkeley. Her sense of hospitality blessed the many who
enjoyed the hospitality of our cathedral rectory. The entertaining of
myriad guests—from significant personalities and beneficiaries of charity and winners of education drawings to servicing diocesan committees—certainly fell into the category of ministry.

Not surprisingly, the first priority the Diocesan Pastoral Council
established was lay leadership formation. At the parish and diocese levels much has been accomplished in that area. A greater challenge comes
from the obligation the Council's *Gaudium et Spes* document placed on
us, namely, servicing the worlds of peace, family, economics, and
culture.

The diocese made great gains in those areas, too. Illustrations
abound: our Catholic Charities work with immigrants and refugees; our
active support for César Chávez and his United Farm Workers; the 1964
campaign on a fair housing initiative; the efforts of Oakland Community Organizations; Family Aid to Catholic Education; the contribution
of UC–Berkeley professors to the U.S. bishops' pastoral letters on nuclear arms and the American economy. Divorced and separated Catholics took it upon themselves, under the tutelage of Sister Marie Wiedner,
to be ministers to those working through such loss alone. Likewise in the
sensitive area of sexual abuse, survivors joined with Carondelet Sister
Barbara Flannery in ministry and support to others who suffered such

violations.

Permit me to add a personal experience. In 1979 I was invited to a two-week seminar in the Philippines. Exposure during the first week took place in Mindanao during the reign of President Marcos and under his imposition of martial law. Dioceses throughout the country had established training programs for catechetical leaders. Those leaders took great care in community formation to be sensitive to the precarious situation of those who were doing union organizing in rural areas. The support, protection, and the sophistication of these leaders was impressive.

The Diocese of Oakland paled in comparison to the world service evident in the Catholic population of the Philippine Islands. Our Catholic colleges and the Berkeley seminaries have laudably made advances on this issue. A singular parish model in this regard is the Lenten luncheon series on business ethics that Father Brian Joyce at St. Monica's in Moraga organized in San Francisco's financial district. His initiative led to regular Saturday morning Masses, followed by breakfast and conversations in the parish.

Lay development in church service has been well documented. Yet, understanding one's secular vocation and integrating one's work in the world with one's spirituality, urgent as this is, has proven to be a difficult assignment. Vatican II's vision is a lofty one. Its explication by experts as French Dominican theologian Yves Congar and philosopher Etienne Gilson fits the contemporary church's emphasis on New Evangelization.

11

Religious Women on the Rise

Sisters Launch Pastoral Initiatives

Women religious have played a wide-ranging role in Catholic education in the Diocese of Oakland in recent years. The ministry of religious women throughout the United States—particularly in the fields of education and health care—is a noteworthy chapter in the history of the church, one that is universally recognized. While their advances in these fields have brought Sisters into major administrative roles, their work for the most part has been known only to the immediate community served. Indeed, St. Paul classified that work as "hidden with Christ in God."

The renewal promoted by the Second Vatican Council offered religious women remarkable encouragement for the redirection and expansion of their ministries in the mid-1960s. Even before the Council, however, the stirrings of a whole generation and more of religious women were becoming evident. One milestone was the urging of Pope Pius XII in 1950 that Sisters renew and adapt their practices to contemporary times in relation to community life, dress, and availability. Two years earlier, Holy Cross Sister Madaleva Wolff opened up the Theology Department at St. Mary's College in Indiana for degrees to women. In the next decade the Sister Formation Conference began urging professional training to enhance the quality of ministry. I have remarked already on the expansion of ministries in the Diocese of Oakland from the older-style institutional involvements to wider ministerial participation—particularly in the host of initiatives the communities themselves created.

Entry into this story begins with Catholic schools in the Diocese of Oakland.

In 1868, six French-speaking Sisters of the Holy Names from Quebec arrived in Oakland through the efforts of Father Michael King of St. Mary's parish in West Oakland. The Canadian Sisters soon augmented their numbers with vocations from California. From their college on 20th and Webster Streets, they developed what I lightly call an "empire" of seven schools in West and North Oakland. Later, the Carondelet Sisters would follow the same path in central Contra Costa County. The Holy Names Sisters expanded their ministry and membership throughout California and then, in a half-century, to Kagoshima, Japan; Lesotho, in southern Africa; and finally Arequipa, Peru.

Reappraising Traditional Ministries

Greater openness to the world—the hallmark of the post–Vatican II years—necessitated a reappraisal of institutional ministries. In 1964 Mary Perkins Ryan wrote a book entitled *Are Parochial Schools the Answer? Catholic Education in Light of the Council.* Eight years later (1972) a collaborative effort of bishops and Catholic school educators, mainly religious women, published "To Teach as Jesus Did," which reaffirmed the heart of Catholic education as message, community, service. At the same time, it embraced change.

In 1978, our diocesan leadership veered from the long tradition of priests as superintendents of schools and chose Dominican Sister Rose Marie Hennessy to be its new superintendent. Their choice was based on Sister Hennessy's experience as principal of St. Elizabeth's Elementary School, her role on the diocesan school board, and her elevated stature in the Mission San Jose Dominican Sisters, whose relationship with Bishop Floyd Begin had long been one of friendship and cooperation. To ensure that she would have to deal with a minimum resistance in her post, I checked with two influential priests in the diocese who were

Sister Rose Marie Hennessy, OP, here listening to first grader Gloria DePaz at St. Elizabeth School, Oakland, was the first woman to become superintendent of diocesan schools, a post she held for fifteen years. (Chris Duffey / *The Catholic Voice*)

known for being uncomfortable with change. The one who would have been the more likely to oppose the appointment of a religious woman as superintendent of schools told me that he would have no objection whatever as long as "it were Sister Rose Marie Hennessy."

Sister Hennessy's fifteen years in the superintendent's office were a time of transition, with laity assuming greater responsibilities and growing in prominence. This change underscored the need for lay training, especially in the philosophy of Catholic education. Sister Mary Peter Traviss, of Sister Hennessy's community and an adviser on education in the newly created Diocese of Oakland, established a degree program for Catholic school administrators at the University of San Francisco.

Large class numbers in our Catholic schools—the result of the post–World War II boom—began to decline as the costs of Catholic education began to rise to cover salaries and benefits for the growing number of lay teachers who were needed as vocations to religious life failed to produce educators in sufficient numbers. Schools in the city, which had provided missionary and evangelical outreach to what we presumed were Christian children, began to enroll people of other faiths. A new generation of pastors, many of whom did not share the convictions of older generations about subsidizing parish schools, faced growing needs for teachers and staff, as well as for religious education programs for public school children. In particular, the diocesan financial committee had to tackle what seemed to be a limitless amount of diocesan aid for inner-city schools, particularly St. Patrick's in West Oakland.

To meet these new needs, the superintendent's office provided teacher training and a variety of other services. To support the diocese's educational needs, Barbara Morrill from St. Theresa's parish, and Holy Cross Sister Sebastian Adza of St. Bernard's parish, suggested to the diocesan office a second Sunday collection to support a new group with the acronym FACE (Family Aid to Catholic Education). The chancery's initial response was that such an appeal would not yield sufficient funds. Not to be denied, Ms. Morrill and Sister Adza, two women with great imagination, organized a FACE event at the newly rebuilt Mission San Jose. Their second was a meeting at the De Young Museum in San Francisco with the exhibit of Vatican art. FACE was successful beyond all early expectations, profiting from work done earlier in the diocese— especially in educational leadership—by pastors among others.

Sisters as Change Agents

In the 1960s, a cadre of principals nicknamed "The Magnificent Seven" stepped forward to make a difference. All seven were religious women from St. Louis Bertrand parish in the east of the City of Oakland to St. Patrick's in the west. The principals lobbied Oakland's public school administration for a share in the resources that U.S. government's Title IX program had made available through the Federal Education Act. These educators were truly change agents; their creativity and persistence brought urban education into the public eye, showcased the excellence of urban Catholic schools, and generated support for Catholic education in the diocese.

The 1980s, however, brought more school closures. Demographic shifts forced the transfer of students from Oakland's Our Lady of Lourdes to neighboring parish schools. Charter schools, which we had looked on favorably—Mary Help of Christians was the site of the first such school in Oakland—proved to be competitive. In the face of the hardest times Catholic schooling had endured since they were mandated by the Third Baltimore Council in 1884, the morale of parents, teachers, and staff remained high. Professional development programs continued and communications were improving, something our priests, particularly pastors, deeply appreciated.

The advances of women religious in educational leadership in the diocese stood in sharp contrast to earlier history in the Bay Area. The makeup of San Francisco's archdiocesan personnel directory in 1959—on the eve of the establishment of the Diocese of Oakland and the opening of Vatican II—was heavily clerical. Diocesan institutions operated by religious would identify only the relevant community and legal titles read only "The Sisters of the Sacred Names of Jesus and Mary, a corporation." Each religious community in those days had a priest listed as an "archdiocesan director."

Individual Sisters in the East Bay were by and large anonymous, especially when they were identified without their family names. The president of Holy Names College was identified simply as Sister Rose Emmanuela; the name of the "superior and superintendent" of Providence Hospital was given as Sister Bonose, SP. Others identified in a similar manner included Sister Mary Aloysius, RSM, "superior" of Our Lady's Home for the Aged in Fruitvale; Sister Beatrice of the Little Sisters of the Poor on East Fourteenth Street, who was somewhat quaintly called "the good mother"; Mother Mary Magdalene of the Resurrection, prioress of the Discalced Carmelite Nuns of Berkeley; Sister Mary Noreen, SHF, who was "in charge" of St. Vincent's Home; and Sister Mary Clotilde, OP, "superior" of St. Mary of the Palms at Mission San Jose.

By 1971, the identities of religious educators were being recorded. Lists of the names of elementary and high school principals included the surnames of Sisters. A year later, Sisters in charge of religious education—mainly Sisters of the Holy Family—would be fully named. The names of Sisters on the diocesan school board were given in full: Sister Clara Anne Budenz, OP, and Sister Rose Marie Hennessy, OP. And Sister Sebastian Adza, CSC, was added to the names of board members of *The Catholic Voice*, our diocesan newspaper.

Religious assumed new responsibilities: Sister Mary Esther Bazzano, SHF, was named director of catechetics; Sister Miriam Thomas

McManus, SNJM, became executive secretary of the Social Justice Committee; Sister Thomas Mary Collins, CSJ, was chosen as an associate director of services for the deaf and hard of hearing. In the department of Catholic Charities that served developmentally disabled members of the diocese, Sister Irene Kobach, SSJ-TOSF, was the executive director and Sister Mary Grace Puchacz, of the same community, was an associate director.

New Opportunities and Responsibilities

In the process of renewal for more effective ministry, many religious congregations voted to allow its members to modify their religious habits or wear secular dress. This change in clothing drew comments pro and con, but permitting the nuns to use their baptismal names in place of the names given them at time of their religious profession caused nary a ripple.

As the recognition of Sisters grew, so too did more opportunities and responsibilities. These followed two paths. One was participation in established institutional ministries. The other was a striking innovation—religious women themselves taking the initiative to respond to the needs they saw. These initiatives were very often inspired by the reclaiming of the original direction of the congregation's institute or charism, as it was called.

In addition to filling already established roles, many religious women became "pastoral associates," among the variety that this term embraced in parish life. Sister Marie Wiedner, an Adrian Dominican, notably became "temporary administrator" of St. Charles Borromeo parish in Livermore, while the pastor took a three-month sabbatical. Shortly afterwards, when the gracefully competent Sister Marian Wright, SNJM, a recent missioner in Peru, was named administrator of St. Andrew's–St. Joseph's parish in Oakland's older area, her appointment made little news at all. Sister Marie Wiedner, OP, established an office for divorced and separated Catholics as an adjunct to her work in Livermore. Following the Supreme Court's Roe v. Wade decision, Sister Maureen Webb, SNJM, of Holy Names University with a doctorate in biology, offered her services to Bishop Begin to promote a Respect Life Office. She became counsel to the California Catholic Conference in Sacramento and was a talented witness before assembly hearings.

Work associated with Catholic Charities abounded. Sister Thomas Josephine Lawler, another Adrian Dominican, developed a program for ministry to the aging that would fit any parish. Sister Elizabeth Lang, OP, exiled from Vietnam, became a recognized expert and a forceful negotiator both with government officials and the newly arrived. Sister Aurora Perez, SHF, created new aspects of the Special Religious Education (SPRED) program for the developmentally disabled and their families. Sister Joan O'Connor worked with Father Ernest Brainard in the ARDOR program, which helped those in need of recovery from alcoholic dependence. In the medical field, Sister Bernice Gotelli, PBVM, became chaplain at Children's Hospital. Sister Antoinette Yelek, CSJ administrator of St. Rose Hospital, firmly rooted that institution in the communities of Hayward and South County.

Education was notably broadened. Religious women theologians joined faculties in Berkeley. Sister Mary Ann Donovan, DC, of the Jesuit School of Theology in Berkeley, became available for diocesan days of recollection as well as counsel on theological issues and proper responses. Sister Sandra Schneiders, IHM, shared theological developments with the bishop, advised on religious and women's issues, and edited episcopal letters. In 1982, with only ten days' notice, she produced a thirty-page presentation on New Testament themes related to nuclear arms for the National Bishops' Committee, which was preparing its peace pastoral.

Religious women served the diocese in multiple ministries. Sister Anne Russell, OP, of Adrian, Michigan, served the Catholic chaplaincy at Mills College and Chabot College, with an office at the Newman Center for California State University at Hayward. Sister Judith Rinek at Holy Names University became director of campus ministry. Sister Karen Stern, SHF, addressed the California bishops on the trends and developments in catechetics. Sister Rita Eileen Dean, OP, in her quarter century of service to the diocese moved from school administration to the diocesan superintendent's office. Later she revived her interest in priestly and religious vocations and became a much-appreciated adjunct staff at St. Patrick's Seminary in Menlo Park.

Sister Barbara Flannery, CSJ, as chancellor, and Sister Felicia Sarati, CSJO, as director of ethnic ministry, carried out major roles in the

Bishop Cummins presents St. Joseph of Carondelet Sister Barbara Flannery to Pope John Paul II as first woman chancellor of the Oakland Diocese, who among other notices won high praise for her work with survivors of sexual abuse and their families. (Vatican photo)

diocese. Sister Flannery, a native of the diocese with an MBA and experience as a school principal and associate superintendent of schools, assumed diocesan responsibility for departments, legal issues, and media response; she also received particularly high praise for initiatives concerning the victims of sexual abuse.

 With carefully calculated steps, Sister Felicia Sarati oversaw the hospitality and service needed by the great cultural diversity of nationalities in the diocese, especially newcomers. Her presence and her interest provided fruitful hospitality. She was much assisted by Sister Rosaline Nguyen, LHC, who directed the Vietnamese office, and Sister Michaela O'Connor, SHF, serving the needs of Khmuu refugees from Laos who were in great need of ministry. Telling evidence of the value of this ministry came from the visiting bishop of Tonga, Patelisio Finau. At one ethnic gathering, Bishop Finau expressed his profound thanks for the welcome his people had received into the Oakland Diocese, especially for the opportunities opened up to them to contribute to the life and health of the wider community.

Initiatives toward People on the Margins

Equally, if not more impressive, have been the initiatives taken on by religious women themselves. Much of these had to do with the familiar expression of people on the margins of the society. With the closing of St. Mary's School in West Oakland, Holy Names Sister Mary Ondreyco established St. Mary's Center, thus continuing the presence of the Holy Names Sisters after a century on 7th Street, while also expanding outreach to the elderly. Holy Names Sisters Cynthia Canning and Rosemary Delaney opened the Next Step Learning Center to give those who had dropped out of education a second chance. The center enlisted help from generous and talented tutors and the Sisters took responsibility for financing a work that through their nurturing has enabled many to acquire a GED certificate and even go on to college.

Sister Maureen Lyons, CSJ, formerly the principal at St. Patrick's in West Oakland, and Sister Carol Anne O'Marie, CSJ, shouldered the financial and personal responsibility for establishing A Friendly Place, which offered homeless women hospitality and a place of safety. Providence House, as an outreach program of the Sisters of Providence, served AIDS patients. In the city of Concord, Sister Ann Weltz, CSJ, set up the Bay Area Crisis Nursery for young children exposed to critical situations. Sister Maureen Duignan, of the Franciscan Sisters of Philadelphia, established and became director of the East Bay Sanctuary Covenant, to respond to the needs especially of Latin American refugees and to offer relief from the misery and fears of immigrants without proper documents.

Under the direction of Sister Maureen Delaney, SNJM, Oakland Community Organizations—a community organizing effort started by Jesuit Father John Baumann—served communities in a number of sites throughout Oakland from its center at the Cathedral of St. Francis de Sales. Sister Delaney, and her sister, Rosemary, also a Holy Names Sister, both worked at forging bonds and improving conditions in the neighborhood community. Sister Maureen Delaney later moved to Tutwiler, Mississippi, to work in a community service project operated by the Holy Names Sisters project in the Mississippi Delta area.

Sister Simone Campbell, SSS, continued a long record of service in the diocese by the Sisters of Social Service—a record that stretched as far back as Sister Patricia Feeley at St. Mary's Social Center in my seminary days. With a professionalism unimaginable in earlier days, Sister Campbell, with her law degree and sense of self-assured confidence, provided legal services for eighteen years to those in the greatest need and with the least opportunity.

Another area of sophistication was housing. Sister Joanna Bramble, CSJ, and Sister Mina Gaskell, CSJ, worked with Jubilee West, a voluntary organization that renovated houses in the area around St. Patrick's parish. Sister Barbara Dawson, RSCJ, joined with Catholic Charities and other interested organizations to establish a housing coalition for the City of Oakland. Sister Elaine Sanchez, SHF, led the Holy Family Sisters through the maze of city regulations to complete an affordable housing project on their property in Fremont. Dominican Sisters of Mission San Jose collaborated with the city to provide a center on their property to serve those suffering from Alzheimer's disease.

The diocese also recognized the contributions of Sister Lillian Murphy, RSM, president of Mercy Housing, a national organization based in Denver. As head of Mercy Housing and one time the director of Mercy Care and Retirement Center in Fruitvale, Sister Murphy came to the rescue of the diocese when three large apartment projects were in danger of failure after the Loma Prieta earthquake in 1989. Our Catholic Charities organization had overextended itself and, if not for the intervention of Mercy Housing, the three projects would have collapsed.

Ministries undertaken by religious women went beyond the urgings of Matthew 25 to help those in spiritual need as well. Sister Marietta Fahey, SHF, opened Holy Family Center in Walnut Creek as a venue for spiritual direction and reflection for those in the immediate area. Sister Fahey was following the example of her own community, which had opened the doors of its motherhouse at Mission San Jose for conferences and retreats. The Mission San Jose Dominican Sisters followed a similar pattern, issuing invitations through their college to groups and individuals who might want to share in the tradition of Dominican spirituality.

Sister Patti Bruno of the San Rafael Dominicans and Father Jude Siciliano of the southern province of Dominicans to promote preaching. Sisters Marcia Frideger and Maureen Hester from Holy Names University made their services widely available in the diocese for the first-ever convocation of Oakland clergy at Clear Lake and the start of what I then thought was a premature Diocesan Pastoral Council. Their leadership dispelled my initial concerns and led to most fruitful outcomes.

In another area, Sister Nancy Teskey of Holy Names University combined the gifts of her religious formation with a doctorate in physiology from UC–Davis to provide services to parishes and institutions engaged in dialogue about science and religion.

Twenty-first-century religious life builds on and extends the work and accomplishments of earlier centuries. The journey of religious women stretches from an era of anonymity to a time of expanded responsibility and recognition. The contents of diocesan directories today reflect the long and, for some observers, rapid growth in services offered by religious women.

Collaboration is a combination of virtue, on the one hand, and initiative, on the other. The strength of religious communities provides the charisms and motivation along with support, moral and otherwise, that favors initiative and can cushion the risks. American religious women have been described as "the best cadre of educated women in the United States." Generations of formation, training, and professionalism have laid the foundation for the growth and further development.

The concerns Rome expressed in the appraisal that took place under Archbishop John R. Quinn in the 1980s may have been a response to rapid change in communities of religious. So, too, was the recent investigation of religious women in the United States by the Congregation of Consecrated Life. The investigation, which was chaired by Sister Mary Clare Millea, ASCJ, left some hurt (especially older religious) and puzzled many in the U.S. Church. The outcome, however, was gratitude and praise.

In any case, I remember the title of an address given by Professor Yvette Fallandy, a lay friend from Mills College, who was later named vice-president of California State University at Sonoma. In the very early days after Vatican II, my brother, a colleague of the professor's in education, invited Professor Fallandy to speak to a group of nuns from

the West Coast. The title of her talk—"Nice Is Not Enough"—anticipated the renewals in religious life that would soon flow from the Council. The evidence, now fifty years later, supports the professor's instincts
about the sustained vitality of religious communities of women.

12

Priesthood Blossoms in New Diocese

Young Priests Given Major Responsibilities

IRISH POET WILLIAM BUTLER YEATS WROTE: "This is no country for old men." That sentiment was somewhat appropriate for the new Diocese of Oakland, for in the days when we were part of the Archdiocese of San Francisco a young priest would have to wait a long time, perhaps twenty years, before being appointed a pastor.

That situation was about to change. One dark morning in late January 1962, Father Jim Keeley, my next-door neighbor in the faculty house at Bishop O'Dowd High School, put his head inside my door and announced, "We are a new diocese. A bishop from Cleveland has been appointed."

I do not remember an extraordinary amount of excitement at the time. Bishops were somewhat distant figures. In the five years I had been at Bishop O'Dowd we never had a bishop visit us nor did we have any hope in this regard. In the wake of the division of the archdiocese that January, we might have expected disappointment from some San Francisco natives who would be left in Santa Rosa or Oakland, and even in far-away Stockton. Monsignor Michael Lucid captured that sentiment later on when he told Bishop Floyd Begin that his mother had come to

terms with her San Francisco–born son being assigned to Oakland because, as he wryly explained, "She always wanted a son in the foreign
missions."

Toward the end of February 1962, Father Pearse Donovan, the
principal at Bishop O'Dowd, knocked on my classroom door during the
second period. I was then dean of boys in the high school, and an inter-
ruption like this usually meant some difficulty. Outside the classroom,
Father Donovan told me, "The new bishop just called. He sounds very
nice. He wants you to be the chancellor." With surprise, particularly
since the bishop had never met me, I asked, "What does that job entail?"
Pearse responded, "I don't know, but it will be good for Bishop
O'Dowd High School."

I was not yet thirty-four years old. Father Michael Lucid was also
young, at thirty-three, when he was plucked from St. Benedict's in East
Oakland, where he was associate pastor and appointed director of religious education and assistant superintendent of schools. He was bright
and administratively competent, but in the exploding post–Vatican II
era he would have to deal with enormous changes in religious education
with the increase in books and other educational materials and new demands for the training of instructors. He worked well with the two Holy
Family Sisters who had already been appointed, the experienced veteran
Sister Mary Esther Bazzano and a very young Sister Joan Derry. Together the two Sisters performed well in the demanding specialty of the
Sisters of the Holy Family, educating Catholic students in our public
schools.

Soon came the announcement that Father Frank Maurovich, 34,
the associate at St. Cornelius in Richmond, was to take over the role of
journalist in the diocese. At that time, this work entailed producing four
Oakland pages in the San Francisco Archdiocese's *San Francisco Monitor*.
Bishop Begin was not sentimental about keeping any connections with
the mother archdiocese, however, and he quickly approved a recommendation to set up his own diocesan weekly, *The Catholic Voice*.

Frank Maurovich was to the manner born. He audited courses at
the University of California School of Journalism and plunged into intelligent reporting on diocesan events and especially, with the excitement surrounding Vatican II, on issues related to events in Rome. He

At the creation of the Diocese of Oakland in 1962, Bishop Begin inherited a sea-soned leadership team from the Archdiocese of San Francisco: (left to right) Deans James Rohan and Thomas Scahill, Vicar General John P. Connolly, and Canon Lawyer Nicholas P. Connolly. (J. Wright / *The Catholic Voice*)

spent time in Rome, where he worked with the influential Cardinal Leo Joseph Suenens of Belgium. At the cardinal's request, Frank arranged for a group of four local Sisters—Sister Gerarda Marie of the Holy Names Sisters among them—to be a resource group in Rome and con-duct weekly lectures entitled, "Co-responsibility after the Council."

Respected Veterans Inherited

The Archdiocese of San Francisco certainly had not divested the East Bay of talent. Bishop Begin inherited two respected deans in Monsignor James Rohan in Contra Costa County and Monsignor Thomas Scahill in Alameda County. Bishop-elect Leo Maher, as interim administrator of San Francisco, assigned two archdiocesan chancery veterans to help prepare Bishop Begin on his arrival in Oakland. Both were experienced canon lawyers. One, Monsignor Nicholas Connolly, pastor of St. Leo's parish, too gentle perhaps to be called a patriarch, assuredly knew the el-ements needed in the central office. The other was Monsignor John P. Connolly, friend of Monsignor Connolly, but not related. They brought to their assignment both talent and interest in temporal administration relating to finance, real estate, buildings, and cemeteries. Rome-trained,

John Connolly opened a social circle for the newcomer from Cleveland and became an intimate of Bishop Begin. He was a much-appreciated companion during the bishop's golf outings on Tuesday.

Oakland was blessed with a number of veteran pastors who were generous to the new bishop. Newly appointed consultors included Nial McCabe of St. Augustine's in Oakland and Monsignor Phil Ryan from San Leandro. Two leaders and sophisticated urban politicians of Portuguese heritage—Monsignor John Silva of St. Louis Bertrand and Monsignor Julio Martens of Hayward—shared their broad experience of participation in archdiocesan leadership. Monsignor James Wade stood out in a younger group of middle-range priests who were creditably managing the diocese's expansive suburban growth. These included Julius Bensen in Danville, Edward Varni in Concord, Robert Adams in Livermore, Martin Eugene Walsh in Fremont, Charles Hackel in Castro Valley, and Louis Dabovich in Pittsburg.

Religious priests were also in tune with the diocese, notably, the long-positioned Father Oliver Lynch, OFM, at St. Elizabeth's, and the more recently arrived Father Jack Kelly, OMI, at St. Mary's, deep in the heart of the City of Oakland. The bond that Bishop Begin forged between religious and diocesan priests would be firm and lasting.

The new diocese inherited priests with particular gifts. Monsignor Alvin J. Wagner, pastor of what became the Basilica of St. Joseph's in Alameda, was the faithful entrepreneur of the daily radio program "Rosary Hour." A distinctive ministry with a gift serving the California School for the Deaf in Berkeley brought forth Monsignor William Reilly and the effervescent Monsignor Michael O'Brien. A providential gift to the diocese came in the charities genius of Father John McCracken who in the months before Bishop Begin's arrival had returned to Alameda County from his post above the Carquinez Straits in Solano and Napa counties. Bishop Begin and Father McCracken would collaborate effectively and congenially both in and beyond the diocese, leading at one point to Father McCracken's being named a finalist as director of the Catholic Campaign for Human Development in Washington, D.C.

Youth Movement Continues

The new Oakland Diocese became more and more a "country" of young men and women. Only a year after he was ordained, Father Jo-

When Cummins succeeded Bishop Begin in 1977, he inherited seasoned young clergy, including (left to right) Fathers Anthony Valdivia, George Crespin, and Donald Osuna, all of whom had earlier been appointed to responsible positions by Bishop Begin. (J. Wright / *The Catholic Voice*)

seph Skillin became the bishop's secretary. Bishop Begin followed with an assignment to the chancery office of the young Father Ivan Parenti. The extrovert ebullience of these two priests put a youthful face on the pastoral center. One year after the establishment of the diocese and his ordination in 1963, Father George Crespin moved from Holy Spirit parish in Fremont to become the judicial vicar in charge of canon law and the marriage tribunal. A year later, Father Jim Bill, fresh from theology studies in Rome, would go immediately after ordination to the chancery office.

The bishop tapped two more men from the talented 1963 ordination class, Fathers Brian Joyce and Dan Danielson, and sent them for theological studies to Manhattan College and Fordham University in New York, respectively. The impact of this decision would later extend beyond the diocese to the national level, with Father Joyce's service in parish renewal and Father Danielson's, in the development of the Jesus Caritas groups and the National Organization for the Continuing Education of Roman Catholic Clergy and the establishment of the Vatican

II Institute for Priestly Renewal at St. Patrick's Seminary in Menlo Park. A year later, Bishop Begin engaged the talents of Father Paul Schmidt in catechetics and Father William Macchi—an economics major from the University of San Francisco with a master's degree in social welfare from UC–Berkeley in social services. Father Tom Gallagher would become the bishop's point man in the promotion of the favored episcopal practice of tithing. Within a decade Father Dick Mangini would succeed Frank Maurovich as editor of *The Catholic Voice*.

The Cursillo movement spread quickly in the diocese, led in Spanish by two young priests, Fathers Antonio Valdivia and Michael Barragan. Motivated by the church's social gospel, the "Flatland Fathers," a name given to socially active priests in the poorer bayside East Oakland district in contrast with the better-off gentry in the surrounding hills, launched projects to empower the powerless. Their broad membership in this work included the leadership of Fathers Ralph Brennan from St. Louis Bertrand's in the east and John Maxwell from St. Andrew's–St. Joseph's in the west and north. Father Mel Hary, early on at the old St. Francis de Sales, campaigned for the enlargement of the student body in his inner-city parish school. The rising consciousness of priests about the needs of inner-city schools complemented the involvement of young religious women. Two young Jesuit priests, John Baumann and Jerry Helfrich, brought a new level of sophistication to our social justice work with the creation of the Oakland Community Organization, together with the beloved pastor of St. Elizabeth's parish, Father Oliver Lynch.

The bishop also added youthful laity to this clerical world with the appointment of a young Clem Finney to the office of manager of diocesan facilities. This new office oversaw building projects in the diocese. Over time the office assumed responsibility for sixteen new parishes, eight elementary schools, and three high schools. Clem's wife, Reggie, would later establish an office for diocesan community relations. The Finneys and other laity came to their positions already trained.

Those who lived through the 1960s remember well the farmworkers' campaigns and the early stirrings of the civil rights movement. Encouraged by the persuasive words of Professor Raymond Sontag of UC– Berkeley, Bishop Begin established the Catholic Interracial Council. This program, which had been created some years earlier by the visionary New York Jesuit John LaFarge, benefitted from the talents of young men such as C. Herbert Clemens, a doctoral student in math from the university, Thom McGowan, who later became a deacon in the diocese, and Father Bill O'Donnell, described by historian Jeffrey Burns as "the diocese's most ardent champion of social justice." Bill's influence was soon felt nationally and even internationally.

Pastors Offer Inspiration and Moderation

Amid the clamor of demonstrations and protests that some younger clergy found enticing, Father Oliver Lynch from St. Elizabeth's offered the blessing of exemplary moderation, while still serving with inspiration. Divine Word Father Clarence Howard, from St. Patrick's, exhibited a spirit of calmness and optimism; his African American heritage increased his effectiveness in West Oakland. In time Father Gus Quinan, the genial builder of St. Paschal's parish in East Oakland, felt the thrust of the Vatican Council. With leadership, both disarming and forthright, coupled with the confidence of a veteran, Gus played a key role in developing the new structures of the Council of Priests and Personnel Committee for an active priestly community.

The year 1964 is particularly memorable for two events that fell into the hands of the younger group—the Free Speech Movement on the UC–Berkeley campus and the repeal of a state law outlawing housing discrimination. In the fall, Bishop Begin took both Monsignor Nicholas Connolly, the elder statesmen of the chancery, and Monsignor John Connolly, to the third session of the Vatican Council. Their three-month absence left me virtually in charge of the diocese. During this period, I made a practice of organizing a week's agenda each Monday morning to be shared with the wise counsel of Monsignor Jim Rohan, dean of Contra Costa County, whose parishioner and friend in El Cerrito was Professor Raymond Sontag—the UC–Berkeley professor who came to be an important influence, if not a mentor, in the lives of a number of us.

In that decade's torrent of activity—with the Free Speech Movement in Berkeley and the hippie movement centered in San Francisco's Haight-Ashbury District—I remember Father George Crespin being particularly perceptive about the significance of what many of us might have thought were local phenomena. Student unrest followed quickly in Europe, as it did in Asia, in Korea and Japan particularly. With caution and questioning we all tried to understand the change that was taking place.

The second 1964 moment had to do with an initiative sponsored by a California realtors group to repeal what was known as the Rumford Act, a bill that outlawed racial discrimination in housing. In the spring, a group of us at the bishop's direction had presented to him the draft of a letter taking a clear moral stand on the proposal. He signed the letter. Bishop Begin's strongest point was his unambiguity on social issues about which other clergy and even some bishops were less clear. We knew he would suffer for his stand. Armed as we were with the bishop's letter, we continued our unwavering efforts against the initiative. To our disappointment, however, the counter-measure passed in November by almost a two-to-one vote. Bishop Begin came home from the Council undaunted; his convictions about racial justice, nourished during his Cleveland days, remained firm.

We who were young appreciated the responsibility the bishop gave us and the confidence he expressed, but he was not always gentle. (One of his secretaries once described him as "volatile.") Bishop Begin's feelings were always close to the surface, and he had little hesitancy about expressing them. On the other hand, he was also quick with compliments, which could come just moments after a criticism.

I remember one episode when a group that was protesting a story in *The Catholic Voice* demonstrated outside of the chancery office. When someone from the bishop's staff told him the reason for the protest, he said, "*The Voice!* I feel like going down myself to join with them." Not long afterwards, he attended a luncheon of Catholic journalists connected with a national bishops' meeting in Chicago. To the bishop's surprise, Father Frank Maurovich—editor of *The Catholic Voice*—was the master of ceremonies and the moderator of the entire event. Bishop Begin admitted to being proud.

There are many stories, too, about the bishop's appointment to St. Francis de Sales Cathedral of the three young men—Michael Lucid, James Keeley, and Donald Osuna, with his unsurpassed liturgical artistry. Soon everyone was talking about the wonderful liturgies at the cathedral. Occasionally the bishop would wonder, "What are they doing down there?" But he knew he had appointed good men and zealous priests. Happily, he lived long enough to see participants in a national conference of liturgists, which was being held in San Francisco, move across the bay to celebrate their closing liturgy in *his* cathedral.

We disappointed him, sorely in some cases. And he had reasons to be annoyed about or to puzzle over our actions from time to time. The memory remains, however, that he loved us all.

13

Remorse in a Healing Garden

Pledge to Victims of Abuse: "Never Again!"

Bıshop ALLEN VIGNERON IN 2005 RESPONDED TO AN INITIATIVE
by survivors of sexual abuse by clergy to establish on the north corner of
the new cathedral campus a "Healing Garden" in remembrance of an
appalling chapter of church history in our diocese and in the United
States. This Healing Garden, representing a broad ministerial community response to the tragic experience, came about through the initiative
of survivors under the leadership of Terrie Light and Jennifer Chapin in
conversation with our chancellor, Sister Barbara Flannery. They found
encouragement from Bishop Vigneron and from John McDonnell,
chair of the Cathedral of Christ the Light project.

Preliminary discussions about a suitable site for the remembrance
eliminated a space *inside* the cathedral as an option, since some survivors
might find it troubling to enter the church building. Craig Hartman, architect of the cathedral, recommended to the enlarged committee the
Japonesque Gallery in San Francisco as a resource for appropriate art.
Jane Lee, an architectural designer with Skidmore, Owings & Merrill,
suggested the design.

The committee selected the work of Izumi Masatoshi as an appro-

priate centerpiece: basalt stone fractured into three pieces. This "described perfectly," according to the survivors' group, "the feeling of
wanting to be whole and healed once more." The curved benches in the
garden each carried plaques that read: "This Healing Garden, planned
by survivors, is dedicated to those innocents sexually abused by members of the clergy. We remember, and we affirm: never again."

Apology Ceremonies

Creation of the Healing Garden climaxed a series of events that underscored the authenticity of the undertaking. In January 2004, within
months of his installation as my successor, Bishop Vigneron presided at
a series of apology ceremonies in parishes where abuse had taken place.
The first took place at St. Ignatius of Antioch with about one hundred
participants. For the bishop it was an emotionally moving experience.
His sensitivity harmonized with the well-publicized charter the National
Conference of Bishops had issued in Dallas in June 2002. The bishops'
declaration ordered annual training sessions focused on the prevention
of child abuse and background checks on all parish and school employees and volunteers who worked with children.

Two years earlier, the celebration of the Jubilee Year had given our
diocese an opportunity for action. In his call for a celebration of the new
millennium, Pope John Paul II also urged the church to take a penitential
stance for its past sins and failures. The diocese responded to the celebratory aspect with a Mass and ethnic pageant at the Oakland Coliseum
Arena, a program overseen by two young priests, Father Stefan Kappler
and Father Mark Wiesner. An estimated 19,000 attended.

Additionally, another planning group, led by Sister Barbara Flannery and Father Dan Danielson, drew up a list of communities whom
the church had not served well. Leadership from these groups were approached to see if there would be benefit in receiving recognition and
perhaps apologies toward some needed reconciliation. They declined
the invitation. Survivors of sexual abuse proved exceptional. They entered into conversations with diocesan personnel that were marked by
confrontation and criticism, on the one hand, but perseverance and acceptance, on the other.

Together with diocesan authorities, plans were made for an apology service as part of the millennial observance. The Leona Lodge in

Fractured basalt rock in the Healing Garden on the
plaza of the Cathedral of Christ the Light symbolizes
the need to heal lasting wounds caused by the clergy sex
abuse scandal. (Artwork by Izumi Masatoshi. Photo
courtesy of blog. timothypflueger.com/)

the Oakland Hills was the chosen site, again out of consideration for the
sensitivities of those for whom an event in a church building would be
troubling. The plan called for a welcome followed by a formal apology,
with survivors given an opportunity to share their own testimonies. On
that March Sunday afternoon, thirty-five priests of the diocese participated. No accurate count was taken of other attendees. As expected, the
event garnered much media attention, but media personnel had been instructed not to approach participants with questions nor ask for inter-
views. No one had to explain his or her participation. Amber Lee, of
Oakland's Channel KTVU, and her crew were particularly sensitive to
our request for privacy.

The event, strenuous as it was, was welcomed with appreciation, and many felt there should be follow-up. An ongoing dialogue led to a gathering in March 2002 at the retreat center in Lafayette. The decision had been made to develop a program of "like-to-like" ministry, similar to the long experience of members of Alcoholics Anonymous. Many years earlier in the diocese, Sister Marie Wiedner had organized a similar structure for separated and divorced Catholics to offer support to those who felt abandoned. The Lafayette group, which called itself "No More Secrets," held monthly meetings with professional leadership and organized a weekend retreat in Los Gatos that proved fruitful.

Forming an Established Ministry

Looking back, I now recall how many in the diocese contributed to the creation of what became an established ministry. The first hints of unconfirmed stories about sexual misconduct surfaced in the late 1970s. Our diocesan lawyer, Richard Logan, provided wise counsel in advising against defensiveness. His concern embraced both the abuse families suffered and the criminal liability of perpetrators. Our chancellors, Father Brian Joyce and later Father George Crespin, along with vicar general Father William Macchi, responded pastorally and personally by visiting the affected families and the accused clergy. Their attention bore fruit, although the difficulty of ascertaining factual information proved troubling. I remember, for example, Sister Felicia Sarati, after attending to an issue in an ethnic community, feeling very constrained by the affected family's demand for privacy.

The dimensions of this appalling problem became obvious in the 1980s. At the national bishops' gathering in 1985, a professor from Johns Hopkins University strongly cautioned against too quickly expelling a priest from diocesan supervision, lest he go on to prey on unsuspecting victims elsewhere. Additionally, whereas we regarded counseling as an effective response, the expert noted that studies showed that even after studied counseling the recidivism rate was 5 percent. This declaration clarified a course of action: no parent or parish or pastor would allow offenders to continue in ministry.

In 1988, our Council of Priests established guidelines for the diocese, stipulating that any report, even anonymous, of abuse involving clergy or church employees would result in administrative leave. If a minor were found to be abused, the perpetrator would be removed from his or her position. Two years later, the national organization of Survivors Network of Abuse by Priests (SNAP) brought us its message of hurt, anger, and the destruction of faith and of lives. In December 1993, following issuance of national directives, the earlier guidelines of the Council of Priests were enlarged to include counseling and other pastoral assistance for those abused. The diocesan community realized that these efforts had priority over monetary claims that so often were contentious in character.

In 1994 Sister Barbara Flannery became chancellor of the diocese. Her work of personal contacts and conversation and of organizing meetings on the sex abuse issue strengthened what was now a clear ministry of the diocese. She steered a generous and understanding course, keeping avenues open between survivors, chancery personnel, priests, and a wide swath of the faithful. In recognition of her outstanding work, Santa Clara University awarded Sister Flannery an honorary degree of Doctor of Humane Letters.

Still, survivors remain hurt. Not everyone we reached has been able to find a way back to the church. In the judgment of those most familiar with this issue, many have not yet been able to come forward. The diocesan finance office in 1999 reported that total settlements reached $60,517,000, about half that amount covered under insurance.

The Healing Garden remains a site of remembrance and hope.

14

Bishops and Theologians Related

Common Pursuit of Wise Decision-Making

I WANT TO SAY A GOOD WORD FOR THEOLOGIANS and, as you might expect from the way I make my living, for bishops as well. This topic is both appropriate and timely because I believe we are in an era of relationship between bishops and theologians that will be quickly seen as a new stage of cooperation and interdependence. At the same time, the years up to now have been prelude to this collaboration, because they do not represent a history of opposition but of positive relationship, perhaps—in the words of a friend of mine—"notoriously so."

Let me illustrate my proposal, first, by three things I know of bishops and theologians from my own experience; secondly, by three things I know from reading and reflection; and, thirdly, by an elaboration of what I see to be the significant change in the present relationships of bishops and theologians in the United States.

First, I want to speak of theologians. Like many priests, I was taught and formed in substantial part by theologians who were mem-

An address Bishop John Cummins delivered in the Diocese of Brooklyn Cathedral series, "Shepherds Speak," May 23, 1982.

bers of the Society of St. Sulpice and who taught in St. Patrick's Seminary of the Archdiocese of San Francisco. I am aware of the lingering and far-reaching effects of writings by theologians. I recall Abbot Columba Marmion's *Christ in His Mysteries* from seminary days and Yves Congar's *Lay People in the Church* from the period immediately preceding the Second Vatican Council. I remain grateful to many theologians in Berkeley, which is in our own backyard, or perhaps more properly, frontyard of the Diocese of Oakland: theologians like Father Joseph Powers, SJ, whose book *Eucharistic Theology* gave me a good sense of moorings in those uncertain times a decade and more ago; or Sister Sandra Schneiders, IHM, whose recent probing of the contemporary problematic of religious obedience has been a helpful contribution and analysis.

I am obliged to acknowledge publicly the breadth of service done in our diocese by the schools of theology at the Graduate Theological Union in Berkeley and by the seminary of the Archdiocese of San Francisco as well. The faculty, and indeed students also, are generous to parishes, to clergy, and to adult education programs, as well as to religious education congresses, diocesan committees, and that convenient but definitely mixed blessing, the telephone.

Blessing from Bishops

My second experience has to do with bishops. I want to note the blessing they have brought to my life. I think of the writings of Emanuel Cardinal Suhard of Paris, influential in our seminary days and whose letter, or really book, on the priesthood has been worth frequent re-readings. I think, too, of more concrete benefits from our first bishop in Oakland, Floyd L. Begin, who led or dragged us beyond the line of comfort in ecumenical affairs and whetted a startlingly ready appetite for the *Decree on Ecumenism* from the Second Vatican Council. I would pay tribute to the Bishop Alden J. Bell of Sacramento, now in his retirement, whose association I treasure, a man who illustrated in troubled times "grace under pressure," an imperturbable openness, tending the whole flock in which the Holy Spirit placed him to shepherd the people of God.

A third point of reminiscing relates to a particular experience of collaboration between bishops and theologians. For six years (1971–

1977) I was secretary to the bishops of the California Catholic Conference in Sacramento, the arm of the California hierarchy for inter-diocesan cooperation and for relations with the legislature and the governor's office.

Ours was an ongoing, changing, and, appropriately for the gold-dust trails of northern California, pioneering work. One decision in 1975 had to do with the repeal of the law governing private sexual conduct of consenting adults. We consulted legal experts, parents, law enforcement people, the English hierarchy's history with a similar demand fifteen years earlier, and our moral theologians in California, who were seven in number.

A studied decision ended up unanimously that the bishops should not oppose the repeal, but should stand aside from any authoritative declaration over this uncertain question of civil law. It was not an easy or well-received judgment on the part of some in the Catholic community in California.

We had in contrast another case a year later. This concerned the law on death and dying, just at the high point of argument over the Karen Quinlan case. Our prejudgment was that the law was not needed, it could spawn more issues than it would settle, and it was alive with uncertain implications. Our moral theologians, by now eight in number, were clear on the moral evaluation of the proposed legislation. The political judgments, however, were divided. They remained so, even to the end when we had to make a decided but tentative decision. It was not so secure or supported that we did not earn the criticisms of some Catholic legislators, some dismayed pro-life people, and a spokesperson for a department of the U.S. Catholic Conference.

What was consoling and enduring was the gracious relation of theologians and bishops all those years. Though our judgments were toilsome and at times inconclusive, the respectful common pursuit of wise decision-making brought a mutual and appreciated satisfaction.

The personal history of bishops and theologians is important to the discussion, and I do not apologize for beginning with it. I believe that my experience coincides with the desirable in the church and even more reflects in great part the reality of ecclesiastical life in our time.

Task of Theologians Today

First of all, with regard to theologians, the office is a respected one in the church and is well defined and described. I believe, too, that the theologian's task today is met with a good deal, not just of understanding, but of sympathy from various sectors of the Catholic community. This is largely because people can grasp the complexity of the theologian's responsibilities today, holding to old questions, moving to new ones, and maintaining equilibrium in an interdisciplinary world of learning and in a pluralistic society.

The International Commission of Theologians that was established by Pope Paul VI outlined in 1976 a succinct and manageable description of the theologian's work covering academic responsibility, freedom of inquiry, and pastoral sensitivity. That described position of predicament of the theologian is also well defined and well documented in official statements of the church. Even from some minor documents of Vatican II such as the *Declaration on Christian Education* come warm compliments and expectations for the theological enterprise.

There are frequent references to the popular remark of Pope John XXIII that the "deposit of faith" is one thing, but its manner of presentation is another. Such a statement found its way into Council documents and into the apostolic constitution *Sapientia Christiana*, issued in 1979 by Pope John Paul II, on ecclesiastical universities and faculties.

There is a harder question, but one equally treated, from similar sources as those above. The *Declaration on Christian Education*, again, talks about "solutions...found for problems raised by the development of doctrine." *Gaudium et Spes* specifies the matter even more clearly: "Science, history, and philosophy raise new questions which influence life and demand new theological investigations." With the serene sense of understatement that should characterize the believer, the same document says that it is "sometimes difficult to harmonize culture with Christian teaching." Pope John Paul II, during his recent visit to the United States, referred at the Catholic University of America to the same theme, the need for theologians in this time and age that is "so profoundly marked by deep changes in all areas of life and society."

The nature of this responsibility demands a quality that is universally conceded to the theologian, that of legitimate freedom. Cardinal

Newman, one and a quarter centuries ago, remarked that "Great minds need elbow room not indeed in the domain of faith, but of thought. And so indeed do lesser minds, and all minds." *Gaudium et Spes* pursues that truth. All the faithful possess lawful freedom of inquiry and "the freedom to express their minds humbly and courageously about those matters in which they enjoy competence." Pope John Paul II, speaking in Cologne cathedral, November 15, 1980, expressed the wish of the church for independent theological research. That same week an article in the *Osservatore Romano* by an Italian priest, Father Battista Mondini, said,

> It seems to me that after the heated disputes that have taken place since the end of the Council to the present time, the following truth is now established…that the theologian enjoys the utmost autonomy and freedom in his and her specific sphere of competence, which is the intelligibility and scientific character of the Christian message.

Bishop's Goal—Unity of the Mystical Body

Secondly, I turn to those who bear pastoral leadership responsibility in the church, the bishops. Let me say that I do not think the satisfactions of the bishop's life center on power and authority. *Lumen Gentium* speaks of other attractive and enriching parts of the bishop's responsibility, the charity and unity of the Mystical Body that are manifested in any community existing around an altar under the sacred ministry of the bishop. It speaks, too, of the joyful experience of anyone in the apostolate, including the bishop, preaching the faith that brings new disciples to Christ.

The same document, however, deals directly and clearly with authority, stating that bishops are authentic teachers, that bishops teaching in communion with the Roman pontiff are to be respected by all as witnesses to divine and Catholic truth. The Council document states:

> In matters of faith and morals, the bishops speak in the name of Christ, and the faithful are to accept their teaching and adhere to it with a religious assent of soul. Their reli-

gious submission of will and of mind must be shown in a
special way to the authentic teaching authority of the Roman
Pontiff, even when he is not speaking ex cathedra. That is, it
must be shown in such a way that his supreme magisterial is
acknowledged with reverence, the judgments made by him
are sincerely adhered to, according to his manifest mind and
will.

We can labor, and are indeed obliged to struggle, over the application and implication of this lengthy paragraph. But its clarity is evident.
The episcopal office is the traditional locus of the magisterium or teaching authority. Though it is only part of the life of the bishop, it is a responsibility he must take seriously.

Thirdly, bishops and theologians with their identifiably different
responsibilities in the church are to be in relationship to one another.
Specialized intellectual competence is the mark of one, and extensive
pastoral authority is possessed by the other. Pope John Paul II said at the
Cologne cathedral, "It cannot be ignored that tension and even conflicts
can arise." I suppose one could say that conflict is built in. We could all
nostalgically reminisce about the glorious early centuries of the church
with men like St. Augustine, St. Gregory Nazianzen, and St. Basil, when
the role of the theologian and bishop was conjoined in one person. We
are, however, no longer in such simple times, and the demands of
full-time pastoral leadership and specialized scholarship will not allow
the combination.

Openness to the Holy Spirit

We can then speak of conflict. Theologians can take stands explicitly or
implicitly in disagreement with accepted church positions. I do not
mean arguments against defined doctrines of faith but postures of policy, direction, or official teaching. The bishop may feel the tension of
loyalty to the church's pastoral authority. At the same time, the bishop
has in his own memory the conflicts on biblical scholarly approaches
and the testing on the question of religious liberty, troubled investigations that eventually were blessed by the Second Vatican Council. Managing the responsibility of authority while remaining open to the
guidance of the Spirit, all the while aware of the possibility of error, is a

delicate and often enough difficult experience.

At this point, however, I would say that conflict is not to be exaggerated. I furthermore raise doubts that clash is the inevitable mark of the relationship of bishop and theologian. Father Raymond Brown's 1978 assessment coincides both with my experience and my reflection that theologians and the magisterium are not the main opponents in the matter of doctrine and that disagreement between them is not the prevailing relationship. I say this well aware of the danger of wrongly stating the case. I remember a well-intentioned prelate years ago speaking to clergy he thought were unduly troubled, "I don't think things are really as bad as they are."

I turn now to an experience of my own. At the second session of the Second Vatican Council in 1963, I was present as secretary to our own bishop. I became acquainted with a gracious and personable gentleman who often sat with me at the morning gatherings. "He wrote *Pacem in Terris* for John XXIII," a friend told me. I mentioned that hearsay to the priest, who was Father Pietro Pavan, and he answered with just a smile. Since then the truth of that statement has been corroborated on a number of occasions. I have no trouble believing it because it seems very much part of a pattern. Leo XIII's encyclical on Thomism, *Aeterni Patris*, evidently was written by the German theologian Joseph Kleutgen. I read, too, the touching memories of Oswald von Nell-Breuning, SJ, forty years after he drafted *Quadragesimo Anno* for Pope Pius XI. With the breadth of vision that comes from age, he looked back with some misgivings about his having written so much that was not precisely the mind and intended meaning of the pope.

Evidence from the last three general councils supports what I believe to be the relationship between bishops and theologians. Jesuit Father T. Howland Sanks from Berkeley, in an article touching on the Second Vatican Council, found it "a high point in the collaboration of the magisterium and theologians." That, I am quite sure, is the assessment of most people.

Father Sanks also finds an illustration, though a limited one, of such cooperation in Vatican I. The declarations of faith and revelation (*Dei Filius*) and of papal infallibility (*Pastor Aeternus*) "are the clearest examples of the cooperation of some theologians with the magisterium."

Then he says with less than a compliment, "Indeed it is perhaps more than cooperation; it is coalescence."

Father Yves Congar, the French Dominican, elsewhere has remarked on the active participation of theologians at the Council of Trent. "The Church," he said, "needs both *inquisitio* and *auctoritas*, that is, research and authority, two different but complementary roles and charisms which exist in the church. Distinction between the two must be kept, even within the parameters of their necessary and felicitous collaboration." He goes on, "A synthesis of the two was fairly well realized at Trent." To the question, "Did Trent then provide a moment of balance?" Congar answers, "Yes."

I recall some years ago the installation of a classmate of mine as pastor of one of our older parishes. The time was the late 1960s, and we were feeling the early disillusionment from the euphoric days of the Council. Standing in the hallway of the rectory waiting to go home, looking up at the single, naked light bulb that hung from a twisted cord, one local clerical pundit said with great, but mock gravity, "John, what went wrong?"

In response, let me attempt to say that not much went wrong. I think of so much collaboration of bishops and theologians. There are promising structures like the International Theological Commission of Pope Paul VI. One must take note of the abundant efforts by theologians and bishops in our country, both in formal dialogue and in studied articles, to establish an optimum mutual relationship. I think of the committees of our national bishops, such as those that drafted the pastoral letter on the health apostolate in 1981, the statement on moral values in 1976, the committee on women in society and the church, and the committee under Archbishop Bernardin that developed the pastoral letter on war and peace. All of these had or have the active participation of theologians. Additionally, my own neighbor, Bishop Roger Mahony of Stockton, in completing a pastoral letter for his diocese in January 1982 on the question of nuclear arms, listed with thanks the theologians who prepared the document with him. I am sure that these instances represent the general experience. Collaboration of bishops and theologians is a pattern, not an occasional event in the life of the church, even in these most recent years.

New Stage of Relationship

Collaboration of bishops and theologians is an appreciated heritage. Our gratitude also has to be extended to those who have engaged in the dialogue over the past several years and who have contributed to the present scene.

One of our Berkeley theologians pointed out to me that the relation of bishop and theologian has changed and has become a more demanding one, largely because of one factor, the development of the teaching role of the American bishop.

The phenomenon represents a growth in appreciation of an idea recovered in Vatican II, namely, the local church. Its evidence is in the large number of pastoral letters written by different bishops on the subject of nuclear arms that do not coincide either in detail or in resolution. There are other illustrations, such as statements on women in the church, the pastoral care of homosexuals, and the matter of dissent within the church.

These subjects come from local initiative and are not direct outflows of documents from the Holy See or from widely deliberated U.S. trends. Furthermore these depart from the character of the era or decade that we are just leaving. These recent years were marked by changes in theology produced by theologians and given impetus by the forces that were sprung from Vatican II. They brought major change in liturgy, in interest in Scripture, the place of Scripture in theology, its incorporation into the liturgy and into the everyday faith-life of our people. It brought different emphases and reflections to such dogmatic questions as the nature of the church and led to the expression that has become commonplace, "We have different ecclesiologies"—with the all-too-human implied understanding, or course, that mine is the better one.

The present change has developed a different agenda. It furthermore has three identifiable dimensions. First, bishops are speaking on topics of immediate and widespread awareness. The office of teaching, therefore, has taken on a force and an authenticity that have been much more the heritage of Europe than of North America.

Second, the issues are specifically American and represent an inculturation of the American Church that has not been so clearly evident before. Again, the war/peace questions are pertinent. So are the roles of women in the church and economic justice. More topics will surely be opened up. John Courtney Murray, in his 1960 work *We Hold These Truths*, set up an agenda that included the church as a community in a pluralistic society, a philosophy of foreign aid, and the matter of censorship.

One item of Murray's that appears to be ripening, an issue with theological dimensions as well as political ones, is the matter of schooling in America. I wish to make a digression here for a moment because I believe in its significance. The present agitation over the range of issues concerning quality of education, the place of values, the means of financing both public and private education, and tax credits represents not merely a contemporary debate. Father Murray would portray these as evidence of a genuine malaise, a pattern of the failure to serve real needs in a country neither vaguely secular not vaguely Protestant. The approach to education must be diversified. According to Father Murray,

> There is an increasing disposition to recognize that the State laws which forbid all manner of public aid to church-affiliated schools are both out of date and at variance with justice...and they realize that nineteenth-century legislation does not solve the problem as it appears in mid-twentieth century.

Father Murray points out the relationship of education and spiritual needs and invites the country to pick up this unfinished agenda of relating schools to spiritual aspirations and provide a system at once more effective and more just.

The third dimension of the present change goes beyond specifically domestic needs. There has been a growth in the consciousness of American international responsibilities. The statement by the bishops on the Panama Canal in 1978 was an object of criticism, and at times derision, by opponents of the bishops' position. The Central American statement, however, of November 1981 was received much more seriously, as have been the testimonies of U.S. bishops before Congress questioning foreign policy toward Central American countries. The time given by the bishops at their annual meeting in 1980 to Bishop Mark

McGrath of Panama, as well as the delegations of bishops sent to Chile, El Salvador, and countries in Africa and Asia in recent years represent a new outreach. Not surprisingly, a Central American rector visiting us recently remarked that the U.S. bishops are the avenue for the third world to reach the conscience of the American people.

I believe that bishops take intellectual competence seriously and respect the directive of *Lumen Gentium* that the officially appointed teachers of the church have to apply the appropriate human means to arrive at the truth. We can expect therefore that bishops will be drawing more and more on theologians for the writing of pastoral letters, for analyzing the American scene, and for synthesizing the dialogue between U.S. theologians and Latin American liberation theologians. The association of bishops and theologians will, by necessity, be more interdependent, even as one has called it "organic." I believe, too, that we bishops will be wise enough to consult not just those theologians with whom we are intellectually comfortable, but even a wider group so that we will have the sense of the broader reflection and experience of the community.

From one point of view, bishops and theologians are independent. Our Holy Father, Pope John Paul II, has said,

> The magisterium and theology have two different tasks to perform, that is why neither can be reduced to the other. Yet they serve the one whole, but precisely on account of this configuration, they must remain in consultation with one another.

Father Joseph Fitzmyer, SJ, writing in *America* magazine, expressed the matter differently:

> As I have often liked to put it, the theologian and the exegete need the magisterium and the faithful to buzz about them like gadflies to make them reflect on "their dedication to intellectual honesty" and "responsible scholarship." But the magisterium and the faithful also need the theologians and the exegetes to buzz about them like gadflies to make them

reflect on their need of "constant updating" and respect for "the deepest and noblest aspiration of the human spirit." This is the role of mutual stimulation, not confrontation.

"Respectfully mutual" may be a softer and happier description. This leads to one more important point. Whether independent or interdependent, theologians and bishops operate within the church. The echo of St. Paul's words surrounds all of our discussion. Bishops are the gift of the Spirit of the church; theologians are the gift of the Spirit of the church. I believe it is true to say that neither forms the community. Rather, they exist within that community of believers and are meaningful only in relation to it. Pope John Paul II, in addressing theologians in Washington, D.C., made the point that they should be sensitive to the role of bishops and to the rights of the faithful. That directive applies equally to all of us and is understood by people like Yves Congar, who says with significance, "I seek no other mandate as a theologian for my duty and my desire to speak of God than my being a friar-preacher in the church.... I have said advisedly: in the church."

The relationship of bishops and theologians is in one sense prayerful as well as supportive. The atmosphere is a respectful family trust, not antagonism that divides the community, which both are responsible to serve. What we can be grateful for is the long history of collaboration and cooperation that has been immensely fruitful for the church over the years. In line with this, I recall an observation made by the director of the bishops' study on the renewal of the parish that has gone on for the last three years. It has come from his research, he indicated, that if one separates out groups from the church, one will experience in that conversation a feeling of isolation, of somberness, and a tendency to complain. Put them together and one will sense with excitement the vitality of our Catholic community as it is today. The relationship of bishops and theologians is lively enough at the moment. It promises to be more vital in the years ahead.

15

Bishops and Scientists in Dialogue

Talks Marked by Respect for Differences

A GRATIFYING MEMORY OF MINE in relation to the National Conference of Bishops is the decade and more that I served on the Committee
on Science and Human Values. I am sure that the invitation came
through a neighbor and good friend, Bishop Pierre DuMaine of San
Jose, whose interest in the relation of religion and science was his avocation, but my relationship with the University of California, Berkeley, and
our annual evenings of intellectual input proved conducive to membership as well.

The committee originated in 1983. Vatican II's *Gaudium et Spes*
must have contributed to its creation. Early on, it was called a Department of Human Values. In 1987, however, Pope John Paul II in an address to the Pontifical Academy of Science, read a quotation from the
Second Vatican Council,

> We cannot but deplore certain habits of mind, which are
> sometimes found too among Christians, which do not suffi-
> ciently attend to the rightful independence of science and
> which from the arguments and controversies they spark lead

many minds to conclude that faith and science are mutually opposed (*Gaudium et Spes*, 36).

Pope Paul VI had referenced this quotation twenty years earlier than Pope John Paul's noting it. The timeliness of Pope John Paul's statement gave a boost to the fledgling Committee on Human Values, championed by Bishop Mark J. Hurley of Santa Rosa, a longtime friend, and particularly by Cardinal James Hickey of Washington, D.C.

By 1995, when I joined the group, the committee, which was chaired by Edward Egan, then bishop of Bridgeport, Connecticut, had a well-established pattern. The scientists had a record of faithfulness, as did the bishops, the latter not restricted by the usual three-year terms of other committees. David Byers, who had a doctorate in English from the University of Minnesota, brought his passionate longing for dialogue between science and religion, even though he served as only part-time staffer. Key to the organizational pattern, Byers was in charge of preparation and follow-up. Bishop William Friend of Shrevesport, Louisiana, was an active participant and a member as well of the Pontifical Academy of Culture at the Vatican. Bishop Frank DiLorenzo, moral theologian from Honolulu, Hawaii, was a faithful contributor, as was the long-serving Cardinal Edward Egan of New York and Auxiliary Bishop John Dunne of Rockville Centre, New York.

The scientists on our committee were led by Eric Fischer, from the Library of Congress, with ties to the National Academy of Science. Fischer held a doctorate in marine biology from UC–Berkeley. His background was American Protestant, but at this time he was delving into Eastern religions. Robert J. White, MD, PhD, a renowned neurosurgeon and bioethicist from Case Western Reserve in Cleveland was a devout Catholic and a member of the Pontifical Academy of Science. Dr. John Burris came from Woods Hole in Falmouth, Massachusetts, the site of several marine science institutions. Another very important player was Dr. Harold J. Morowitz, a man of extraordinary erudition from George Mason University in Virginia and an enthusiastic participant. The name of Paul Berg, from Stanford, a Nobel Prize winner and member of the Pontifical Academy of Science, was prominent as was that of Dr. Maxine Singer from the Carnegie Institute in Washington, D.C. Father

James Salmon, SJ, professor of chemistry from Loyola in Baltimore, served as moderator. The core group was consistent, but occasional visitors included Rev. Dr. James Miller from the American Association for the Advancement of Science and others, particularly from the association's department of science and religion.

Pattern of Discourse

Committee meetings convened annually (at times semiannually) on weekends from Friday noon until Sunday afternoon. Dr. Byers would forward material to participants prior to each meeting. Some of the material was quite challenging, such as on the issue "Brain, Mind, Spirit," which we discussed during a weekend at Notre Dame, Indiana; other materials dealt with more familiar topics, such as end of life issues. The first day featured presentations by quality experts. The entirety of Saturday was given to responses characterized by a spirit of genuine dialogue, the pattern of discourse exemplified in Pope Paul VI's 1964 encyclical *Ecclesiam Suam*. However much I knew of any topic, I learned and valued more because of the respect, goodwill, acceptance of differences, modesty, friendship, and good humor that marked our conversations.

By Sunday afternoon, Dr. Byers would have drawn up—in consultation with his executive committee—a summary of common-ground understandings on the topic under discussion, a recap of areas of differences, and a listing of issues that needed more development. After the meeting, Dr. Byers would produce a summary of the discussions for the bishops along with a substantial leaflet on the state of the question that had been treated. The leaflet was made available to bishops and to schools. I found this a useful service, opening up newly developed questions, with an appraisal that was quite objective and not dwelling on critical aspects.

My first meeting focused on genetic testing and screening, led by Dr. Michael Kaback, from the University of California, San Diego. Besides being a medical doctor, Dr. Kaback had a doctorate in genetic counseling. The topic of this meeting disturbed me at first, because I sensed a challenge to the bishops to defend controversial issues in the public arena. But Dr. Kaback's presentation allayed my apprehension. The details he discussed came from his own practice. They concerned two developmentally disabled young people, married, living on property owned by the wife's parents. Their first child was disabled; the second was healthy; the condition of a third pregnancy then unknown. While I felt uneasy about having so many thorny issues wrapped up in the one case presentation, I was pleased with what resulted, namely, a genuine search for the moral issues involved with high regard for Catholic heritage. Desirable issues in public policy surfaced. Dr. Kaback also shared the agonizing professional dilemma he faced regarding specific genetic issues about which he was professionally bound to keep confidential, but which would have had tragic consequences if he failed to speak up to prevent them.

Part of the second day was an explanation of sickle cell anemia. We learned about the great promise in new research underway at that time, such as the Human Genome Project under the direction of Dr. Francis Collins. Hazards loomed, however, particularly concerning the impact on insurance options if genetic screening revealed negative information.

The day's discussion was intensely engaging, yet at the same time easy, friendly, and even humorous. Participants found common ground in the sacred dignity of the human person. Dr. Morowitz lightly commented, however, on the failure to agree on the definition of person. At one point in the midst of vibrant discussion, Morowitz commented to Bishop DuMaine alongside him, "We are creating new problems for you, Father. Suppose someone comes to confession and says, 'Bless me, Father, for I have sinned. I changed a gene'." Without a moment's hesitation, Bishop DuMaine adopted a confessor's pose, with elbow on the table and hand on forehead, and replied, "For your penance, recite your DNA code."

An additional service from our Committee on Science and Human Values was the occasional seminar on a day that preceded our general assembly in Washington, D.C. In one such presentation, Dr. Francis Collins, head of the Human Genome Project and a professed Christian, served us well with a clear outline of his work, both the anticipated blessings and the expected difficulties. A professor from the University of Maryland, well attuned to Catholic moral theology, spent a day with us on stem cell research, clarifying the issue long before the topic became politicized and gave rise to some misunderstanding of the church's viewpoint on this controverted issue.

Uneasiness from Outside

The topics our committee addressed made some members of other conference committees uneasy. In March 1998, Bishop Anthony Pilla, as president of the Bishops' Conference, wrote to then Bishop Edward Egan urging careful cooperation between our committee and the Committee on Pro-Life Activities and the Committee on Doctrine. Further, he asked that committee reports be distributed to bishops only, not to the general public.

In October 1999, Cardinal William Keeler, chair of the Committee on Pro-Life Activities, wrote to Bishop Egan, commenting on some of the sentences in the summary of the state of the question for the topic of that year, which was cloning. Specifics were not mentioned. My own hunch is that the uneasiness came from the staff of the Pro-Life Committee, who were the church's public voice on life issues and were concerned that the conference not have two voices on issues within their responsibility. Cardinal Keeler courteously asked for a meeting of bishops from three committees—ours, Pro-Life, and Doctrine. The timing of that meeting extended into my becoming chair of the Committee on Science and Human Values. Our members felt open to whatever changes proved suitable, but we did want to preserve the positive aspects of our dialogue with science and the benefits of the consultations in which we were engaged. The dialogue did not continue, however, and our offer of editing was left without further response from the cardinal or the Pro-Life Committee. Meanwhile, we felt no sense of discouragement about the future of our committee, although we were still obligated to restrict the publication of our summaries.

We spent the next two years on the topic of evolution. Dr. Sara Via of the University of Maryland, vivacious and clear, took us through one day of what might be called Evolutionary Biology 101. She stimulated questions that the process of evolution brings to the surface, and we couldn't help but be reminded of the musings of Teilhard de Chardin. The presence of theologian Jack Haught from Georgetown, with his penetrating insights into the legacy of Charles Darwin, provided a rich contribution. The committee sensed that their deliberations might lead to a USCCB publication, particularly with the richly contextualized and oft-quoted statement of Pope John Paul II in 1996, "the recognition of evolution as more than an hypothesis."

With the prospect arising of Dr. Byers moving to other responsibilities in the conference, members of our committee began to hope for enlarged secretarial staffing. Dr. Byers had the responsibility for the Committees on Mission, Family Life, and Youth. We were seeking a stronger bioethical committee in order to have a greater moral influence at the public and national levels.

Unexpected alignment and encouragement developed from my engagement with St. Mary's College here in the diocese. Those who had been attending our Berkeley dinners were very interested in the bishops' Committee on Science and Human Values. After I became committee chair, six young Berkeley professors—all from the physical sciences—offered to be of whatever assistance they could. In particular, Dr. Tom Hayes from UC–Berkeley's Donner Laboratory and Dr. Ron Olowin, an astrophysics professor from St. Mary's College, were anxious to participate.

In the late 1990s, St. Mary's formed a dialogue committee on the issues in Catholic higher education that Pope John Paul had raised in his letter, *Ex Corde Ecclesiae*. The neuralgic issue was the "mandatum," the requirement that every professor of Catholic theology had to have the approval of the local bishop. The focus of the pope's letter, however, centered on the meeting between Catholic higher education and the contemporary world. The discussions became a fixed element in the administration of St. Mary's and resulted in what became the Bishop John S. Cummins Institute for Catholic Thought, Culture and Action.

Dr. Olowin served on this Institute and continued to show his interest in the bishops' Committee on Science and Human Values. One fruit from our relationship was an invitation he sent me to attend his astronomy class, which was discussing the possibility of extraterrestrial life. My first instinct was to pass up the invitation for obvious lack of competence. About the same time, however, I was having lunch with an adjunct professor of astronomy, Dr. Margaret Ailes, who was a NASA director. "We are moving into new areas," she told me, "involving new moral questions, but when we turn around to look for the church, it is not there." With Martian exploration underway she listed a number of

St. Mary's College science professor Dr. Ronald Olowin, holding book, stands with *Gael* collegians (left to right) Justin Robinson, Leland Moore, and Samantha Shultz. (R. Olowin photo)

moral issues that might arise: Should life or the remnants of life be found, can it be experimented with? Can it be brought back to earth for research? Can it be destroyed?

After further reflection, I accepted Dr. Olowin's invitation to speak with his students about the history and relevance of the bishops' committee. The students were more than complimentary about the bishops' involvement in such scientific discussions. Some expressed enormous satisfaction; others were happily surprised.

In addition to interest in the bishops' work, concrete suggestions began to be made about further connections with our committee. Our national group at the time had representatives from three other universities besides my role at St. Mary's College: Georgetown, with Jack Haught; Notre Dame, with Dr. Phillip Sloan, head of the Program of Liberal Studies; Loyola of Baltimore, with Jesuit Father James Salmon, professor of chemistry and moderator of our committee discussions. Faculty and others at St. Mary's saw an opportunity to suggest topics for the committee's work. I saw the universities as a vehicle for publicizing the existence of our committee along with the dissemination of the results of our dialogues.

Meanwhile, our National Conference of Bishops had decided to revise its committee structure with economy and efficiency in mind. Speculation arose about our group. We saw difficulty in losing our freestanding position. Three groups had the potential to envelop our work: the Committee on Ecumenical and Interreligious Affairs—though our efforts went well beyond Christian unity and interfaith understanding; the Committee on Pro-Life—though its involvement in political advocacy was not part of our agenda; and the Committee on Doctrine. We eventually became part of the Committee on Doctrine, which typically had not included an appraisal of scientific developments in their work.

In due time, consultation on the part of our committee led to a report by our chair, Bishop John Dunne, to the Committee on Doctrine and to the Committee on Priorities and Plans. The report had a concise quality though it embraced the value of our dialogue, its history, and its accomplishments. It also provided concrete steps for stability and continuity and even estimated the budget for the coming year. Its recommendations included the appointment of a member of the Doctrine Committee to promote consultation with the scientists as well as to pursue the recommendation of relationships with one or more universities. It outlined clearly the methodology of dialogue between scientists and bishops, which Pope John Paul II had recommended in 1984: "A dialogue should be set up which is unprejudiced by undue passions.... Such a dialogue should above all try to clarify the problems in question to discover a possible convergence of the various groups involved." Bishop Dunne announced at the close, "I am convinced that this dialogue and its outcomes will truly be one of the most important matters the doctrine committee will be attending to."

Father John Strynkowski, a priest from Brooklyn who was the theologian for the Committee on Doctrine and had earlier experience with the Congregation of Bishops in Rome, responded positively to the deliberations of our committee. He was soon called back to his diocese, however, and was replaced by Father Thomas Weinandy, OFM, Cap. Bishop John Dunne and I at our first opportunity lobbied Father Weinandy on the hopes of our committee. The conversation was short on satisfaction. Undismayed, we arranged for Bishop Dunne and Father

Weinandy to stop in Oakland on their way to the spring assembly of the bishops in Los Angeles. At St. Mary's College we reviewed with them the thinking of the Cummins Institute in relation to the dialogue between science and religion. Present were Dr. Ron Olowin, Dr. Steve Woolpert, dean of St. Mary's College of Liberal Arts, and Brother Ronald Gallagher, FSC, president of St. Mary's, among others. Father Weinandy did not engage in the conversation.

There was another intervention during the spring assembly in Tucson, Arizona, where I sought a meeting with the chair of the Committee on Doctrine. I noted how pleased I was that science and human values had been retained as a responsibility of his committee. I was specific in suggesting that the chair of our committee become one of his consultants as suggested in Bishop Dunne's presentation. The conversation ended abruptly.

A change in tenor was evident in the last meeting of our committee, which took place in 2006. The subject was stem cell research. Dr. William Gearhart, a prominent leader in that work from the University of Maryland, gave a presentation, though he was initially hesitant to accept the invitation, uncertain about his being welcomed. Responses came from Professor William Hurlburt (Stanford), Dr. Maureen Condic (University of Utah), and Dominican Father Nicanor Austriaco (Providence College). Whereas earlier dialogues had been marked by respectful exchange, the atmosphere this time was argumentative. Dr. Gearhart did not stay for lunch.

A Regretful Demise

A prominent bishop once told me not be concerned about the demise of the Committee on Science and Human Values, indicating that universities could pick up the dialogue. I maintain that such conversations are not the same. The authority of bishops in the dialogue is enlightening for science majors. Bishop Pierre DuMaine has put it well,

> The church is seen as a red light to scientific research. It should be reduced to a yellow light, only pointing out concerns, dangers and problems, but affirming the worth and the value of scientific research.

Scientists on our committee have spoken with deep conviction. Dr.

Robert J. White from Case Western Reserve said,

> I would like to suggest a time is appropriate to argue the importance and crucial nature of this specific committee. Certainly the development in recent days, even in recent years demands, in my opinion, direct involvement of the church and its leadership in science, specifically biotechnology. I see this committee, because of its history, staff and activities, in a pivotal position to offer linkage between the scientific community and our bishops.

Speaking from a Jewish heritage, Michael M. Kaback of UC–San Diego wrote,

> I have been actively involved with the committee over the last five or six years and have found this to be an extraordinary venue for the communication and discussion of critical issues relating to science and theology.... This is a critical time in the development and applications of science with enormous social and ethical implications.... I must also say that it has been incredibly enlightening for me, a non-Catholic, to understand the enormous energy, commitment and humanity of the bishops in this process. I am not sure which group actually gains more from these interactions.

Committee member Dr. Eric Fischer wrote,

> When I began to work with the Committee on Science and Human Values in 1993, I hoped that the effort would lead to a series of useful and constructive dialogues between members of the conference and the scientific community on scientific issues with a strong moral and ethical dimension. The success of the dialogues has fully met and even exceeded that initial expectation.... The committee has chosen to address a number of difficult and timely issues and has done so in a manner that has educated all participants and led to sub-

stantial mutual respect among them. Several of those issues increased in national prominence subsequent to the dialogue, and I believe that both the scientists and bishops who participated were better prepared to grapple with them as a result of frank and open discussion. Examples include end of life, cloning, and stem cell research.

"Scientists," Fischer continued,

have recognized the importance of these dialogues and few of those approached to participate have declined. Several did express some initial trepidation because of their prior perceptions about the teachings or positions of the church on the issues, but virtually everyone has stated after participating that he or she found the dialogue fulfilling and informative and had come to a greater understanding of and respect for the views of the church on the issues discussed.... It would, I believe, be particularly beneficial to the scientific community and I would hope to the conference as well, if a way could be found to disseminate more broadly the kind of enhanced mutual understanding and respect that these dialogues have brought to participants.

Dr. Maxine Singer from the Carnegie Institution of Washington, D.C., wrote, "The growing importance and influence of science and technology in people's lives means that the committee work and study will continue to increase in the years to come."

Harold Morowitz adds,

I think it is an act of hubris for an outsider like myself to make suggestions to the bishops. On the other hand, I think that Dr. Robert White has a very good point, so many issues of both theological and pastoral importance go back to their scientific roots, but it seems clear that the church for reasons of relevance is going to have to devote more and more time and effort to background considerations of these matters.

The New Evangelization

I realize that the letters cited above may sound self-serving, but I remain convinced that in this new era when we speak of New Evangelization, formal dialogue between science and the Church in the United States at its authoritative level should be restored. The field is opening up with examples from the Center for Theology and the Natural Sciences of Dr. Robert Russell in Berkeley, Brian Swimme on ecology from this Bay Area, and Sister Nancy Teskey of Holy Names University, a physiology professor gathering thoughts on faith and reason. These and others grasp the classic apostolic exhortation of Pope Paul VI's *Evangelii Nuntiandi* (1975), the need of engagement with culture. There is place for the bishops in this engagement.

16

Ministry with the Church in Asia

Part I: Vocation and Avocation

My years as diocesan bishop in Oakland (1977–2003) were largely concurrent with my role as "fraternal delegate" to the general assemblies of the Federation of Asian Bishops' Conferences (FABC)—a collegial gathering of twenty Asian countries that the bishops established to continue the dialogue they experienced at the Second Vatican Council. Pope Paul VI warmly encouraged this initiative.

I chose the word "avocation" in the chapter subheading with purpose. The common understanding of the term contains the notion of "something one does in addition to one's vocation and regular work, and usually for fun." The definition represents a good fit in my case, along with another extended term I enjoyed with the U.S. bishops' Committee on Science and Human Values. The Asian memories are filled with satisfaction and enjoyment. The opening invitation and appointment came in 1979 with the welcomed accompaniment of Bishop Howard Hubbard of Albany, New York, with his well-deserved reputation for international justice and peace. The overture reunited me as well with Maryknoll Father Edward Malone, whom I had encountered memorably at Maryknoll's headquarters in Ossining, New York, in his early

Maryknoll Father Edward Malone, right, who worked closely with Asian hierarchy, arranged an orientation tour of southern Asia for Bishop Cummins before the Oakland prelate assumed his role as fraternal delegate from the U.S. bishops to the Federation of Asian Bishops' Conferences, a post he held for twenty-two years. (FABC photo)

days as professor of theology. He taught me much about how to adapt to the world of Asia and about the history of the Federation, sprinkling in much unvarnished commentary during our meetings in Hong Kong, which was his base, and eventually in San Francisco, Rome, and New York.

The extended years belie a prodigious investment of time. The FABC general assemblies convened every four years. Remarkably hospitable, the Asian bishops offered welcome to me and to my accompanying staff. They returned visits to our Diocese of Oakland, which during my years as delegate experienced a burst of Asian newcomers. Episcopal visits confirmed my relationship with the newly arrived peoples and provided enrichment to the family of our diocese.

Not surprisingly the years occasioned some mutuality. A Hong Kong businessman whose family attended UC–Berkeley asked me to serve on the board of his American school. The bishop in Mongolia, who earned a master's degree with the Jesuit School of Theology in Berkeley, hosted us graciously on two occasions. The heavily burdened young bishop Carlos Ximenes Belo from East Timor visited us. Our

Korean people organized a pilgrimage to the Eucharistic Congress in 1989 in Seoul. Twice I participated in a group visiting Mindanao in the Philippines, studying the intense conflict between Christians and Muslims in that region. Twice while I was in Rome for synods I noted with some astonishment the diversity of the church in Asia augmented with its Eastern rites. Rome, too, introduced me to an admired friend, Archbishop Giovanni Cheli, whose pastoral sense I admired, aligned with that of Roman Curia acquaintances Cardinals Stephen Hamao, Jozef Tomko, and Eduardo Pironio.

I am particularly grateful to have experienced how the church can bring together such diversity of peoples, languages, and cultures—a pattern proposed at the Vatican Council for the unity of the entire human family. The experience has been a strengthening of faith.

Early Conditioning

I grew up on the West Coast with a Japanese population, dispersed unhappily during World War II. Chinese and Filipinos were significant population segments in our East Bay. *Maryknoll* magazine with its accent on mission in the Far East was always on our family table. We shared a back fence with the Shea family, whose second son, Thomas, entered Maryknoll to become an overseas missioner. I recall when I was nine years old, going with Tom and my own family in 1937 to the San Francisco waterfront to wave farewell to James Thornton, a young California Jesuit originally from my mother's place in Galway, Ireland, as he sailed for Japan for his theological studies and priestly ordination. He would be imprisoned by the Japanese and repatriated in 1943 on the Swedish ship, the *Gripsholm*. After the war, he returned to mission in China, only to be expelled during the Mao Revolution. Undaunted he later returned to serve in Japan.

My seminary days were shared with candidates for Maryknoll. We had diocesan seminarians from Hawaii and Guam, Chinese, on the one hand, and Chamorro, on the other. Fellow seminarian Joseph Wong, native of San Francisco and alumnus of St. Mary's College, Moraga, served as acolyte at my first Mass in 1953.

By way of interest if not curiosity, in 1968, my brother and I with four other priests took advantage of a World Airways charter offer of a round trip from the West Coast to Tokyo for $345. In Japan, we called on a Maryknoll classmate, Father Tony Brodniak, who was caring for developmentally disabled children in Yokkaichi. We walked through Hiroshima streets feeling self-conscious as Americans, but nonetheless welcomed in the afternoon by a grammar school classmate, now Jesuit Father Walter Brennan, who was principal of a high school there. In Tokyo, we caught up with aforementioned, redoubtable James Thornton, SJ, then teaching a course on Shakespeare at Sofia University. Technically we were tourists, but contacts built over our still young years gave us access to places and people to which an ordinary traveler had no access.

In Hong Kong, we caught the very different flavor of a rushing but assured Chinese world. Rupert Li, the owner of Swindon Books, a major Hong Kong distributor of school books, entertained us one Sunday afternoon. (His two daughters had attended Oakland's Mills College.) He led us by ferry to Lan Tao Island, now the site of Hong Kong's enormous airport, but in those days a rocky hill giving parched evidence of too little water. The site, however, proved adequate enough for a Trappist monastery, whose monks, exiled in 1949 from Beijing, had in our student days spent three months with us at St. Patrick's Seminary in Menlo Park. We were warmly welcomed and treated to water, beer, and lychee nuts, as a monk smilingly told us, "courtesy of Mao." One moment of that warm summer provided the chilling experience of standing on the site of the boundary of the New Territories, peering into the expanse that was mainland China and sensing what in 1968 was awesome and ominous silence.

We rounded out our trip with a week in Taiwan, enjoying the hospitality and the experience of a parish in Lukang, in the diocese of Taichung, then under the Maryknoll Society's jurisdiction. Father Edward Quinn, MM, a native of San Jose and classmate of my brother from college seminary days, served Lukang's Chinese Catholics. The community had a vibrancy that included Taiwan's indigenous peoples, forced into the mountain territories by the flood of mainland Chinese fleeing the Red Revolution. We concelebrated a Mass with them, enabled by a still Latin Eucharistic Prayer. The festivities afterwards included an exchange of songs, including our own. The situation was reminiscent of what we had known with the "displaced persons" who arrived on the West Coast from Eastern Europe after World War II.

In 1972, at my urging, Frank Maurovich, the editor of our diocesan paper, which had a trade arrangement (advertising in exchange for travel) with American President Lines, extended what would initially have been a cruise to Hawaii all the way across the Pacific to Asia, home to 60 percent of the world's population. The transfer resulted in a demotion from a deck-side cabin aboard the *President Cleveland* (incidentally the proud ship's last voyage before decommissioning) to a lower-deck bunkroom for Frank Maurovich, Father Jim Keeley, and me all the way to Yokohama. The thirteen-day voyage of more than 5,100 miles also gave us a graphic experience—so many times superior to an air flight or even a map—of just how vast an ocean separates us from our Asian brothers and sisters. In Japan we nurtured again Maryknoll and Jesuit connections in Tokyo and Kyoto.

Proximate Preparation

In 1979, Monsignor Thomas Kelly, OP, general secretary of the U.S. Bishops' Conference, sent a congenial invitation to the competent Bishop Howard Hubbard of Albany, New York, and me for a two-week commitment in Asia. We were invited to attend "The Fifth Bishops' Institute for Social Action," sponsored by the Office of Human Development of the recently formed FABC. The first week of the assembly, called "immersion," offered a choice of one of seven areas to visit: Hong Kong, Bangladesh, Thailand, Indonesia, India, Sri Lanka, or the Philippines. In the second week all participating bishops and some staff and theologians would gather in Bangalore, India, for reaction and reflection. Invitees included prelates from eight Asian countries, seven parts of Oceania, and eight Western countries—Canada, Finland, Germany, Spain, Ireland, England, France, and the United States.

I chose the Philippines for my immersion because when I returned to the Oakland Diocese only two years earlier after a six-year assignment in Sacramento I had the impression, later profoundly verified, that the Filipino population in our Alameda and Contra Costa counties had grown extensively during my absence. On the first evening of our visit, we gathered at the Jesuit East Asian Pastoral Institute (EAPI) in Manila. I ended up being the sole American presence, since Bishop Hubbard, unfortunately I felt for me, had an intervening date that required his participation in the ordination of his classmate Matthew Clark as bishop of Rochester, New York.

Arriving in the Philippines, I happily renewed the acquaintance of another New Yorker, Father Edward Malone, a Maryknoll missioner, whom I had met a dozen years before when he was teaching dogmatic theology at the Maryknoll seminary in Ossining, New York. Stationed now in Hong Kong, he was named the assistant secretary general of the FABC. In this post, this quiet, unassuming priest played a key role in establishing the organization's structure and functioning process for twenty-five years. The EAPI in Manila, an institution in the development of which he shared, was only one of the many ways he promoted understanding of Asian affairs with bishops worldwide and friendships among Asian bishops themselves and their brothers in the universal church. Father Malone would be nurturing my Asian association into the twenty-first century. A welcome as well came from Filipino Bishop Francisco Claver, SJ, who would be part of my life for some thirty years, a most competent expositor of the church's theology and social teaching. The Christian Brothers at De La Salle College provided lodging and more. An international group, they enjoyed singular freedom at extended breakfast conversations to express opinions and judgments about Ferdinand Marcos's martial law regime.

My assignment for the week sent me to the southern island of Mindanao. I was delighted to move beyond the Metro Manila area. Accompanying me were two Spanish bishops, one a Basque, explicitly so, from Pamplona, and Andreas Henrisusanto, a congenial young bishop from Sumatra. In the city of Davao, the Maryknoll center house offered us hospitality, courtesy of regional superior Father Jim Ferry who, as director of the Maryknoll house in San Francisco, had served the Diocese of Oakland some years previously.

Bishop Federico Escaler, SJ, of Ipil was hospitable, but challenging. He began with an innocent sounding question, "How many Filipino priests do you have?" I responded, "Three." He replied rather sharply, "What are they doing there?" He followed with what now is a dated response, "There are 222 Filipino priests in the United States. They should be home." Bishop Escaler, on the border of the mountain territory, some years later suffered being kidnapped. He visited us once in Oakland on his way to Guelph in Canada to serve on an Ignatian thirty-day retreat, promising that he would consider very seriously leading a retreat for the priests of Oakland.

I held very special our visit to the Diocese of Tagum, with its Bishop Joseph Regan, native of Massachusetts and a Maryknoll missioner exiled from China. I mentioned in Chapter 1 that he had been a passenger in the same row with me on the Alitalia charter returning to New York from the second session of the Vatican Council in December 1963. The name given to his young, motorcycle-riding priests, "Regan's Raiders," was perhaps related to the protest the mild bishop and his priests had registered after the "disappearance" of a catechist. Catechists and labor organizers seemed to be objects of the diocese's special attention and protection.

After the immersion week in the southern island, we gathered in Manila to prepare for the following reflection week to be held in Baguio. Baguio was chosen to replace our original site, Bangalore, India, after the Indian bishops reportedly expressed discomfort with the international quality, as well as possible political overtones, of so large a group. From Manila, we were bussed to the mountains and the cooler and more beautiful countryside. As we passed near Clark Air Force Base, our Filipino host made critical remarks about the atmosphere surrounding the American military base. The U.S. naval installation at Subic Bay was a postscript.

All told, we were thirty-seven delegates. Ireland had two—Michael Murphy, auxiliary bishop of Cork, who had served in the Peru missions, and Derry's bishop, Edward Daly, of "Bloody Sunday" fame, who while gathering some of us for Jameson each night exhibited a profound belief in nonviolence in pursuit of political change. The Dutch-born bishop of Finland humorously attended to the report of a Bangladesh bishop who noted that in his diocese "Catholics were zero point three percent [0.3%] of the population." The bishop of Finland thought he could do better, "We are point zero three percent [.03%]." Eight prelates came from the South Pacific—Australia and New Zealand, Papua New Guinea, Fiji and Tonga, this last of whom we would later entertain on a visit to Oakland. I innocently inquired of Bishop Hubert Coppenrath of Tahiti whether he was a missionary. With some edge, he countered that his family dated back three generations in the South Pacific Islands.

Theologians Tissa Balasuriya, an Oblate priest from Sri Lanka, the verbose Father Samuel Rayan from India, and his colleague Father Amalorpavadass, were resource people. I also remember well Anita Fernandes from India, a laywoman whose manner called to mind Katherine de Hueck Doherty of Canadian and Chicago fame.

The close of the symposium with its dazzling interchange did not signal the end of my Asian experience. Some months before, I had noted an advertisement for travel into the newly opened People's Republic of China—from Hong Kong to Canton for $350 for five days. I turned to Matt Connors, a member of our parish in Oakland and a travel agent for Kaiser Industries, who, despite initial hesitation about my travel proposal, successfully obtained a visa for me. I was to bring it to China International Travel in Hong Kong in care of Eddie Chang. A disturbing phone call followed my depositing my passport: "You have a Roman collar on your passport picture. Visa has been refused." Father Malone, by now my instructor in culture as well as host, explained Mr. Chang's failure to serve me ended with his "losing face."

Afterwards, Father Malone introduced me to Dr. Thomas T.S. Liang, a gentleman whose family lived in the Diocese of Oakland and who would be my friend and benefactor for many years. The extended week in Hong Kong gave me a chance to take a hydrofoil trip to Macao in the company of a De La Salle Brother visiting from Cuba. I found the atmosphere around Macao's highly touted casinos several levels below those of Lake Tahoe. Bishop Arquiminio R. Costa, hospitable and thoughtful, explained that it was time for a Chinese bishop rather than a Portuguese prelate in Macao. The appropriateness of his observation was rapidly gaining support. The prelate became my tour guide and instructed me to leave my camera in the car. I discovered why when we walked to the end of a path where a small waterway, not as large as the Russian River in northern California, separated Macao from the People's Republic. Across the border, a seated young sentry, looking bored and smoking a cigarette, rose as we approached and moved to a small station tower, where he proceeded to display a rifle barrel through a narrow slit.

My lengthy report to Washington after this trip was anything but tentative. Reflecting much of the broad perspective and commentary of Father Malone, I advised our national office to make formal contact with the large world that was Asia, specifically with the FABC. Consideration, I urged, should be given to inviting an Asian bishop to address an assembly of our bishops, as Panama's Archbishop Mark McGrath, CSC, had done on behalf of the Conference of Latin American Bishops (CELAM) at our meeting in November 1978.

Furthermore, I urged that other U.S. bishops be invited to the next FABC Institute for Social Action. I sensed that we needed to familiarize ourselves with Asia and the church there. They knew much about us—so many of their bishops having visited as well as studied in the United States—yet we knew little about them. At the EAPI, some Asians had bristled about the regional effects of U.S. politics and businesses, especially corporations. They also noted that immigration operated only in one direction. I pressed my case that more U.S. bishops should consider travels to Asia beyond the typical tourist junkets, and they should ask for assistance from the knowledgeable Father Malone in planning their visits.

U.S. Church Envoy to Tokyo on behalf of Kim Dae-jung

Another step into Asia came in December 1980 with a phone call from Monsignor Daniel Hoye, asking if I would be able to attend a meeting in Tokyo called by the National Christian Council in Japan, a Protestant group paralleling our National Council of Churches here. The subject concerned Korean activist Kim Dae-jung, who had been kidnapped out of Japan, tried in a Korean court, and sentenced to death.

Accepting the invitation took me into unfamiliar territory in terms of politics and personal involvement. Father Bryan Hehir, from our bishops' office in Washington, sent me several pertinent articles, which I read on the plane, as well as the recent encyclical of Pope John Paul II, *Dives in Misericordia*. All of these materials proved both relevant and helpful.

Maryknoll missioners, particularly Father John Vinsko, welcomed me at their Tokyo center house and continued my preparation. I remembered the unexpected mildness of the weather as well as the view from the Maryknoll house of a surprising block-long portrayal of Santa Claus and reindeer at the Akasaka Shopping Center in that notably non-Christian world.

Bishop Augustine Nomura from Nagoya, chair of the Japanese hierarchy's Justice and Peace Commission, arranged a meeting with the
members of the commission, along with Jesuits from Sofia University
and the archbishop of Tokyo. Of particular help to me were two gentlemen from Washington, D.C.: Donald Ranard, formerly of the U.S. State
Department, and Pharis Harvey, a United Methodist ordained minister,
with an international reputation on union rights, child labor, and protes-
tations against sweatshops. The group made it clear that I was to make a
presentation.

At the gathering, the chair of the National Christian Council invited me to speak first. More preoccupied with my presentation, I found
the microphones and television cameras notable but not disturbing. My
presentation included testimony given by the U.S. bishops to Congress
on the situation of Kim Dae-jung, a repetition of the stance President
Carter and President-elect Reagan had both taken, and the words of
Pope John Paul II, which included the quotation, "Violence is a prelude
to continuing violence." The quality of the day-long meeting was admirable. Later in the day I would twice hear my voice broadcast on car
radio.

One can assume that the gathering in Tokyo, well ordered and well
publicized, contributed to the growth of international sentiment in support of Kim Dae-jung. In time he was exonerated and he went on to become the eighth elected president of South Korea, incidentally, the first
Catholic in that post. Undoubtedly because of my participation in the
Tokyo conference, I received a Christmas card from Kim Dae-jung for
many years afterwards.

Radio Veritas in Manila Calling

My Asia experience was not yet at an end. In the spring of 1981, Monsignor Daniel Hoye, associate general secretary from our national office,
called. Father Edward Malone, on behalf of the FABC, had requested a
bishop from the United States to participate in an appraisal of Manila-
based Radio Veritas. From my limited knowledge of that facility I anticipated that it would be "Vatican Radio East," a shortwave radio station
that could reach much of Asia.

The action station exceeded my expectations. Risen some years after World War II, Radio Veritas had found a welcoming home in Manila. Cardinal Rufino J. Santos, archbishop of Manila, promoted the project with strong leadership. Support funds came mainly from Germany. Archbishop Edward O'Meara of Indianapolis, from his mission experiences, reminded me later that in the immediate aftermath of World War II, the Office of the Propagation of the Faith of the United States had much to offer in rebuilding and expanding the missionary efforts of the church. A decade later it would providentially fall to the church in Germany to be a resource for overseas activity.

Giving me my directions, Monsignor Hoye made it clear that no money would be available from the National Conference of Catholic Bishops for this project. The bishops' position had been carefully thought out. Needless to say, upon my arrival, the director of the station, Father Hugo Delbaere, a priest of the Immaculate Heart of Mary Order, also known as the Scheut (pronounced *skirt*) missioners from Belgium, greeted me and then expressed his expectation that the church in America could be depended on for perhaps $2.3 million. German Divine Word Father Franz Joseph Eilers, with whom I would be in conversations for some decades to come, lobbied for the request with some impatience.

Germany was well represented on the review team in the persons of Monsignor Norbert Herkenrath, from the Misereor aid agency in Aachen, and Monsignor Bernd Kaut, who represented the German foundation known as Missio. These two groups had built the station on the grounds of the University of the Philippines in Manila. The history of the project was somewhat cloudy regarding its early vision and questionable expenditures. After so many years and with such great liberality, both German operations wanted to move on to other projects.

I was favorably impressed by the station's daily operations. Notable was the work of the Vietnamese-language unit in providing theology courses for would-be seminarians in a country whose seminaries were shut tight. Among the station's five other languages, broadcasts in Chinese delivered courses in the Scriptures; programs were offered in Hindi as well. I remember particularly the Korean division, staffed by two Korean nuns who were almost stereotypical in their politeness and the diffidence of their gestures. But when one of the German monsignors asked the nuns whom they represented, the reply was delivered in a rather steely manner, "We are here by appointment of the Korean Catholic Bishops' Conference."

Despite some reasonable criticisms of its operations, my evaluation of Radio Veritas was positive. The Asian bishops concurred, describing the radio service through the years as a worthy cause.

A memorable aside happened on a Sunday afternoon helicopter journey with Manila resident Lee Telesco, whom I had engaged in casual conversation some months earlier in Washington's Dulles Airport. As welcoming as he was surprised by my call, he invited me to lunch at his home in the Makati area of Manila with his wife, the daughter of a German pharmacist who had arrived in the Philippines in 1901. A native of Fresno, California, and at one time a Jesuit scholastic at the Los Gatos novitiate, Lee Telesco had served behind Japanese lines in the Philippines during the war. With the GI Bill, he earned a degree in international law from Stanford University and was coaxed back to the Philippines after the war by the well-known Ayala family. He was now vice-president of San Miguel Beer. More to the point, while we toured the island of Corregidor and spoke of the Bataan Peninsula during its 1942 drama, he praised fellow guerrilla Ferdinand Marcos for his bravery. Even though critical of Marcos's politics, his appraisal was in contrast to the martial law president's reputation in California. So, too, was the contrast between the afternoon wartime conversation and dinner that evening with his wife and family at the Manila Hotel, once the headquarters for General Douglas MacArthur, with a seraphic concert from the chorale of the University of the Philippines.

On my arrival back in the States I felt obligated to make some effort to raise funds for Radio Veritas. Cardinal Terence Cooke, of New York, with his ongoing interest in Asia, expressed encouragement, "If you do not follow through with supporting the project, no one else will." Archbishop Edward O'Meara added his support, "Just because a thing is difficult does not mean it should not be tried."

I enlisted the two of them as names on a national committee to seek funds. Archbishop Joseph Bernardin of Chicago readily agreed. So, too, did Archbishop Edward McCarthy of Miami and six others. I did not visit foundations or other groups, but I did write letters. The response was $67,000, meager according to the wishes of Radio Veritas, yet remarkable given the process of the fund-raising.

Orientation for Service as a Fraternal Delegate to the FABC

The year 1982 brought further opportunities for Asian involvement, with an invitation to participate far beyond my experiences during the three previous years. Both Bishop Howard Hubbard of Albany—this time happily available—and I received an invitation to become "fraternal delegates" at the Third Plenary Assembly of the FABC to be held in Bangkok, Thailand. My familiarity and friendships with so many in Asia assured a quick affirmative response on my part.

I did note in my acceptance, however, that given that so much time and money went into these travels there should be somebody in our Washington office to whom I could report back in a format beyond the written summaries I sent to the general secretary. Calls quickly came back, one from Monsignor Daniel Hoye, another from Father Bryan Hehir, asking, "Did you not know that you are our liaison to the Asian bishops?" Not only didn't I know this, but no official letter of appointment had ever been sent. This omission resulted in a puzzling and disappointing inquiry twenty-two years later when it was time for me to retire the liaison position. One reason for this slipup—no criticism of staff intended—was that Asia was low on the priority ladder of American church concerns.

Through the graciousness of Father Malone, the invitation became expansive. At my suggestion, he made allowance for Father Anthony McGuire, who had become the overseer of ministry to the ethnic communities in the Archdiocese of San Francisco, to accompany me. In sync with Father Malone's intention of broadening knowledge and solidarity with and within Asia, Father McGuire would join a larger group of international participants—priests, theologians, religious, lay men and women, ecumenical representatives, and occasionally one or two who had some interreligious connection. The boundaries of the group did not stop at bishops but embraced a style of the "people of God." San Francisco's Father McGuire would later move into ministry to Asian peoples, first becoming a Maryknoll Associate priest and learning Chinese in Hong Kong at the age of fifty, and later at the national level when he directed the U.S. bishops' Office of Pastoral Care for Migrants and Refugees.

With the aim of familiarizing U.S. bishops with the church in Asia, Father Malone arranged travels for me on the way to Bangkok that included stops in Kathmandu, Nepal, in Varanasi (Benares), India, and Yangon (Rangoon) in Myanmar (Burma), this last a wish of mine.

Nepal: On my arrival in Kathmandu, Maryknoll Father Adam Gudalefsky awaited me with an immediate plan for the day. He connected me with Father Cap Miller, the provincial of the Jesuits, and then we met an impressive Loretto Sister from Bavaria who had served in Little Rock, Arkansas, during the integration of public schools in the 1960s. Her current work was managing an impressive elementary school of 3,800 well-uniformed girls. Father Gudalefsky himself was in the process of outfitting a home for Nepal's developmentally disabled children.

Nepal became my first experience of Hindu culture. Cows wandered the streets, appearing undernourished compared to the animals I'd seen in Alameda County or in County Mayo, Ireland. Poverty was evident, reflected in the street people's grim demeanor. I mused whether the Christian presence would seem revolutionary.

In Nepal, Bishop Cummins took this photo of Sister Anna Maria, SCN, (red sweater) with one of her charges. Behind them are two U.S. airline attendants who took year off from their jobs to work with the nun. A native of India, Anna Maria is a member of the Sisters of Charity of Nazareth, Bardstown, Kentucky. (J. Cummins photo)

Father Adam took me along with a Nepalese doctor into the brilliant morning sunshine of the mountain territories. The Nepalese medic, who had enjoyed a residence year at the University of Minnesota, spent his practice admirably administering shots and medicine at the tea houses that dotted the countryside.

During my last evening with the Jesuits and Maryknollers, I asked: Since Christianity was proscribed in Nepal and the preaching of the gospel illegal, how come church activity is so abundant? The answer came, "They don't bother us, and we don't bother them."

India: While a friendly face met me in Kathmandu, no one awaited my arrival in Varanasi's sunbaked airport near the Ganges. A short taxi driver accosted me, inquiring, "Are you Christian?" I responded affirmatively and asked how far it was to the Catholic bishop's house. "Twenty-four kilometers" was his quick response. I checked with a young airline official nearby and he confirmed that the distance was "about twenty-three kilometers." Pointing at the taxi driver, he then asked, "Is he taking you?" I said he had offered. "Don't give him more than sixty rupees," he said both to me and firmly to the taxi driver.

I had to note that in that area of 13 million residents with 13,000 Catholics, the bishop's place of residence seemed so well known, much better than mine in Oakland. Of course, the episcopal compound in Varanasi had outstanding recognizable features—cathedral, school, nursery, and clinic, and the site of other services, plus the bishop's rectory. Father Joseph, a priest from Kerala with thirty years of ministry in the city, took welcoming care of me in the absence of Bishop Patrick D'Souza, who had already left for the Bangkok meeting.

I learned about Varanasi's significant interreligious importance. Regarded as the spiritual capital of India, the city is held sacred by Hindus, Jains, and Buddhists. Hindus regard it as the holiest of its seven sacred cities. The northern Indian city also played a critical role in the development of Buddhism.

Activity in the city exhibited the intensity that media from home would have predicted. Father Joseph commandeered a boat on the Ganges River, and thousands of people performing their morning ablutions proved a spectacle, as indeed did a walk through a bazaar, where I sus-

Water buffalo rest in Varanasi, a city in northwestern India that
Bishop Cummins visited. Located on the banks of the Ganges
River, worshipped as the goddess Ganga by Hindus, Varanasi is
often called India's holiest city, sacred to Hindus and Jainism and re-
portedly near the site of Gautama Buddha's first sermon. (Sean
Sprague photo)

pected I was the only European face. Visiting the Little Sisters of
Charles de Foucauld and two other convents gave me a good sense of
the church in the midst of that immense and ancient culture.

Myanmar: Last came a visit to Yangon, the renamed capital of the renamed nation of Burma. My wish to visit this nation, whose name was
imprinted on our memories during World War II as a country with a famous supply road, to say nothing of a bridge over its River Kwai, had
arisen from a dinner arranged the summer before at our home in Oakland by Brother Patrick Moore of St. Mary's College.

Surrendering willingly to his avocation for Anglican/Roman Catholic dialogue, thirteen of us sat at dinner that evening with Brother
Moore's friend, the Anglican primate of Rangoon, Archbishop Alexander, as guest of honor and overnight resident. Perhaps overwhelmed by
the crowd at dinner, the prelate relaxed afterwards, nursing a glass of
brandy, with just Father Joe Carroll and myself. At one point in the conversation I indicated that I might be somewhere in his neighborhood in
the fall of the following year. "Come up," he said. "Can I get in?" I inquired since I knew of Burma's xenophobia. "We'll get you in," he re-

sponded. Later I told Father Carroll that I had an unasked question, "Can I get out?"

Yangon was crowded and busy. I stayed at the house belonging to the Bishops' Conference. Bishop Paul Graung, very young, who would years later visit us in Oakland, was solicitous, as was Archbishop Matthias U. Shwe, who also spent time later in the Bay Area. The archbishop one evening remarked with sad resignation that they had none of the freedom of speaking and writing that American bishops enjoyed. Bishop George Yod Phimphisan, a Redemptorist visitor from up-country Thailand, who had studied in Wisconsin, was an articulate expositor of the situation in southern Asia, including the Burmese church.

The effects of persecution were clear. A brick wall with broken glass atop separated the cathedral from its once accompanying school. The Christian Brothers and the priests proved reluctant to talk about politics, but the alumni of their schools were not. A Sister who ran a home for the elderly exhibited an entertaining boldness, "Even the Holy Spirit does not know what this government will be doing next."

I visited the seminary with its 220 students in philosophy and theology. Given that number in relation of the Catholic population of Burma, I realized that the proportionate number for us in the Diocese of Oakland would be 440. At that time we had perhaps twenty seminarians. The rector asked me to come Sunday evening to give a talk. I told him I was not a theologian. He pleaded, reporting that the last visitor, Cardinal Cooke of New York, had come nine months earlier. "I cannot send the priest professors out of the country for additional studies," he cried. "The government would never give permission." I came on Sunday evening and spoke slowly and deliberately—very conscious of my American accent—on the nature of authority in the church after the Second Vatican Council.

I had lunch with Primate Alexander on the patio of his very Asian-looking house and met his two children. A welcoming host, he told me that he did not expect to see me again after the Oakland visit. His freedom, he explained, was very restricted. I understand that he was arrested later because of guns suspiciously discovered in the basement of his church. The last word I heard was that he died not many years after our visit.

Part II: Fraternal Delegate to the Asian Bishops

Bangkok, 1982. "The Church: Community of Faith in Asia"
When I finally arrived in Bangkok to join Bishop Hubbard and Father Anthony McGuire for the FABC Assembly, seventy-seven Asian bishops were already present. The full number of attendees easily doubled with the addition of theologians as well as other men and women, both lay and religious, in an easy mix. The minor seminary in Samphran, outside the city of Bangkok, was the assembly site. Beds were short and lightly mattressed. A crocodile farm was within walking distance.

The meetings lasted ten days in what I learned was a well-developed pattern. The first half consisted of presentations and reflections on the agreed-upon theme. This third assembly had chosen "The Church: Community of Faith in Asia." In 1974 in Taipei, the first FABC gathering had reflected on "The Church's Task in the World." In Calcutta four years later, the bishops chose "Prayer: The Life of the Church in Asia," a reflection on the interior life seen as an Asian heritage.

The fifth day of each assembly was set aside for sightseeing and cultural exposure, while a writing team began analyzing the theme of the conference. Bishop Hubbard and I were surprised to be invited to join the writing team, but Hubbard graciously but firmly turned down the offer, insisting that he and I were present to listen and learn. The last days were given to discussion of the proposed draft, which was inevitably literary, rich in spirituality, and invariably bearing a confident tone.

Daily liturgies and prayers exhibited the cultural flavor of the groups. Mission Sunday in the nation's capital city cathedral that October took on profound meaning with seventy-seven bishops from all parts of Asia gathered around the altar. In later years, Brothers from the Taizé community of France came to lead morning and evening prayers.

Evenings during the assembly were for special reports, often behind closed doors, examining political tensions in places such as Pakistan and Bangladesh. Participants from Sri Lanka felt the force of Christian community from bishops who came from both sides of the ethnic conflict there.

I was impressed by the amount of activity that took place between plenary assemblies. Under Father Malone's direction, offices had been created for laity and family, one for theological concerns, others for consecrated life, ecumenical and interreligious affairs, and social communications. Furthermore, he had directed that offices be sensitively and prudently located in different Asia countries. His insight had further developed a program of publications that comprised a library of information on theological, spiritual, sociological, and social issues to promote clerical and lay leadership. From its earliest days, the FABC had insisted on the need for threefold dialogue: with cultures, with world religions, and, especially, with the poor.

Father McGuire pointed to Stephen Cardinal Kim as the outstanding personality during the Thailand gathering. While the church in Korea registered over two million Catholics, a story passed around claimed that almost 700,000 had been baptized in the six previous years. During an evening social hour Cardinal Kim was asked to explain how the church had prospered so well. "We don't do anything. They just come to us," he said. To a follow-up question about the Rite of Christian Initiation of Adults, he said, "We really don't have time for that."

After the general assembly, Archbishop Renato Martino, the Vatican's apostolic nuncio to Thailand, arranged for Bishop Hubbard, Father McGuire, and me to cross the country into Cambodia to visit a camp for refugees. Maryknoll Father Tom Dunleavy was our guide, together with John Clink, a Santa Clara University graduate who was directing Catholic Relief Services in the region. "Are we in Cambodia?" I asked Tom. The answer was affirmative. I also asked, "Where are the Khmer Rouge?" "From that tree north," he lightly pointed out. People in the camp welcomed us. They were tolerant and even pleased to pose for pictures. At midday a truck came distributing sacks of rice to people waiting patiently. Bishop Hubbard lent a hand to the process, along with entertaining youngsters, few of whom were shy.

On our return trip we visited another camp operated in Thailand by the military. Facilities there were much more up-to-date with hospital and dentistry and a much better organization. The sight of young children with arms and legs missing was horrifying. Bishop Hubbard observed that the first camp we visited in Cambodia, although lightly

Father Laurence T. Murphy, M.M., second from right, with colleagues at the opening of a Catholic seminary in Seshan, China. Father Murphy played a key role in opening the doors of the Catholic church in mainland China to the world. (Maryknoll Archives photo)

equipped, appeared a remarkably more contented place. The military's presence in Thailand made the camps there feel less homey.

Two years after the Bangkok assembly, our U.S. bishops' Washington office asked me to respond to an invitation from Dominican Bishop Joseph Chang to represent our conference at the 120th anniversary of the Archdiocese of Kaoshiung in Taiwan. A participant in the celebratory Mass was Bishop Stanislaus Luogang, once the chancellor of Fujian University in Taipei. He prevailed on me to change my ticket home so that I could spend several more days at the university, conversing about religious and political concerns of the church in Taiwan.

The scheduled FABC Assembly in October 1986 nurtured a lingering desire in some of us to attach a tour of mainland China. While that thought developed, Dr. Thomas T.S. Liang invited a diverse group to the inauguration of an American school, a long-standing desire of his, in Hong Kong. The group included Terence Bell, former director of the U.S. Department of Education, others from the political world, and educators from the West Coast, particularly Sister Lois MacGillivray, president of Holy Names University. I came on the invitation list along with Father Joe Carroll, a friend of the Liangs, our school department leadership Sister Rose Marie Hennessy, OP, Carondelet Sister Barbara

Flannery, CSJ, and Father Dan Danielson. Attaching the China visit provided us a full two weeks of time, though we did not expect any underwriting from Dr. Liang. He quietly arranged our entire tour and sent as our guides his wife, Billie, and daughter, Rose. Shortly beforehand, Father Larry Murphy of Maryknoll, who had been an early respondent to the opening of the People's Republic, called. He listed a number of bishops we might encounter and offered words of caution. We came in touch with three: the bishop from Guangzhou, Joseph Yi Yinyun, who had replaced Archbishop Dominic Tang Yee-Ming; Michael Fu Tieshan of Beijing; and Bernadine Guangqing Dong of Wuhan. The day after my return home, Father Murphy dutifully called. I gave him our appraisal: Guangzhou received a seven, since we thought the bishop there was doing the best he could; Bishop Dong in Wuhan received a ten; Bishop Fu in Beijing we rated a two. Father Murphy agreed with our estimate.

Our contacts with the Chinese bishops continued. Bishops Dong and Fu both visited UC– Berkeley the following October in response to earlier visits to China by Father Murphy, then president of Seton Hall University. Sometime later Father John Vaughn, a California priest and friend, once my confessor, then minister general of the Franciscan Friars, shared a matter of great confidentiality with me: Wuhan's Bishop Dong had reconciled with the Holy Father. At the next plenary assembly of the FABC, an Indonesian bishop told me that 80 percent of the irregular episcopal appointments, i.e., those made by the so-called Patriotic Church, had reconciled with the Vatican, including Bishop Dong.

Father Murphy's creative initiatives to reopen roads to the church in China deserve special mention. Within a year of Beijing's announcement of a reform period in the People's Republic of China, Father Murphy, as president of Seton Hall University, acquired visas for twenty-one top-level education, business, and church leaders, including the governor of New Jersey, to visit China. The visit proved so fruitful in establishing education and business ties, as well as allowing friendly meetings with Chinese clergy, that the Maryknoll missioner put together another inclusive group for a visit in the following year. At the urging of his fellow Maryknollers, Father Murphy went to Rome to confer with the Vatican's top diplomat for China. During a breakfast meeting with Pope

John Paul II, Father Murphy described the restrictions still in force on the Catholic Church in mainland China and he explained that some Catholics had reached an accommodation with the Beijing government while others were refusing any political cooperation. There was "only one church in China," he stressed, a church united in faith but divided in strategy. The Holy Father asked the missioner to continue being a "bridge" to the Chinese people and to report to him regularly.

Tokyo, 1986. "Vocation and Mission
in the Life of the Church and in the World of Asia"

Bishop Hubbard, pressed by new commitments with our national conference, could not attend FABC's Fourth General Assembly in Tokyo in 1986, but Father Anthony McGuire was able to join me again. Cardinal Eduardo Pironio, from Rome by way of Argentina, opened the assembly with a remarkable presentation of the Vatican Council II's teaching on the laity. He addressed the matter of structures of collaboration and participation and pointed to the value of basic communities and the need of formation for ministry. He urged "effective and affective communion with the bishop."

Drawing also from Vatican II, Sri Lankan theologian S.J. Emmanuel delivered an equally magnificent presentation, outlining in the broadest of strokes and with the richest of international theological input the vision of laity in the church. Father Emmanuel and I continued correspondence for many months after the assembly, I, in the hope that he might visit us in Berkeley.

Father Felix Wilfred's talk outlined Asian realities challenging the church, among which was the ideological divide between capitalism and socialism, "Neither of which," he noted, "are Asian."

The education committee delivered a surprising and unusual statement about overemphasis on education in Taiwan and Japan. Archbishop Dario Castrillon Hoyos, representing CELAM, remarked publicly on the similarity of concerns from both federations of Asian and Latin American bishops. Bishop Howard Hubbard's visit in Thailand in 1982 was recalled.

FABC's Tokyo gathering took place two years after I participated in a twentieth-year evaluation of the *Constitution on the Sacred Liturgy*

Arriving for the 1990 FABC Assembly in Indonesia, Jesuit Father Albert Poulet-Mathis of FABC staff, far right, greets (left to right) Filipino Archbishops Leonardo Legaspi, OP, and Orlando Quevado, OMI, and Auxiliary Bishop Teodoro Bacani. In 2014, Pope Francis appointed Quevado, now the archbishop of Cotabato in Mindanao, one of nineteen new cardinals of the Catholic Church. (FABC photo)

(*Sacrosanctum Concilium*) as chair of the U.S. bishops' Liturgical Committee. I brought to the meeting several issues related to liturgical reform from our experiences in the United States. One issue centered on the need to develop a sensitivity regarding inclusive language. Resistance on this matter was clear in comments from the staff of the Congregation for Divine Worship and Cardinal Virgilio Noe that this was a concern only in North America. I wish the cardinal had been with me in Tokyo when Archbishop Antony Selvanayagan of Panjang, Indonesia, remarked to all at our breakfast table that when we had more experience of women in political and social life, we would better able to understand their place within the church.

After the Tokyo meeting, Father Malone, passing through San Francisco, informed me that I would receive an invitation to the Bandung Conference in Indonesia in 1990. I wrote to Monsignor Daniel Hoye, saying that whereas I was content to continue in the post, the Asia experience was so rich that perhaps we should let other U.S. bishops have this opportunity. Monsignor Hoye's succinct response was, "The Asians like familiar faces." What sounded like a bit of Confucian wisdom to me then, I took later on to be confirmation of my valued, though informal, role in Asia.

Bandung, Indonesia, 1990. "Journeying Together toward the Third Millennium"

More than 200 participated in FABC's Fifth General Assembly in Bandung in 1990; 120 were bishops. Delegates from Vietnam were expected, but did not arrive. Through the courtesy again of Father Malone, Father George Crespin, our vicar general, accompanied me to Bandung. This was providential because of the important role Father Crespin played during my visit to East Timor after the assembly. I was touched by the appreciation the assembled bishops exhibited for diversity: we are "a communion of communities," one bishop declared. Laity, religious, and clergy, the prelate stated, are to recognize and accept each other as brothers and sisters.

Again the confidence of the Asian church showed itself. Evangelization was emphasized, while the force of the great religions, Islam, Buddhism, Hinduism, was duly recognized. Catholic education in the region was praised. In Indonesia one million students attended Catholic schools, slightly more than half of them non-Catholic. Japan, with its mere 400,000 Catholic faithful, provided for 13 Catholic colleges, 115 high schools, and 530 elementary schools. I recalled from my grammar school days a mission of our Sisters of the Holy Names, with Sister Edith Christine, opening a school in Kagoshima, Japan, in the 1930s.

Filipino Jesuit Catalino Arevalo, long associated with the FABC, opened the FABC's Fifth General Assembly with a presentation on dialogue as a means of interior development in the church and as an instrument of evangelization and outreach. Earlier I alluded to the contrast between the tone of Arevelo's talk and that of the next presenter, the Vatican's Cardinal Jozef Tomko, who focused on the need for proclamation. He remarked that Jesus came into the world despite the existence of world religions at the time of the Incarnation. Alan De Lastic, later to become archbishop of Delhi, India, whispered to me, "There is a war going on that neither you nor I know anything about."

Manila, 1995. "Christian Discipleship
in Asia Today: Service to Life"

Participants in the 1995 FABC Assembly increased to 234, including three from Myanmar and four from Vietnam. I found Cardinal Thomas Williams of Wellington, New Zealand, delightful company. (He remarked that he made himself available for the twenty-three-hour flight to Rome just once a year.) New attendees included representatives from Focolare in Hong Kong and Young Christian Workers in Japan. Through the courtesy of Father Malone, I brought along Monsignor James Petersen, secretary of the California Catholic Conference of Bishops, and Sister Felicia Sarati, who worked with our ethnic communities. Some topics discussed in this assembly were the usual ones such as dialogue, ecology, family, women, youth, arts, and media. New discussions arose about the rising number of displaced persons, internal in some countries, but spreading across boundaries in other cases. Jesuit Father Ismael Zuloaga, formerly provincial of the China apostolate, pleaded for an international response to the ongoing toll from land mines left in rural areas of Vietnam and elsewhere after the wars.

The final statement notably was written by three bishops, Orlando Quevedo, Luis Tagle, and Telesphore Toppo. Their concern centered on what they called the globalization of economics. I was reminded of an observation by Dr. Robert Bellah of UC–Berkeley about "a deracinated global elite who know how to use new technology and information systems that are transforming global economies.... Not communities but 'networks', they do not have the moral qualities of communities."

The FABC's executive committee had postponed the sixth assembly from the summer of 1994 until January of the New Year in order to coincide with Pope John Paul II's participation at the World Youth Day (WYD) celebration in the Philippines. Father Malone, privately to me, expressed his disagreement, seeing it a distraction that would narrow time for FABC's work. He had a point because the WYD event attracted over four million people to Manila's Rizal Park in the middle of the ten-day FABC gathering. (The pope arrived for the event quite late, causing the young crowd to alter their early chant, "Pope John Paul II, we love you," to "John Paul II, where are you?")

The pope did address the FABC delegates at their meeting. Looking toward the third millennium, the pope observed that the first thousand years of the church focused on Europe and second millennium, on the Americas and Africa. The third, he declared, will look "particularly to Asia toward which the church's *missio ad gentes* is to be directed."

At breakfast one morning, Vietnamese Archbishop Francis Xavier Van Thuan (later cardinal, now "venerable") and Bishop John Chang-Yik of Chunchon, Korea, remarked that the Pacific was the new Mediterranean Sea. It was bound on the east and west by the large countries of China, Indonesia, Mexico, and the United States. It contained ten of the eleven fastest-growing economies in the world.

Bangkok, 2000. "A Renewed Church in Asia: A Mission of Love and Service"

I expected that my return to Bangkok for the FABC Assembly in 2000 would be the last of my formal visits. I therefore asked permission, perhaps with some sentimentality, to bring along three of the veterans who had accompanied me on earlier visits, Father George Crespin, Father Anthony Maguire, and Sister Felicia Sarati. Father Maguire was greeted with enthusiasm because of his role with Asian pastoral care from the national office in Washington, D.C. All of us were embraced on our arrival; we had become part of the family.

The Thailand archdiocese, under the leadership of Cardinal Michael Michai Kitbunchu, had visibly expanded from the time of my visit in 1982 for the FABC Assembly. The 2000 event took place in the diocesan center, with its contemporary five-story hotel, its meeting halls, and a central pond, from which, the cardinal jested, the crocodiles had been removed "much to the satisfaction of the fish." He continued in a wry manner by welcoming the delegates to stay after the assembly and then adding that, of course, they would have to pay rent.

At the Sunday jubilee celebration for the church in Thailand, a solemn Eucharistic liturgy in the stadium followed performances by young people accompanied by lilting Thai music. The dark of evening produced an impressive pageant done in lights, silhouettes, and fireworks.

The ten days in Bangkok were filled with an optimism that came from the Synod of Asia and from Pope John Paul II's apostolic exhorta-

At World Youth Day in the Philippines in 1995, which coincided with an FABC Assembly, Bishop Cummins compares notes with Martinus Situmorang, OFM Cap., bishop of the Diocese of Padang in western Sumatra. Sumatra is the largest of the 900 inhabited islands in Indonesia's sprawling archipelago, which stretches some 3,200 miles, a comparable distance would be from Oakland, California, to Bermuda. (FABC photo)

tion. In the mix were thoughts about countries freed from colonialism together with traditional topics such as the tripartite dialogue, collaboration, and role of laity; warnings about globalization, which was accelerating secularization and spawning extremist fundamentalists; and international economic restructuring and urbanization brought on by these same global economic forces. The Synod and the papal exhortation promoted an Asian image of Jesus "through stories, images, symbols, parables, myths and the chanting of sacred texts."

Our final evening together included music, song, and congenial socializing. The bonds of that diverse gathering had been well developed. Sister Sarati responded favorably to the request of Auxiliary Bishop Paul Mori of Tokyo for a lesson in dancing. In my report to Washington I wrote, "They really exemplify hope and they keep their faith in the context of the community. There is nothing parochial in their mindset."

Daejon, Korea 2004. "The Family: Toward a Culture of Life"

My roundabout way to the plenary assemble at Daejon, Korea, my last participation in the FABC, reminded me of my circuitous trip around Asia to my first assembly in 1982. On the way, I visited Hong Kong to seek funding for the building of our cathedral from Dr. Liang, a long-time, generous friend. Then, I spent five days in Nha Trang, Vietnam, with the family of our diocesan Vietnamese leader, Sister Rosaline Nguyen, LHC. Her sister, also a Holy Cross nun, operates a lively pre-school with 170 students. On the second day, before the Mass in "the library," I asked whether this gathering was illegal. "Oh yes," she said very calmly.

On the way to Korea, my third stop was a renewed visit to Mongolia, where I met up with Frank Maurovich, editor of *Maryknoll* magazine, and his photographer, Sean Sprague. Once again Bishop Wens Padilla graciously hosted us. One had to be impressed by the growth of the young church itself and especially its outreach. Fifteen priests, two Brothers, and thirty-one Sisters (all missioners) ministered to only 210 Catholics, but their ministry directly reached more than 3,000 needy, young, infirm, and older Mongolians.

My fourth stop took us to Jilin, in northern China, where Frank Maurovich, Sean Sprague, and I spent three days with Maryknoll Father Brian Barrons, who introduced us to the church in Jilin City and its bishop, Zhang Hanmin, who resides in Changchun. (Bishop Zhang died in 2009.) The dynamic Maryknoll missioner teaches English at Beihua University, as do some forty Maryknoll priests, Sisters, and lay volunteers at other universities throughout the Middle Kingdom. They are hired by the Chinese government, but not allowed to proselytize. The missioners witness to their faith by their lifestyles, helpfulness, and friendliness. Beside his classes, Father Barrons has acted much more publicly with city officials, teaching English to young Chinese working in the hotel and tourist industry, opening an office to teach English to prospective college students who must pass a difficult English exam to qualify for admission, and, with his fluency in Mandarin, serving as a cohost on a popular radio talk show. He is surrounded by an impressive group of young people in addition to friendly hospitable Bishop Zhang, and a lively group of young Chinese Sisters and priests, a continuing

Before heading to South Korea for his final FABC
Assembly in 2004, Bishop Cummins observed mis-
sionary work in Mongolia and in Jilin City in northern
China (above), where he visited with Maryknoll Father
Brian Barrons and Bishop Zhang Hanin. (Sean
Sprague photo)

witness to the vitality of the church in Asia.

The assembly in Daejon, ninety miles south of Seoul, focused on
family, anticipating the concerns of the Synod of Bishops in Rome a decade later. The summary paper spoke of "listening to God and to the
voice of Asian families" and of the Christian ideal of marriage as God's
gift and blessing to all of Asia. It was long in theological reflections
about "covenant," declaring the family to be "a sanctuary of love and
life, communion and solidarity." Topics discussed included the vocation
and mission of family spirituality, prayer, the paschal mystery, and the
place of the Eucharist. The document urged a vision of family ministry
with regional planning to help make more effective the role of family in
social transformation.

The assembly welcomed Atlanta's Bishop Wilton Gregory, president of the U.S. Catholic Conference of Bishops, in the company of the

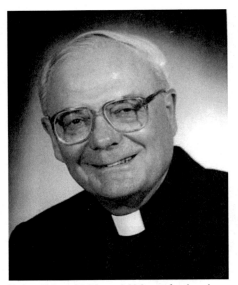

Father Edward Malone, M.M., used cultural sensitivity in helping found the FABC and its related offices. (Maryknoll Archives photo)

Conference's general secretary, Monsignor Bill Fay, and the director of its Asia desk, Tom Quigley, with whom I had worked for many years. The two weeks in Korea were a time of nostalgia for me. This was not only my last participation in an FABC Assembly, but it turned out to be Father Malone's final assembly as well. In fact, the FABC's associate general secretary and its architect made only a token appearance in Daejon before returning to the Maryknoll house in Seoul for health reasons.

Father Malone's absence gave me pause to reflect on what he had accomplished. Professor of theology in New York for eighteen years, he achieved the wish of every Maryknoll missioner, namely, to be appointed to the field afar. By sending him to courses in cultural anthropology at prestigious Columbia University, Maryknoll had indeed imbued him with a developed sensitivity to the vast complicated world of East, South, and Southeast Asia, and to the new enterprise of the FABC. He exhibited a remarkable ability to promote meaningful participation of *all* the bishops. He once said to me, in half-jest, "I wish I could get the Japanese bishops to speak more, and the Indian bishops to speak less." Examples of his inclusive efforts included suggesting that the presiding bishop have the title of general secretary rather than president, in order to emphasize service instead of authority, and choosing Hong Kong as a neutral place for the FABC's center, while at the same time locating the organization's pastoral and social action offices in other countries so as not to accentuate the power of the central office. He was not afraid of talent; he could spot it and cultivate it. He also introduced members of the assemblies to a "happy hour" before dinner each evening, where bishops and guests could enjoy a libation and conversation.

Father Malone did not operate in solitary: the description of him as being in harmony with the bishops he served was the reality. He was not wedded to his own ideas; yes, he planned and suggested, but he never encroached on the bishops' authority. Thus the general secretaries from Cardinal Stephen Kim of South Korea in 1973 through archbishops Mariano Gaviola of the Philippines, Henry D'Souza of Calcutta, Oscar Cruz of the Philippines, and Oswald Gomis from Sri Lanka in 2004 treasured the respect he gave them and often voiced words of appreciation.

Ed Malone and I last met at Maryknoll, New York, over lunch at St. Teresa's, the Maryknoll Society's retirement facility. He had lost much of the brusque vitality that marked the rapt attention he usually gave to everyone to whom he spoke. As we ate he would stop and ask what we were just talking about a few minutes ago—without the least embarrassment. He walked me toward the Society's main building and while saying our goodbyes in the parking lot I said to him, "You must enjoy great satisfaction with all that you have accomplished." He said quickly and easily, "What *we* accomplished," with a strong accent on we.

Asian Theology and Spirituality: Impressions

My participation in the FABC's plenary assemblies—from Bangkok in 1982 to Daejon in 2004, combined with numerous other experiences throughout the continent—left me with rich impressions of Catholic life in Asia. The following themes emerge as examples of how the universal church will be enriched abundantly as it gets beyond its Western boundaries.

First, the sense of the Holy Spirit stands out. Years ago a theologian friend of mine pointed out the Asian richness of the concept of the Holy Spirit, a reality almost tangible. I recall conversations I had as a campus minister with an Arab exchange student of Muslim background, who referred graphically to the Spirit of God. Asians find the Holy Spirit in creation and in history. The Spirit has sown the seeds of truth and grace among all peoples, philosophies, cultures, and religions. Asians see the Spirit as the inspiration of gospel enculturation, ecumenical and interreligious dialogue, and human development. They view the church as a communion of communities united in the Holy Spirit. Asia's bishops urge their colleagues as well as their priests, religious, and laity to be alert to what the Spirit is saying to the respective churches.

Second, the Asian approach to Jesus appears poetic, no doubt echoing St. Paul's words about the presence of the Father "shining in the face of Christ." Paul was Asian, of course. Jesus is the Good Shepherd and indeed the Good Samaritan; also, he is a compassionate friend of the poor, as well as the enlightened one, the teacher of wisdom, the possessor of life. In this regard, I recently noted a reference by Father Robert Imbelli in *L'Osservatore Romano* on a recommendation of the philosopher Charles Taylor regarding the New Evangelization. Father Imbelli wrote,

> He [Taylor] sees the need for a fresh, more creative language, capable of communicating the Gospel, a language that is more affective and poetic than the prevailing prose of a one-dimensional technology, a language that taps the aesthetic dimension of experience, whether through music, art or literature.

He continued,

> As examples of the ability to craft a more integral and evocative language, Taylor sites the great Catholic poets: the English priest, Gerard Manley Hopkins, and the French layman, Charles Péguy...the sacramental sense of a world "charged with the grandeur of God"...a living sense of the communion of all the saints, uniting earth with heaven.

I believe that the church in Asia presents Jesus in the context of which Taylor speaks.

Third, the Asian church regards highly what we call religious experience, coupled closely with a special devotion to Mary. "Eyes, not ears," said the bishop of Nagoya, Japan, expressing the very clear Christian tradition of witness rather than words, but informing us that, in the Asian interpretation, humanitarian action must somehow be perceived

Cardinal Joseph Zen, SDB, of Hong Kong is one of the many bishops from the FABC who accepted an invitation from Bishop Cummins to visit the East Bay diocese and meet their respective ethnic groups. Together at a luncheon in Berkeley in 2004 are (left to right) Bishop Cummins; Father Stanislaus Poon, a priest of the local diocese from Shanghai; Sister Felicia Sarati, CSJO, diocesan director of ethnic ministries; Cardinal Zen's secretary; Cardinal Zen; and Caroline Wong, secretary of Berkeley's Catholic-sponsored International Friendship Association House. (IFAH photo)

as coming from an interior life. Therefore, the Asian culture has its special devotion to Mary, the mother of God. We experience this with our Asian peoples here on the West Coast, where a spectrum of Asian and other cultures gather now annually in the diocese was facilitated by placing the first meeting on the feast of the Assumption. As a bishop in Bangkok noted, "It is in Mary that all faiths of Asia meet."

Fourth, particular reverence for our Holy Father is evident, an ecclesial bond felt particularly by those in small Christian communities in societies that are overwhelmingly non-Christian. Rome is seen to be an avenue of grace and life. The spirit is not one of diffidence; rather it expresses the confidence of those small communities.

Fifth, the high value placed on harmony is another dimension of all the general assemblies that remains with me. I believe that that value led the Catholic Church in China to work out an accommodation with Beijing, uncomfortable as it may be for those who still resist and demand full freedom. Critics of that accommodation have to concede,

During the 1998 Special Synod for Asia in Rome,
Bishop Cummins greets Cardinal Ricardo J. Vidal of
Cebu City (Philippines), a friend from the FABC.
Bishop Cummins also participated in the Rome Synod
for America in 1997. (FABC photo)

however, that churches in China are now open and many thousands of
new Catholics have walked through those portals to embrace the faith.

Benefits from My Asian Experience

My years in Asia as fraternal delegate enriched the ministry of the Diocese of Oakland and served the wider church as well. The immigration
law passed in 1965 by the U.S. Congress gave Asians rather generous
opportunities. Filipinos, Chinese, and Japanese who had long been part
of our northern California community were joined in the last quarter
century by new Asian immigrants and indeed refugees: Vietnamese, Koreans, Cambodians, Laotian Khmuu, Indonesians, Thais, Indians, and
Sri Lankans. Immigrants also came from the Pacific Islands: Samoans,
Tongans, and Fijians. Chinese who had early on built the railroads and
later so many of the farms and cities in the West increased in numbers

with the change in governance of Hong Kong. They were joined by immigrants from mainland China.

Our first bishop, Floyd Begin, recognizing the diocese's abundant diversity, had set up five centers that he called "vicariates." One was Asian—an easy step to take because we had a native Chinese priest in the diocese, Father Matthias Lu. By my time we had the benefits of the far-seeing vision of our chancellor, Father George Crespin, and the abundant pastoral giftedness of Sister Felicia Sarati, CSJO, of Filipino and Panamanian heritage. Reluctant to leave parish ministry, Sister Sarati nonetheless proved particularly adept at offering hospitality to the breadth of our newcomers.

The many Asian bishops I met at FABC assemblies and the reports I sent back on my experiences in Asia generated a warm and embracing response from our local Asian communities. When I left for my first travels to the Philippines in 1979, for example, a large contingent of Filipinos from St. Anne's parish in Union City came to San Francisco Airport to see me off. Our new sense of community was greatly enriched by visits from Asian bishops who were in the States on holiday or business travel. Many of these bishops came to Oakland in response to invitations I had extended during my own visits in Asia.

Filipino archbishop Orlando Quevedo, OMI, phoned from Minneapolis one Wednesday to say he would be in the Bay Area on the weekend. We filled the church at St. Joseph's in Pinole for a Saturday evening Mass and report on the state of the Philippines, at the time under martial law. The archbishop remarked to me, "You have many Filipinos in the diocese." I told him that this was largely just one parish. If he had given us a month's notice, we would probably have needed the Oakland auditorium.

Both Philippine cardinals, Jaime Sin and Ricardo Vidal, passed through. Francis Xavier Van Thuan now ("venerable"), exiled from Saigon, was a cordial visitor. Bishop Yves Ramousse, MEP, added immeasurably to our pastoral outreach to the Cambodian community. Bishop John Chang-Yik from Chunchon Diocese in Korea, a frequent visitor, provided a Korean priest for the diocese for years. Father Paul Graung and a companion from Myanmar spent some days relaxing barefoot in our cathedral rectory. Visiting a supermarket was the first of their

American sightseeing goals. Archbishop Joseph Ti-Kang of Taipei, along with Bishop Joseph Zen, coadjutor of Hong Kong and later cardinal, enriched our Chinese community with their visits.

I have an especially fond memory of Tongan Bishop Patelisio Finau's visit. At the end of Mass at a diocesan ethnic gathering he whispered quietly to me, "May I say something." His words to his own people were encouraging, but he added special thanks for the welcome that the diocese had provided the newcomers. He made a particularly gratifying point about the ways the diocese had encouraged Tongans to make their contribution to the health of the local church. The bishop commented on the steadfast ministry of Sister Felicia Sarati in bringing to the fore such talented leadership from the various ethnic groups.

Benefits beyond the Diocese

The benefits of my Asian experience extended far beyond the diocese. The 1980s, for example, witnessed a rising consciousness among Asian-American Catholics about their place in the church. Leadership in this community was in the hands of women such as Ruth Doyle, of Japanese heritage, from the Archdiocese of New York, with a doctorate in sociology from Fordham University; Chicago's Terry Nuval, of Filipino heritage; Seattle's Veronica Barber, a Samoan; and Sister Lucia Tu, a Chinese-American Sister of Social Service from Los Angeles. Our own Sister Felicia Sarati, whose own credentials were considerable, maintained contacts with these women. Over time, we recognized the appropriateness of the church in the United States recognizing the achievements of these women in their communities.

As chancellor of the Oakland Diocese in the 1960s, I sympathized with and supported such efforts. I had witnessed the formation of the National Office of Black Catholics under our national bishops' conference, but lamented that its office had to be located a block away from the bishops' main office in Washington, D.C. In the 1970s, as secretary to the California Catholic Conference, I was frequently involved in the *Encuentro* process, with its painful airing of examples of the lack of hospitality accorded to our numerous and varied Latino Catholics over many years. There was no need, it seemed to me, to duplicate the slow pace of these earlier experiences.

The Asian situation was unique. In the latter part of the twentieth century, for example, twenty-eight of the fifty states had no measurable Asian populations. David Gibson, who edited *Origins* for many years, remembered that in the bicentennial year diversity in America meant only African Americans, Latinos, and Native Americans. Asians were not in the consciousness of so many in positions of church leadership. Bishop Bill Hughes of Covington, Kentucky, once said to me, "John, when you speak of diversity I can listen, but in Northern Kentucky we are pretty much Irish and Italian Catholics and German Lutherans."

Something of this same realization was evident in the wider U.S. church. Toward the end of the Bishops' Synod of Asia in 1999, I was having a cup of coffee with Cardinal Roger Etchegary and he asked how I had been enjoying the month. I responded favorably and then asked for his appraisal. He stretched out his hands and flattened them a bit, mimicking this action with the words: "Asia is very far from Rome." I replied, "Asia is very far from California, too. That is a big lake out there."

Sometime in the 1980s, Archbishop John R. Quinn of San Francisco suggested to the leadership of our bishops' conference that they set up a desk focused on the church in China. Asian-American concerns at the time fell under the Committee for Migration and Refugees, with the name Pastoral Care of Migrants and Refugees (PCMR). Father Anthony McGuire of San Francisco staffed this position. Coupled with his involvement in ethnic diversity issues in San Francisco, he brought to this work the experience he gained from two FABC assemblies, one in Bangkok and one in Tokyo. His credentials also included visits to Vietnam and Cambodia and particularly Hong Kong, where at fifty years of age he went as a Maryknoll Priest Associate to learn Cantonese. PCMR in the 1990s was appropriate for newcomers, but hardly for Filipinos or Chinese, whose presence in the United States spanned more than a century.

Of great help in establishing Asian-American consciousness in Washington were the general secretaries of the bishops' conference, Father Thomas Kelly, OP, Monsignor Daniel Hoye, and Monsignor Robert Lynch, along with their staff, Father Bryan Hehir, Father Bill Lewers, CSC, and Tom Quigley. Most responsive, and perhaps providentially placed, were the conference president, Anthony Pilla, from Cleveland, and vice-president, Bishop Joseph Fiorenza of Galveston-Houston.

Bishop John Tong of Hong Kong received the red hat of a cardinal from Pope Benedict XVI in 2010. (Sean Sprague photo)

Their perspectives embraced the rising sentiments of Asian and Pacific Islanders and led to the document, "Welcoming the Stranger among Us: Unity in Diversity," published by the Bishops' Conference in 2000 and celebrated at the national congress in Los Angeles at the close of the millennium.

The national climate grew more hospitable in the 1990s and Vietnamese, Koreans, and newcomers from other parts of Asia took advantage of the changed climate to organize themselves. In 1993, Filipino Americans gathered for a congress in San Francisco, with Cardinal Joseph Bernardin of Chicago as keynote speaker. I had that role at the second congress, which was held in Chicago. (I joked in Chicago that conference organizers would have saved on airfare had they reversed the order of speakers: asking me to address the San Francisco congress, and inviting Cardinal Bernardin to the Chicago assembly.)

In 1986, Father Ismael Zuloaga, SJ, recently appointed Jesuit provincial for Hong Kong, Taiwan, and Macao, came to ask if I would organize the U.S. bishops to hear about the growth and potential of the church in China. I disappointed him by saying I did not have the capacity to draw together all the American bishops, but would be able to bring together bishops from cities with significant Chinese populations. Our Berkeley people responded to this initiative with enthusiasm, particularly Father Lyn Farwell, president of the Jesuit School of Theology, and Fathers Kenan Osborne, OFM, and Joseph Chinnici, OFM, from the Franciscan School of Theology.

We decided on San Francisco as the site for the first meeting on this important issue. The meeting took place in 1997 at the Holiday Inn in San Francisco. Ninety-seven persons, all approved by their bishops, came from around the country. Sixteen U.S. bishops participated; they were joined by several bishops from Canada. We also determined to have some of the Asian bishops from Hong Kong and elsewhere. Recognizing that this conference amounted to their first formal acknowledgment from U.S. church leadership, Chinese faithful attending the conference from Brooklyn, New York, welcomed the gathering with tearful expressions of joy.

Two years before the meeting in San Francisco, I briefed Father Zuloaga in Manila on our project. In contrast to his enthusiastic urging of a decade earlier, he sat with his arms tightly folded as I described our plans for a meeting. He was worried that we would be interfering with Vatican diplomacy in China, as well as drawing unwanted attention to the Catholic clergy who were then working in mainland China. He relaxed when he heard that we were inviting Chinese-American Catholics only.

Keynote speakers at the 1997 conference were Father (later Cardinal) John Tong Hon, from Hong Kong, who came at great and generous personal inconvenience; Father Jeroom Hendryx, a Vincentian missioner and China expert from Louvain; and John Kamm, a businessman who was intensely involved with human rights in China. The speakers outlined very clearly the Vatican position on the unity of the church in China, both "above ground" and "below." Their exposition anticipated Pope Benedict XVI's sober and judicious letter to the Catholics in China in 2007.

Later, at the suggestion of Bishop Jerry Barnes of the diocese of San Bernardino, my name was suggested by our region to participate in the Synod of America in 1997 in Rome. I was to bring to the attention of the delegates the significance of the Asian presence in the United States. (At the time, editor Frank Maurovich estimated this presence to be greater than seven million, "equal to the population of Bolivia and greater than the populations of Paraguay or Uruguay.") Two years later, I was appointed, along with Bishop Frank DiLorenzo of Hawaii, to attend the Synod of Asia, again to raise the awareness of Asia's bishops and of the church at large to the significant Asian presence in the U.S. Church. The editor of *America* magazine, Jesuit Father George Hunt, and the editor of *Maryknoll* magazine, Frank Maurovich, invited me to submit articles.

To say the least, recognition of the church in Asia during the last quarter of the twentieth century had been productive.

Part III: Persons and Personalities

I RETAIN SPECIAL MEMORIES OF MY ENCOUNTERS with three very special personalities mentioned in this narrative, namely, Archbishop Dominic Tang Yee-Ming, SJ, bishop of Guangzhou (Canton), China; Bishop Emeritus Carlos Filipe Ximenes Belo, SDB, of Dili, East Timor; and Bishop Wenceslao Padilla, CICM, head of the prefecture of Ulan Bator, Mongolia.

Archbishop Dominic Tang Yee-Ming, twenty-two years a prisoner in China.

On a March morning in 1980 I had a doctor's appointment. Anticipating some waiting time, I brought a copy of the (London) *Tablet* to read. One article in the Catholic newsweekly dealt with a Chinese bishop who had recently been released after twenty-two years imprisonment to receive treatment for cancer in Hong Kong. The article called him "the most important person in the church in China," since he had been appointed to Guangzhou by Pope Pius XII before the 1949 revolution.

China's indomitable Cardinal Tang Yee-Ming spent twenty-two years in prison in China.

At 1:30 P.M. on that very day, our own Chinese Father Matthias Lu came to the chancery office with the bishop, whom my secretary announced to me simply as "Tang." I was stunned, remarking to her, "He is the most important person in the church in China." Taken aback, she asked, "How do you know these things?" Missing the chance to appear all-knowing, I replied, "I read it this morning."

Apprehensive about how we would be able to converse, I welcomed the archbishop to my office. No need to worry: his English was excellent. He informed me that he had studied at the University of London. I was full of questions.

"What did you do in solitary confinement for eight years?"

"I went back to the seminary," he said, "and did a holy hour every morning and every evening."

"Did you suffer physical punishment?"

"No, but I had to go to instruction every morning on the subject of Marxism. They thought they would convert me."

"Is there hope for the church in China?"

[His silence indicated the inanity of that question.]

"What about the Patriotic [government-sponsored] Church?"

"Everyone [in China] knows who the pope is," he stated firmly. "Furthermore after thirty years without the sacraments, one gets hungry," he said, referring to the Catholics who had worked out an accommodation with the government in order to have their churches reopened.

As I walked him to the front door of the Chancery Office, he told me to return to my office since I was a busy man. I didn't realize it then, but that morning was the beginning of friendship that would last two decades. Whenever he visited San Francisco, Archbishop Tang would have dinner with us in Oakland, usually on very short notice. When he came to dinner on one occasion, we had already invited Robert and Theresa Hill, an esteemed African American Methodist minister and his wife. Supposed to be our guests of honor, the Hills were enthralled by the courage and personality of Archbishop Tang.

On another of his visits, I invited some of the Berkeley Jesuits to have dinner with him. One of them was Louie Shen, a Chinese seminarian scholastic. I had never met Shen, but had heard that he also had been in prison. At dinner I was struck by his dark black hair and smooth complexion. "How many years were you in prison?" I asked. "Twenty-six," he answered. I turned to the archbishop and said, "You were in jail twenty-two years in addition to your school years in Portugal and England." Charmingly and brushing aside any sense of burden or bitterness, he said, "I was in the Mao University, but I did not receive any degree." As Father Bob Manning, the Jesuit rector in Berkeley, was leaving, he whispered to me at the door, "I feel deeply honored to have been at this table tonight."

Archbishop Tang and I met again at the Eucharistic Congress in Korea in 1989. At other times, we had dinner together through the courtesy of Dr. Thomas T.S. Liang in Hong Kong. One particular memory I have was an evening after a group of us returned from a two-week tour of mainland China in 1986. In Guangzhou we had met the bishop who was then in Archbishop Tang's rightful place. I hesitated to mention this at first because I thought it might be a sore point. But after I told him about the meeting, he said of the current bishop,

> He suffered so much. He was born in the north, in the farmland. He had to come to the city to study. He served the people up in the north in the villages. When they exiled me, they brought him down as bishop. He has suffered very much.

That same evening before dinner was finished at the Shangri-La Hotel, I told him that I had learned that UC–Berkeley had 267 Chinese students, second only to the University of Michigan. His response was immediate and strong. Raising a hand he said, "You must contact those people. The only contact they will have with the church will be what you can give them. They will come back here as leaders."

Our obligation was clear. I discussed possibilities with some of the Chinese priests in San Francisco. One remark surprised me, "Nobody did anything for us when we came here." Another reacted strongly, "They are all Marxists; they will not be open to the Gospel." Our Oakland priests were more encouraging. Providentially, Father Bernard Chu, SJ, the former Jesuit provincial for Taiwan, Hong Kong, and Macao, was doing a sabbatical at that time in nearby San Jose. With the aid of the congenial secretary in the Department for Asian Studies at UC–Berkeley, a list of names enabled conversation and exploration.

Father Chu gathered a group of young Chinese men and women, mostly from the San Jose area, and purchased a house of hospitality in Berkeley, close to St. Joseph the Worker Church. Friends in time helped pay off the mortgage. The house offered hospitality to Chinese scholars, whose alumni now number well over 400. The center—known as the Inter-Friendship House Association (IFHA) or Fuyou (its Chinese name)—keeps in touch with alumni through email. One convert was in

Shanghai teaching at Fudan University. Through their contacts with Berkeley—and with help from Dr. T. Paul Lee, whose work took him to Beijing—alumni have been setting up Catholic academic centers in Shanghai and Beijing. Archbishop Tang's charge to us has already borne fruit. He would have been pleased.

Carlos Felipe Ximenes Belo, SDB, Bishop of East Timor.

In spring 1990, while I was preparing to attend the fifth FABC Assembly in Bandung, Indonesia, Monsignor Robert N. Lynch, then general secretary of our U.S. Bishops' Conference, asked me to inquire about a possible visit to a troubled part of the Indonesian archipelago, namely, East Timor. Monsignor Lynch indicated that in 1986 the Bishops' Conference had published a statement of concern about the situation of the church there. In a veiled way he said that some were worried that the young bishop in East Timor was being far too outspoken and perhaps politically immature. Providentially, Father George E. Crespin, our vicar general, had been approved to attend the Bandung conference with me.

Both of us had much to learn about East Timor, which for centuries had been a Portuguese colony. In 1975 Lisbon decided to relinquish control over its former colony, but with little preparation. Three groups, including a leftist faction, formed in a struggle for control. Fearing a communist uprising in neighboring Indonesia, U.S. Secretary of State Henry Kissinger reportedly signaled U.S. approval for the Indonesian military invasion of East Timor. An estimate of 100,000 Timorese killed as a result of the invasion stands among the lower numbers. From 1976 to 1989 the area was cut off from communication with the rest of the world. Persecution continued for years with politically motivated "disappearances" an ongoing experience. Meanwhile, the role of civil service, the military, and the organization of commerce fell to the hands of immigrants from the Indonesian island of Java. With Indonesia's large Muslim population, East Timor's capital, Dili, in this overwhelmingly Catholic country saw its first mosque.

Dili's Bishop Martin de Costas Lopez, a Portuguese, was removed from his post, ostensibly because of his constant public support for East Timor's independence. In 1988, the young Carlos Belo, ordained to

Bishop Carlos Belo stands in a group photo with Maryknoll Sisters who serve in his diocese. The Sisters are wearing the widely distributed tee-shirt that honors the bishop as a co-winner of the 1996 Nobel Peace Prize for his consistent efforts to peacefully win East Timor's independence from Indonesia. Bishop Cummins visited Bishop Belo twice and also greeted the Maryknoll missioners serving in the small mountain town of Alieu. (Sean Sprague photo)

the priesthood only eight years earlier, was named apostolic administrator. A native of East Timor, born in 1948, he had been educated in the seminary in Dili run by the Salesians, but had studied abroad in Portugal and Rome. In 1989, he wrote letters to the president of the UN, to Pope John Paul II, and to the president of Portugal, asking not just for aid for East Timor but for help in obtaining a referendum on freedom for the community. The world he served had never identified itself as Indonesian. Languages spoken in East Timor were Portuguese and the native Tetum. Indonesia's invasion and the influx of "foreign" Indonesians, most of them Muslims, burdened, if not grated upon, the sensitivities of the natives of East Timor. Bishop Belo welcomed a visit by Pope John Paul II in 1989.

Father George Crespin and I landed in Jakarta on July 15, 1990, for two days of orientation at the center house of the Indonesian Bishops' Conference. There we met the young Bishop Belo. At ease in conversation, he wondered why we were interested in going to East Timor. We responded by relaying the interest of the American bishops.

Whereas Bishop Belo in Jakarta was appropriately noncommittal at first about our request to visit his country, the U.S. ambassador in Indonesia, John Monjo, made himself accessible to us and urged us to go to East Timor. Others who recommended our visit included Valencia-born Jose Carbonell, the provincial of the Salesians; Pak Florentino, director of an agricultural development project in East Timor; the Apostolic Pro-nuncio in Bandung, Francesco Canalini (who told me he processed my appointment as bishop when he served at the nunciature in Washington, D.C.); Cardinal Jozef Tomko; and Jesuit Cardinal Julius Darmaatmadja, of Jakarta. The cardinal would speak to the issue only in the presence of Bishop Belo, a condition that indicated to us the tension among the bishops of Indonesia about East Timor.

My recollection is that three or four days after we asked to visit, Bishop Belo graciously replied that we should come. What remained was to obtain tickets to fly into Dili. A Jesuit priest, Father Marcus Winandy, boastfully indicated he could take care of us. Apparently, he had two brothers in the Indonesian Parliament. Father Crespin and I were wary, but he got us the tickets from Tuesday through Thursday of the following week. This schedule allowed us time to spend in Bali, Indonesia, with Father Ed Malone and Cardinal John Baptist Wu of Hong Kong. The cardinal was not used to taking vacations, but after savoring some of the sites in Bali, he admitted that taking a few days off occasionally was a good thing to do.

At home Bishop Belo was particularly good company; his hospitality was very relaxed. We stayed with him while he arranged meetings with some significant personages. One was the appointed governor, Mario Carrascolão, a native of East Timor who had trained as a lawyer in Portugal. The governor displayed vitality and a genuine interest in his people, speaking of the needs of health and education and the lack of preparation of his people for positions both in civil service and commerce. He spoke no word of independence or the tension existing in the people, although we later learned he leaned in favor.

Bishop Belo likewise set up a meeting with the military commandant, Brigadier General R.S. Warouw. We had half an hour with him, with a young soldier translating for us and being corrected a few times by another military. We felt free to ask how long the heavy visible military presence would continue. The general, who we later found out was a Celebese Protestant, responded that two years would be a reasonable estimate.

The full day we had on the island was marked by whatever delight one could feel in that world. We traveled across the island to the other large town of Baucau, and beyond at Fatumaca, where a Salesian center functioned with an extraordinary secondary school. Across the island we spoke to some of the parish priests. Military seemed everywhere, but did not stop to check us. The driver was typical third world, operating with a heavy foot and a loud horn, trying to disperse carabao off the road or anything else in the way.

My impression was perhaps of Hawaii in 1850. The Portuguese government seemingly had not taken much out of the island colony but neither had they put much in. Apparently we were on the only road across, servicing us easily enough but providing as well safety for the rebels who still were hiding in the mountains without much accessibility or perhaps genuine hope. The high school band welcomed us with "Meet Me in St. Louie, Louie." Brother Andres, a Salesian from Andalusia, took us through the school with all the curricula for which the Salesians were renowned—carpentry, automotive, computers, and particularly television repair and electrician skills—looking forward to the day when those workers would be employed and vital parts of the life of East Timor.

Meanwhile, the center, which also included an orphanage with a Salesian Sister, a native of Orange County, California, had the use of what they called "big generators." The manager of that part of the operation was a Father Locatelli, cool and competent. He had a fleet of tractors that were serviced by the students but put out to the farmers in the area during the several harvests throughout the year. Father Locatelli seemed well connected to the rebels, facilitating sending their children for education both at Fatumaca and elsewhere. He also clearly stood against the military, who occasionally proposed some hope of reconciliation and amnesty, but the priest did not believe a word of it. The whole compound was charmingly alive amid so much tension. I remarked to Father Andres on the extraordinary behavior of the young men students. I inquired if they were threatened with capital punishment. He smilingly replied, "They know they are lucky to be here."

I sent an eleven-page report to Monsignor Lynch on my return. I stated, "I was more than favorably impressed with the bishop of Dili. At forty-two years of age, he has a matured calmness, an assured step, and a large sense of hospitality." I noted that his English was good, but that he found a special ease and congeniality with our Spanish-speaking vicar general George Crespin. He felt the presence of George as tonic and indicated that there was advantage in his being both native and Salesian, but that this brought the burden of pained empathy with his own people.

A flood of emotion flowed in a direction other than reconciliation. I noted only one reference to Catholic Relief Services. The governor especially was critical of their absence. The Salesians in Fatumaca wanted CRS to return, but without all the paper work. "Trust the competent," was the statement. I forwarded the message to Archbishop Edward O'Meara at CRS, who graciously and quickly accommodated the wishes from East Timor.

An incorrect observation of mine was the not altogether firm conclusion that there was no hope for independence. The Indonesian forces seemed so overwhelming in an archipelago that extended as far as the distance from Seattle to Tampa Bay. Furthermore, a rumor existed that the UN wanted to drop the long-standing East Timor issue from the table. By some sort of decision the UN hoped to open up East Timor to more embassies than merely Canada and the United States. The Indonesian pro-nuncio visited despite the Vatican's lack of acknowledgement. Incidentally, Bishop Belo indicated to Father Crespin that I was the first bishop from outside who had visited. The Australians, however, were sending a group of bishops the following October.

The report I sent to Monsignor Lynch was not the end, nor really did I wish it to be. There was an appreciated cordiality that had been the fruit of the weeks with the bishop. First came an inquiry from an Arnold Kohen, a Cornell University graduate who had a passionate interest in East Timor and its bishop. A journalist by profession, he had access to *The Washington Post, The Boston Globe,* and *The New York Times.* He sent the retired Episcopal bishop Paul Moore, of New York, to visit me. The bishop had spent a month in East Timor in a period more tense than what we had experienced. He was hoping to promote scholarships for the Fatumaca students at his alma mater, Yale. He inquired about the possibility of similar welcome from Catholic colleges and universities in the United States.

Arnold Kohen promoted an ambitious vision. He had already taken steps to nominate Bishop Belo for the Nobel Prize. Within two years he had organized an international visit by the bishop that included the United States in 1995, and he was instrumental in arranging a meeting between the bishop and President Bill Clinton. Bishop Belo also was welcomed at the spring meeting of the U.S. bishops in New Orleans. Unhappily, he did not make the presentation to the whole body, but he did make himself available to meet those American bishops with particular interest in the cause of East Timor. Also, the bishops' Committee on International Justice and Peace hosted Bishop Belo at a well-attended luncheon. During that visit, he stayed three days with us in our Oakland cathedral rectory. He made himself open to the local press. We had the experience of hosting an international celebrity—concerned phone calls came from Lisbon, Rome, Washington, and even Bangkok, largely centering on the bishop's security. My secretary, Judy Fellner, with her remarkable international background, put her language capabilities, particularly French, to good use.

Bishop Belo gained even more international recognition when he was awarded the 1996 Nobel Peace Prize, along with Jose Ramos-Horta, Timorese leader of the independence movement. In December, I was sent to Oslo to represent the American bishops. Bishop Belo's extensive remarks were impressive. He spoke warmly of Catholic heritage, including *Gaudium et Spes* (*The Church in the Modern World*) from the Second Vatican Council, and the unmatched impact of Pope John Paul II. He spoke of contemporary heroes for human dignity, Mahatma Gandhi, Desmond Tutu, Aung San Suu Kyi, and Martin Luther King Jr. He praised the Indonesians as well as his own people who suffered for the cause. He was gracious toward the UN and Alfred Nobel. He pleaded for a dialogue for peace for which, he insisted, his people were ready.

There was still more to come. In 1999, the torch for freedom that had burnt so low burst upon East Timor with the UN referendum on independence. The votes were overwhelmingly in favor. At that same time, a group of us were scheduled to make official visits, first, to the Conference of Bishops of the Philippines and then especially to a

With Vietnamese children in Ho Chi Minh City (Saigon), Bishop John Ricard, SSJ, above, accompanied a group of four U.S. bishops from the U.S. Catholic Conference observing conditions in the Philippines and Vietnam in 1999. Other bishops in the group were Joseph Fiorenza, president of the USCC, and committee chairpersons Theodore McCarrick, of International Justice and Peace, Cummins, of Committee for Migrants and Refugees, and Ricard, of Catholic Relief Services. (J. Cummins photo)

week's gathering in Vietnam to meet with both church and civic officials. Bishop Joseph Fiorenza of Houston represented the presidency of our conference. Archbishop Ted McCarrick was delegated as the chair of International Peace and Justice. Bishop John Ricard of Tallahassee–Pensacola was chair of Catholic Relief Services. I was chair of the Migration and Refugee Committee, which included pastoral care of Asian-American Catholics. Ted McCarrick and I were delegated to visit East Timor after the week in Vietnam.

In Vietnam, our last days were in Saigon, now called Ho Chi Minh City, where the American consul, a large burly man, said to us, "I am going to be blunt with you. Gentlemen, you cannot go to East Timor. We cannot guarantee protection. You are also hostage bait." When we reached the sidewalk outside, a broad walkway along a very busy boulevard, Ted McCarrick asked, "What do you think?" I was taken by his courage, but I responded that the directions appeared strikingly clear. It was only during dinner at the hotel that evening that a fax came to Archbishop McCarrick that settled him about the travels. We did not go, but

Tom Quigley, who had accompanied us as staff from the bishops' conference, did go. He later reported the experience as predictably harrowing.

In January of 2000, the Federation of Asian Bishops' Conferences had its meeting scheduled in Bangkok. I presumed it would be my last assembly and therefore brought with me those who had gone to earlier meetings, Father George Crespin, Sister Felicia Sarati, and Father Anthony Maguire of San Francisco. This time it seemed both agreeable and convenient that we should return by way of East Timor to represent interest and support on behalf of the American bishops.

The landing at Dili was startlingly depressing. Street after street exhibited violent destruction, especially by fires. Apparently the armed militias with the connivance of the army and the police had watched gasoline trucks go up and down streets spreading fires. Estimates were that half of the country's population had fled by every kind of transport for refuge into West Timor.

On the evening of our arrival we had dinner on the outside porch of the bishop's damaged house. His home gave evidence of vicious havoc. The chapel, large enough to have perhaps 100 at Mass in the morning, had the appearance of an abandoned inner-city establishment, with walls defaced and statues broken. Reports of the destruction are well depicted in Arnold Kohen's book, *From the Abode of the Dead* and the later book of Geoffrey Robinson, *If You Leave Us Here, We Will Die*. At dinner, the bishop exhibited signs of exhaustion, but he was his calm self for the whole evening and gave every evidence of enjoying our presence and conversation.

The next day we drove up the mountain side above the city to visit Sister Susan Gubbins and the other Maryknoll Sisters in the village of Aileu. The same sickening destruction met us. The convent was destroyed, their clinic badly damaged. Destruction defaced the town center. Indonesia with cruel deliberation had punished the population for choosing independence. We saw UN officials in the mountain town, apparently negotiating with some visiting Australians and others about rehabilitation and rebuilding. The young people, however, especially the young men, gathered idly on street corners, surely a recipe for trouble.

The second evening, however, in the midst of so many remembrances of suffering, the bishop ordained a young man for the Society of the Divine Word. A native of East Timor, he was destined to be a missionary in Paraguay. We raised our eyebrows about his travels only to be told that the church in East Timor was several centuries old and indeed was mature enough to be sending missionaries.

At the reception that night, it was easy to admire the manner of the bishop and the presence also of Xanana Gusmão, the heroic resistance figure who had become commander both of political and military wings of the unconquered. Soon to be elected the first president of the free East Timor, he was quiet and agreeably cordial. He made it clear that our visit was cherished.

In 2002, Bishop Carlos Belo, himself weakened from the stress of almost twenty years asked to be relieved of his administrative burdens. He went to Portugal for treatment. He later requested a missionary appointment to Mozambique and a return to the Salesian tradition of education. After a brief time, however, Bishop Belo returned to Dili. There was a new bishop there as well as a new diocese in Baucau. Our emails, as can happen, became fewer, but memories, appreciation, and admiration remain.

Bishop Wenceslao Padilla, CICM, Prefect of Urga, Ulan Bator, Mongolia.

In the spring of 2002, a call came from Rome from an admired and esteemed Jesuit friend, Keith Pecklers, a professor of liturgy both at San Anselmo and at the Gregorian University. The professor, who studied his theology here in Berkeley, inquired whether I would be interested in accompanying him to an interreligious dialogue meeting in Japan in September. I indicated interest.

Within weeks came a time extension: Father Pecklers could get ten days off before the conference in Japan. We juggled a few Asian sites until he asked, "Can we do China?" "Yes," I wrote back, "we can do the East Coast of China, but I have an obligation at this time to pass through Hong Kong on business related to the building of our new cathedral in Oakland." His quick answer was affirmative. My follow-up was just as rapid. "If we go to Beijing, we should also go to Mongolia."

My interest in that unusual part of the world came with my meet-

Bishop Wens Padilla, CICM, of Mongolia intrigues residents of an orphanage for girls founded and administered by his Congregation of the Immaculate Heart of Mary. His congregation, founded in Belgium and popularly known as the Missionhurst Fathers, sent the first group of Catholic priests to serve in Mongolia in 1991 after the Soviet Union lost its political stranglehold over this Asian nation. (Sean Sprague photo)

ing the then Monsignor Padilla in his native Philippines at the FABC gathering in Manila in 1995. Wens Padilla, high personality as well as high energy, meets people easily. His experience of gaining his theology degree at the Graduate Theological Union in Berkeley bolstered that capacity for friendship. His memory of the Diocese of Oakland and of the Cathedral of St. Francis de Sales in particular waxed rhapsodic. The flattering reminiscence was beguiling. Within an hour after I wrote him, his email came back from Ulan Bator. Yes, he would be home the weekend of September 20, looking forward to the reunion.

Keith Pecklers and I met in Hong Kong, and the next morning's trip found us in Shanghai. We went to the cathedral and introduced ourselves to the renowned Chinese Bishop Aloysius Jin Luxian in his simple living quarters. The bishop, who had spent two decades in a government prison, ordered us back the next day for a visit to the seminary, where we would meet the arriving Hong Kong Maryknoller Peter Barry, who would be teaching English there. The seminary was not enough; the bishop also wanted to show us his pride and joy—a newly built retreat house.

Beijing was next. Doreen Huang, a former eighth grade student of our Sister Felicia Sarati and now second in command of UNESCO in Beijing, met us at the airport. She provided us her driver with a large black Mercedes Benz and set us up in a five-star Hyatt. Our hostess was most generous with time and judicious with objects to be seen. We visited both seminaries and met Beijing's Bishop Michael Fu, a man with a poor reputation for loyalty, who did not even try to remember that we had met in 1986. The diocesan and the national seminary hospitality, however, proved unequivocal. The three priests of the seminary faculty who took us to lunch were trained at the University of Chicago, at the Catholic University of America, and at the Gregorian University in Rome.

Doreen Huang took us to dinner. Afterwards she led us to a street fair. We thought we needed parkas for the weather that was to come. What started at $24 ended up after some tough bickering at $12. I remarked when I arrived home how cheap North Face jackets were in China. "They make them there," I was told. Back at our hotel, Keith asked me where we were staying in Mongolia. I told him I had made no inquiry. He proceeded for the first time to look in his guidebook. "The best way to see this country," he read, "is by horse or camel."

The flight took two hours, first over the Great Wall, then over the mountains and finally over a desert that—to the unaccustomed eye—lacked beauty. Suddenly, over a short rise the expansive city of Mongolia's Ulan Bator appeared. The airport was perhaps Oakland, 1938. The horse or camel turned out to be the bishop's black and chrome Ford SUV. The bishop drove us quickly into the city. Keith's first observation noted that there were many dogs in the place. "We do not eat them here," came the explanation.

Keith followed with the affirmation that there were only eighty-six Catholics in a population of one million. Almost with a tone of offense, Bishop Padilla replied, "No, 130." We passed through a large open plaza in the central city and arrived in the city's southern part at the five-story Catholic Center. We were given spacious room downstairs. Close to six o'clock, Keith and I met in my room with the Johnnie Walker brought from the Beijing duty-free shop. Immediately, the phone rang to summon us to the top floor where the Congregation of the Immaculate Heart of Mary missioners, often more simply called Missionhurst had gathered—Bishop Padilla, plus one from the Philippines, two from the Congo, and one from the Cameroons. The evening was long and lively.

The next morning's temperature hovered around the freezing point. After Mass, we crossed the city to see a new church in construction, the future cathedral, to be circular-shaped with a round dome, similar to a ger, the round homes of the native people. A high school, newly built by the Salesian Fathers, stood alongside the church. The principal, who had family in Sacramento, California, was from the Philippines, and worked with two other Salesian priests, one from Slovenia, the other, from Vietnam. In a room given over to computers, we walked to the windows without looking, as the principal had directed us. Turning around, we saw the whole wall in front was mirror so that the teacher could patrol easily the computer screens.

In the late morning, we went to a Korean immigrant parish on a special day of celebration. The buffet luncheon was extensive. From there, we visited a farm close to the city, operated by the Salesians for young people. At mid-afternoon, the bishop's bright and accommodating secretary, a lawyer and convert for some years, drove us downtown. Both of her parents were medical doctors who lived in another city. She had a brother working toward a medical doctorate in Tokyo. She pointed out "the supermarket," a four-story department store with full shelves —but no elevator.

The evening was unanticipated. Apparently, the UN had called for a day of prayer for peace. We gathered on the second floor of the Catholic Center, which had been arranged to serve as a chapel. The experience was indeed interreligious—representatives from different Zen communities participated with other Asian religions, whose names were unfamiliar to me. Bishop Padilla was the host, but I, as the oldest, had to preside for the Catholic community. One had to be impressed. The Catholic Church, only ten years present, served as convener of this diverse group. The evangelical, but especially the diplomatic skill, of the Catholic leadership stood out in evidence.

In the new Cathedral of Saints Peter and Paul in Ulan Bator, Mongolia, Bishop Cummins concelebrates Sunday Mass with Bishop Wens Padilla and the international group of missionary priests who serve with him. (Sean Sprague photo)

The Sunday morning Mass, with many worshippers in the congregation from the embassies, was celebrated in a number of languages, including sufficient Mongolian words as well as dress. Afterwards, we had lunch at a restaurant run by German immigrants. An afternoon trip carried us along bumpy roads away from the city to see a retreat center, which the bishop had converted from what once served as barracks for Russian soldiers. On the return trip, we visited one of the two groups of Mother Teresa's nuns serving in the diocese. In a simple neighborhood, the Sisters lived in a modest house that served as home for the frail elderly and open to all the neighborhood youngsters.

We made another stop at a center for abandoned children, ages three to nineteen. A nun from the Philippines ran the center, aided by one of the Missionhurst priests. Spirits were high, and the bishop was the object of noisy and enthusiastic affection. We learned that the Asian reputation for a strong, family life suffered in Mongolia, affected in no small part by the introduction of ample, cheap Russian vodka. Thirty-four of those 103 children enrolled in the center had no known relatives.

On the way to the airport Monday morning, both Keith and I were aware of experiencing the vitality of the young church in Mongolia. "I am not a cheerleader," said Keith, "but I am very proud to be a Catholic." He followed that up with continued correspondence with Bishop Padilla, which twice resulted in his return to spend a week instructing the community leadership in liturgy. Keith also brought the experience to Rome, to the father general of the Jesuits, Hans Peter Kolvenbach. The Jesuit curia gave consideration to the possibility of a high school in that remote world, but the decision was made not to move on it at that time because of the lack of adequate Catholic elementary education.

Three weeks after I arrived home, I celebrated Mass at the alma mater of Bishop Padilla's graduate work, the Catholic schools at the Graduate Theological Union. When I remarked that I had recently offered Mass in Mongolia, I observed puzzlement, indifference, amusement. (I wasn't surprised that they would be amused.) My homily centered on the vitality of the Holy Spirit with God's grace so evidently present in the life of that tiny young community. I suspected that those missionaries in Mongolia would see difficulty rather than accomplishment. My hypothesis was that, were Mongolians visiting us, they might perceive the Spirit as sharply among us as I felt we did among them.

My homily did not close the Mongolian chapter. Three years later, I had a phone call from Frank Maurovich, editor of *Maryknoll* magazine. He sought verification on Mongolia's missionary character for a cover story. I told him 130 people out of a million would confirm his conjecture. In July of that year, on my roundabout trip to the FABC Assembly in Korea, I flew to Ulan Bator to meet Frank and photographer Sean Sprague at seven o'clock in the evening. In contrast to my previous winter visit, the temperature was ninety-seven degrees Fahrenheit. Ulan Bator also had changed, showing stylish newer buildings, a tribute to what people given their freedom can accomplish. Once again, the bishop offered us generous hospitality at the Catholic Center.

On Sunday morning I celebrated Mass with Bishop Padilla and a half-dozen other concelebrants, three of them recently arrived Consolata Fathers from Italy, still learning the language. The venue was the nearly completed cathedral, round-domed like the native gers, and comfortably filled with worshippers. The large choir wore elegant purple robes. Of those who came up for a blessing only one I noted received communion. I asked the bishop later whether these were really catechumens. He said they had not instituted the RCIA, very sensitive to allowing the people to move at their own pace—for some as long as three years.

With the magazine crew, I revisited most of the places I had seen with Keith Pecklers, but at a much slower pace, as Frank interviewed individuals and Sean shot photos. Each ministry had flourished; the Salesian farm, for example, had grown into a Mongolian version of Boys Town, alive with youngsters. I watched them working in the fields, tending seedlings in a long hothouse, and feeding the animals, laughing at the table manners of young pigs. The retreat house an hour out of the city was elegantly finished and had a large contingent of young people attending for the weekend. Both during our coming and going the horses for which Mongolia is renowned were very visible. This time cattle were more in evidence than on our first visit. The fields had much more grass because of a happy rainy spring.

The last part of the story occurred in April of 2012. Vincent Resh, a researcher in the life sciences at UC–Berkeley, emailed me that he would be in Ulan Bator for two weeks in June, measuring among other things the level of mercury in the drinking water. He inquired whether I knew people whom he should meet, though he did not want to burden me with the request. I told him how distressed I would have been had he not asked me. I told him he would enjoy Bishop Padilla as much as the bishop would enjoy him. The bishop's email response to me was rich in usual hospitality. He also enclosed an invitation to me for July 8, "if you are in the neighborhood." It was the weekend of the twentieth anniversary of the establishment of the church in Mongolia. *L'Observatore Romano* later quoted Bishop Padilla, "A young church entrusts the future to young people." I was not there, but attendees included Archbishop Hon Tai-Fai, secretary of the Congregation for the Evangelization of Peoples, and Bishop Lazzaro You Hung-sik of Daejon, Korea, along with the twenty-one priests and eighty-one lay and religious missioners that now serve the prefecture of Ulan Bator. The bishop and his fellow missionaries have presented the faith in most attractive form. The presence of the Spirit is perceptible.

Other Impressive Persons Meriting Mention

While the three men I mention above stand out in my esteem, I would be remiss in not naming, as least briefly, some of the many other persons who impressed me by their work and personalities:

Bishop Bernadine Dong, OFM, of Wuhan, China, was most welcoming to us in his home diocese in 1986. He visited the Graduate Theological Union in October of the same year. One of the first ordained with government sponsorship and reconciled quietly with Rome, he connected easily with the Franciscan minister general, Father John Vaughn, OFM, former California provincial.

John Baptist Wu, cardinal of Hong Kong, also treated me with gracious hospitality at his cathedral center. When we were together in Kaohsiung, Taiwan, he told me to put my pectoral cross where people could see it. I attended the conclave that elevated him to the cardinalate. I felt included in his entourage.

Bishop Francisco Claver, SJ, of the Philippines, creative explicator of Catholic social principles, seemed to me more given to scholarship than to administration. I had privileged years of association with him, the last at Georgetown University in Washington, D.C.

Bishop Francis Xavier Hardisumarta, of the Discalced Carmelite Order and president of the Indonesian Bishops' Conference, and also a missionary bishop in the Diocese of Manokwari in West Papua (Irian Jaya), showed in his own words that "people from Java could really be missionaries." With happy fortune I sat next to him at the Synod of Asia in Rome in 1999. He made an intervention, speaking of a need of an intermediate level of authority between Rome and the church in Asia, such as the patriarchical pattern of the early church (an intriguing subject covered in the book *Ever Ancient, Ever New: Structures of Communion in the Church,* by John R. Quinn, retired archbishop of San Francisco).

Cora Mateo, based in Taipei serving the FABC by working creatively in education and youth ministry, was only one of several impressive women I met attending FABC assemblies. She contributed generously to the library of the federation, particularly in the theology of the laity.

Virginia Saldanha, impressive and articulate from India's Archdiocese of Mumbai, was an intelligent promoter of the role of women in the church. She brought an articulate voice to the assemblies, moved easily with the bishops, and was a familiar participant on FABC committees.

Rita (Ting) Nolesco, a Focolare member, excelled as secretary and collaborator with Father Ed Malone, MM, in Hong Kong.

Sister Luise Ahrens, MM, former president of the Maryknoll Sisters Congregation, has done admirable work as vice-president of the National University in Phnom Penh, Cambodia, restoring the university after the tragic Pol Pot regime. Undaunted by obstacles in her aim to professionalize the school of higher learning, she commented, "To work here, you really have to believe in everlasting life."

Sister Anna Maria, a native of India and a Sister of Charity of Nazareth, Kentucky, exhibited competence and poise amid Hindu society in Kathmandu, Nepal. She had gathered some volunteers to assist in the house she had established for neighborhood service amid rice fields south of the city. At a wedding rehearsal almost twenty years later, one of those volunteers, who had taken leave from American Airlines to work with Sister Anna, pointed to me from amid a crowd to announce, "Nepal 1979!"

The mention of Nepal reminds me of **Anthony Sharma**, SJ, bishop in Kathmandu and a builder of churches, oppressed by the Maoists and still cheerfully living in danger.

At the Rome synods I attended, I recall exemplary Vatican participants: **Cardinal Eduardo Pironio** of the Council of Laity, an expert on the ecclesiology of Vatican II; **Cardinal Jozef Tomko** of the Congregation of the Evangelization of Peoples; **Archbishop Giovanni Cheli**, cheerful and accommodating secretary to the Council of Migrants and Refugees and a genuine friend; **Stephen Hamao**, formerly bishop of

Yokohama, Japan, prefect of the Council of Justice and Peace. **Adolfo Nicolas**, SJ, cheerful and careful appraiser of the Asian scene, recorded in my diary after our first meeting in Tokyo 1986 as "a delight" and now father general of the Jesuits in Rome.

I met, of course, many others, clergy but especially laity, whose names I did not record but who nonetheless impressed me profoundly with the vitality of the church in Asia and its hopes for the future. I remain forever grateful.

17

A Blessed Half-Century

Gifts of Magi as Historical Metaphor

This Eucharistic celebration of the Epiphany of Our Lord in 2012 becomes a fitting feast to open this fiftieth anniversary year of the founding of our Oakland Diocese. Memory bonds our golden jubilee with the Magi. From memory the Magi drew the expectation of the birth of a special king, that birth to be marked by a sign in nature.

The Magi were an important story for the early church. Seemingly, Matthew was writing for his own community, which had accepted substantial numbers of gentile peoples. Tensions arose between the two groups, about which of the inherited Jewish customs were obligatory. In the *Acts of the Apostles*, we recall the spirited conversations between Saints Paul and Peter.

The story of the Magi tells of good-willed, gentlemanly scholars from the exotic, mysterious East. They not only read the sign in nature but followed as well the scriptural promise to Bethlehem. Meanwhile,

---

An edited version of the homily Bishop John Cummins preached in January of 2012 in Oakland's Cathedral of Christ the Light at the beginning of the diocese's jubilee year.

the assembled Scribes and Pharisees had the word but did not let it bring them to life. Matthew's story is a compliment to the gentiles.

The early church embraced devotion to the Magi, who went through some romanticizing. By Tertullian's time at the end of the second century, they are regarded as kings. In the 400s, the emperor brought relics attributed to the Magi from Persia to Constantinople. By the Middle Ages, the Magi had a number, and the three royal personages even had names: Balthazar, Caspar and Melchior. Early artworks show great diversity of age and ethnicity.

Along with romanticizing, however, there developed a poetic and catechetical interpretation of the Magi—much more to our purpose today. I speak of the poetic imagination related to the three gifts. St. Irenaeus in the second century saw the gifts instructing us on the life and mission of Jesus. Gold announced his kingship over all creation. Incense signified his divine nature. Myrrh associated with burial indicated a redeemer who would suffer and die.

The gifts taught the faithful about their responsibilities for Christian living. For one commentator, gold symbolized rich virtue. Incense with its fragrant smoke ascending signified prayer. Myrrh reminded the faithful of cross and suffering endemic to Christian life. A North African theologian, a contemporary of St. Augustine, saw gold as the wisdom of faith, by which one can believe the divine utterances correctly. Incense reflected the works of mercy, which the Lord has set before sacrifice. Myrrh became mortification rising above worldly values out of love for Jesus Christ.

A variation from that heritage serves our golden jubilee reflection: Gold signifies the divine and our reaching to that divinity through prayer. Incense carries respected reverence and touches the demands of charity. Myrrh is the fragrance overcoming death—hope with the theme of resurrection.

Gold Stands for Prayer

Gold draws our attention to the manner in which we reach and touch God, especially through prayer and worship. For the last half-century we have had the blessing of the Second Vatican Council which was opened by Pope John XXIII the same year this great pontiff established the Diocese of Oakland. The Council's first document focused on public prayer and worship, favored by the Council bishops by an overwhelming vote of 2147 to 4. Profound and pervasively reformed liturgy has marked our diocese.

Key renewal concerned the Mass, untouched for five centuries. The role of Scripture was enlarged and with it the restoration of the traditional understanding of the Eucharist as both table of Sacrament and table of Word. Most notable, Mass was now celebrated in the language of the people. I remember the emotional thrill at the first example of vernacular when Bishop Floyd Begin offered with us at St. Francis de Sales Cathedral. Looking back, no one was aware that the old cathedral would become such a sign of acceptance and warm embrace of the new liturgy by the people of our diocese.

In many ways the timing of vernacular language suited us well. Bishop Begin had established five ethnic centers in his time. Through the leadership of Father George Crespin as chancellor and Sister Felicia Sarati as ethnic coordinator, the five centers grew to fifteen. Liturgical inculturation was an extraordinary blessing. We welcomed the change of language. Only later did we realize the difficulty when a parish required two, three, even four vernaculars.

We welcomed people from various lands, including Eritrea. Father Donald MacKinnon, one of our Redemptorist priests and native of the diocese, along with Holy Family Sister Michaela O'Connor, learned the language of Khmuu refugees from Laos, serving our own Khmuu people, as well as developing from this community persons who rose to national leadership.

I would add more than a word about Sacred Scripture. The rich development in biblical awareness since the Second Vatican Council has been well received. Only people my age remember that first part of the Mass was not regarded as even needed to fulfill what we called, in those days, "Sunday obligation." In these intervening years we have learned the traditional understanding of the presence of God in the Word, as St. Paul pointed out so sharply.

With that came the important role of lector. Preaching loomed in importance and raised high expectations, even preaching at daily Mass. Beyond the Mass, Scripture moved with ease to enrich much of our prayer. Scripture, woven into catechesis, became the focus of study for many of our people. Newer forms of prayer arose—charismatic prayer, *lectio divina*, centering prayer. Courses on Ignatian Spirituality as well as Carmelite and Dominican Spirituality followed. Happily, San Damiano Retreat House in Danville offered varied opportunities for prayer and reflection, joining the welcome of the Mission San Jose Dominican Sisters for Taizé prayer, along with the invitation from the Holy Family Sisters in Mission San Jose to promote religious experience for our people.

Along with the new, traditional Marian devotions remained, with the rosary prominent along with devotions, such as Our Lady of Perpetual Help. Devotion to Our Lady of Guadalupe also grew greatly. Our Vietnamese people introduced us to Our Lady of Lavang. The devotional Marian patterns of our ethnic people brought us together for the first gathering of *Chatauqua* on the Feast of the Assumption in 1992.

As a postscript, we became accustomed to ministries at the altar. Lectors, Eucharistic ministers and acolytes, no longer known as "altar boys," served. Piety was enriched by the service of Eucharistic ministers, especially in bringing communion to the homebound. Beyond that, we note the fruitful ministry of permanent deacons, unhesitatingly established by Bishop Begin.

Frankincense for Human Dignity

The development of so many ministries leads us to a poetic reflection on incense. We not only incense the table of the altar, which represents Christ; we also incense persons. It is a sign of respect and reverence. A theme traceable to the Second Vatican Council becomes explicit through the teachings of Pope John Paul II, namely, the dignity and the sacredness of the human person.

The steady and prayerful upholding of the sacredness of life in the womb, spoken of in the Second Vatican Council as an unspeakable violation if not protected, has been the clearest witness by the church. The diocese has been blessed to have Sister Maureen Webb of Holy Names University. Scientifically and politically competent, she established our Respect Life Office, extending concern to threats to the life of the elderly or the ill and reflecting the clarity of Pope John Paul on the immorality of capital punishment.

Dignity of person is a foundational heritage pointing our attention to those among us in need. The St. Vincent de Paul Society, long and well established in the East Bay, carried a national reputation even in my college years. It moved beyond parish work and even thrift shops after the Second Vatican Council. With patriarchs, such as Michael Hester and Cyril Gilfether among so many, the Society opened a dining room for the homeless and needy, a rehabilitation center for released prisoners, and Casa Vincentia for the care and training of single pregnant women.

In the 1960s, Professor Raymond Sontag from the University of California History Department, keynote speaker at the welcome for Bishop Begin, remarked with passion that racial division had brought down empires. It was he who prevailed on the bishop to establish the Catholic Interracial Council. The advent of the AIDS epidemic stirred Mother Teresa's Brothers from southern California to help form here a center of care and concern—in recent times carried on quietly by Providence House. The Sisters of St. Joseph of Carondelet reached out to homeless women.

At the institutional level, Bishop Begin and Monsignor John McCracken, inspired by renewed vision after the Council, enlarged the older patterns of Catholic Charities. Its outreach became more flexible and adaptable, opening up new services and closing down those that had served their purpose. The proud work of resettlement and welcome of refugees has marked our diocese. At one time we also responded to the needs in Sacramento and the San Joaquin Valley. The very sophisticated Mercy Sisters Housing program came to our rescue after the 1989 earthquake.

Steady attention was given to the role of inner-city education. Important initiatives in adult literacy and care of marginal young students came through the efforts of the Sisters of the Holy Names and the Christian Brothers of St. John Baptist de La Salle, two of the pioneering religious communities serving in this diocese for more than a century.

The Vatican Council stressed the dignity of people in need but also reminded us to recognize the dignity of those of mature talent. Thus grew the diversity of consultative bodies at the level of parish and of diocese. Committed to pastoral direction and finance, the pattern did not develop without resistance, but it is indeed a holy work.

Before its time, through the recommendation of the senate of priests and the work of Father Brian Joyce, we developed a Diocesan Pastoral Council composed of priests, religious, and largely laity. A gathering of 400 people at Holy Names University in 1983 promoted five priorities. They stressed lay leadership, youth, social justice, education, and evangelization.

What surprised me somewhat was the united emphasis on social justice. Perhaps it should not have since what the delegates promoted was a century-old teaching of the church. The council identified inner-city schools as a matter of justice, and Catholic hospitals in their pursuit of universal health care, also St. Vincent de Paul Society in its work with prisoners. Credit for this consciousness must be given to congregations of religious men and women, who developed such awareness as part of their ministries. When I requested of Olga Morris, an officer in St. Vincent de Paul Society, to become part of the committee to carry out the work, she resisted the invitation. "I do not picket," she said. "Neither does John Paul II," I reiterated. Social justice was not just for activists. It was mainstream.

Dignity of person related as well to new roles in church government. What once was the realm of clergy became much more diffuse. I remember one day at a meeting of department heads in our chancery office. Almost without notice there were more laity than clergy and more women than men. These talented lay women and men were directing education, charities, the diocesan newspaper, community relations, canon law and the role of chancellor.

Parish administration because of immediate need fell to deacons, to religious women, to lay men and women, to whom the diocese owes great appreciation. Such developments affected relations in regard to authority and obedience. Again the example and instruction from our religious men and women opened up the understanding of discernment. The old pattern of authority and obedience was holy, "not to be mocked by caricature," as one delegate said so well, but the present insight into the will of God in community had to give full play to mature freedom.

Again by way of postscript, dignity of person included those beyond the church. The Second Vatican Council in a strong document required Catholics to embrace their fellow Christians in prayer and dialogue. Clergy began to prepare homilies together. The teaching of Scripture was in common as well as ecumenical prayer services.

Bishop Begin modeled much of this. Four months after his arrival and shortly before he traveled to Rome for the first session of the Vatican Council, he invited 150 Protestant ministers and their spouses to the Claremont Hotel for dinner. He did so only, as he told them, because he loved them—words remembered through the half-century.

Also ecumenically significant, he of all the California bishops was the one who witnessed and promoted the development of Roman Catholic participation in the Graduate Theological Union in Berkeley. The GTU is a singular experiment in training Christian leaders across denominational lines, leaders who were enriched by resources, generously made available by accord with the renowned University of California.

Bishop Begin as well assimilated the words of the Council calling for new relations with Judaism. A famous picture was his preaching from the pulpit of Oakland's Temple Sinai at the request of the popular and renowned Rabbi William Stern. The bishop might have been surprised that within relatively few years we would have mosques in our diocesan neighborhoods along with the opportunity for promoting dialogue and understanding with our Muslim neighbors.

Myrrh Proclaims Promise of Hope

Lastly, the poetry of myrrh is associated with burial. We remember Mary Magdalene and the other Mary coming to the tomb on Easter morning with their spices. The fragrance of perfume stood against the odor of death and decay. For Christians it would translate to resurrection and therefore hope. And hope is an indispensable virtue for us in the run-up to our golden jubilee year.

Violence in our city, not unrelated to growing poverty, has called for the best in diocesan pastoral leadership, a leadership undoubtedly wounded by the clergy sexual abuse scandal. Added to that were the natural disasters, the Oakland fire and the heroism of Monsignor Bernard Moran and the parish of St. Teresa's. In addition to its human toll, the earthquake destroyed two churches, but the centrality of cathedral experience in the diocese enabled the rebuilding of Sacred Heart Church and the inspiration for the Cathedral of Christ the Light.

We face difficult economic times. We note the effect on parish life and the challenge for parish leadership. We remember how the recession of 1989 dislodged so many careers, especially in the San Ramon Valley. We recall jobs lost with the almost simultaneous closing of Ford and General Motors factories in our diocese plus the 30,000 military positions lost in the Bay Area with the demise of bases. More than faceless statistics, these were jobs lost and careers affecting our parishioners and neighbors.

The Vatican Council's document, *The Church in the Modern World*, urged broad Christian responsibility for issues of family life, for war and peace, for economic morality and human culture. The document cast the light of the gospel on all human society. This ambitious burden or responsibility was met by the last of the directives from our Diocesan Pastoral Council, namely, evangelization. Paul VI's 1975 Apostolic Exhortation, *Evangelii Nuntiandi*, left us a classic outline of mission as, above all, Christian witness, plus interreligious dialogue and human development as integral parts of evangelization along with proclamation of the gospel.

A missionary sense in the diocese is reflected in the October collection as the largest of the special requests. More important, however, is the realization that our response as a people begins with ourselves. In the decade of the 1990s, parishes engaged in the RENEW program, some groups of which are still meeting, reflecting and praying. Twice we developed strategic plans for the sake of religious renewal. Youth ministry added experience to instruction and made catechetics real by organizing service activities.

We are on the edge of the developments, so long spoken of by Pope John Paul II and by his successor Pope Benedict XVI, calling for "New Evangelization." That program will be in our midst in a short time. Our experience as diocese should have prepared us well for this.

In conclusion, we look over the fifty years not as a question of whether it was the best of times or the worst of times. The Vatican Council pointed us to see it as *our time*. In this connection I remember an evening at St. Cornelius parish in Richmond for the ordination of a priest. Bishop Begin began his homily with praise for hope. He indicated that we were like the butterfly coming out of the cocoon with perhaps moist wings but clear of the vision to come.

With St. Paul it would serve us well to remember in this holy year those who have gone before us, who brought us the faith. It will be a golden jubilee year to remember and therefore refresh us as to who we are. The words of Samuel Johnson, a pious and wise observer of society some centuries ago, indicated that we need not so much by way of instruction, we just need reminders.

Index

Ad Hoc Committee on Ecumenical Affairs, 57
Adams, Philip, 54, 56, 58, 61, 154
Adenay, Bernie, 101
Adza, Sebastian, 142–143
Aeterni Patris, 171
Agagianian, Grégoire-Pierre, 8
Agius, Joseph Mary, 59
Ahern, Barnabas, 10
Ahrens, Luise, 248
Ailes, Margaret, 182
Alexander (Archbishop), 204
Alma College, 58, 64, 66, 71, 77
Amalorpavadass, D.S., 196
American Association of Catholic Colleges and Universities, 117
American Baptist Church, 121
American Bishops' Committee on Science and Human Values, 124. *See* Committee on Science and Human Values
The American Ecclesiastical Review, 3
American Freedom and Catholic Power, 4
Anderson, Mel, 38, 40
Anderson, Stuart Leroy, 48, 76
Andres (Brother), 235
Anna Maria (Sister), 248
apology ceremonies, 161
Archdiocese of San Francisco, 28, 30, 166
ARDOR, 145
Are Parochial Schools the Answer? 140

Arevalo, Catalino, 125, 212
arms race, U.S. bishops and, 95
Arrupe, Pedro, 69
Arthur D. Little Corporation, 58
Asian mode of operation, 125
Asian theology and spirituality, 219
Associated Students University of California, 55
Association of Catholic Trade Unionists, 131
Athenagoras (Aristocles Matthew Spyrou), 124
Atherton, Faxon, 128
Austriaco, Nicanor, 185
Avery, Clarence, 131

Bacci, Antonio, 13
Baker, Joseph, 10, 47
Balasuriya, Tissa, 196
Barber, Veronica, 224
Barnes, Jerry, 227
Barragan, Michael, 156
Barrons, Brian, 216
Barry, Peter, 241
Barth, Karl, 75
Bascom, Duke, 35
Baum, Bill, 10
Baum, William, 10, 17, 47
Baumann, John, 147, 156
Bay Area Crisis Nursery, 147
Bay Area Rapid Transit, 46
Bazzano, Mary Esther, 143, 152

Bea, Augustine, 5, 12, 45, 75
Beatrice (Sister), 143
Begin, Floyd L., 8, 12, 17–19, 23, 27, 31, 42, 46, 49, 57, 59, 62, 75–76, 85, 88, 112–113, 129, 133, 166, 223, 252
Bell, Alden J., 166
Bell, Terence, 208
Bellah, Robert, 100, 104, 213
Belo, Carlos Filipe Ximenes, 190, 229, 232, 240
Benedict XV, 97
Benedict XVI, 123, 127
Bensen, Julius, 154
Beran, Josef, 15
Berg, Paul, 178
Berkeley Farms, 35
Bernardin, Joseph, 95, 122, 172, 200, 226
Beyersdorf, Larry, 54, 55
Bill, Jim, 155
Bishop John S. Cummins Institute for Catholic Thought, Culture and Action, 182
Bishop O'Dowd High School, 1–2, 5, 9, 45
bishops and scientists, relations between, 177
bishops and theologians, relations between, 165, 171, 173, 176
Blakely, Ed, 35
Blanshard, Paul, 4
Bloom, Allan, 25
Boeddeker, Alfred, 130
Boedekker, Marie, 130
Bonose (Sister), 143
Botelho family, 127
Bousma, William J., 105
Bowker, Albert, 87
Boyle, Jack, 58
Brainard, Ernest, 145
Bramble, Joanna, 148
Brennan, Ralph, 156
Brennan, Walter, 192
Bridston, Keith, 53
Brodniak, Tony, 192
Brown, Paul, 100
Brown, Raymond, 171
Brown, Robert McAfee, 5, 12, 19, 43, 46, 76
Bruere, John, 42

Bruno, Patti, 148
Bruyere, John, 78
Bucher, (Father), 28
Buckley, Michael J., 118
Budenz, Clara Anne, 143
Burghardt, Walter, 12, 108, 110–113
Burke, Daniel, 117
Burns, Cornelius, 72
Burris, John, 178
Bush, George H.W., 101
Byers, David, 178

Calatrava, Santiago, 38
California Catholic Conference of Bishops, 91, 144, 167, 213, 224
California School for the Deaf, 154
California State University (East Bay), 86
California State University (Hayward), 85
"Called and Gifted," 133
Campbell, Jack, 90
Campbell, Simone, 147
Canalini, Francesco, 234
Canning, Cynthia, 147
Canning, Mary, 31, 38, 127
Caporale, Rocco, 58
Carbonell, Jose, 234
Cardijn, Joseph, 4
Carnegie Foundation, 54
Carondelet Sisters, 140
Carrascolão, Mario, 234
Carroll, Joe, 98, 106, 208
Carrone, Gabriel-Marie, 117
Casanave, Rose, 130
Cathedral of Christ the Light, 28, 29, 105, 256; dedication of, 41; establishment of, 29; naming of, 38
Catholic Campaign for Human Development, 154
Catholic Charities, 137, 148, 254
Catholic colleges and universities, identity of, 117; intellectual life of, 18; nature of, 117
Catholic Daughters of the Americas, 128
Catholic education, role of women religious in, 139
Catholic Interracial Council, 131, 156, 254

Catholic Ladies Aid Society, 128
Catholic Social Teaching, 95, 104
Catholic universities, intellectual life of, 18
The Catholic University as Promise and Project, 118
The Catholic Voice, 89, 94, 134, 143, 152, 156, 158
Cecconi, John, 41
Center for Theology and the Natural Sciences, 188
Cento, Fernando, 121
The Challenge of Peace, 95, 122
Chamberlain, Owen, 99, 102
Chang, Eddie, 196
Chang, Joseph, 208
change agents, women religious as, 142
Chang-Yik, John, 223
Chapin, Jennifer, 160
Chávez, César, 103, 137
Cheli, Giovanni, 191, 248
Chenu, Marie-Dominique, 119
Chet and Helen Soda Foundation, 35
Chew, Denise, 95
Chew, Geoffrey, 94
Chialvo, Felix, 129
Chinnici, Joseph, 93, 226
Christ in His Mysteries, 166
Christ the Light, 38
Christian Family Movement, 4, 131
Christiansen, Drew, 98, 100
Christine, Edith, 212
Chu, Bernard, 231
Chunchon Diocese, 223
church authority, 108; elements of, 111; history of, 109; understandings of, 109
Church Divinity School of the Pacific, 48
The Church in the Modern World, 257
church, concepts of, 5; doctrinal guidelines for, 11; laity in, 127; newfound interest in, 87; penitential stance of, 161; servant to the world, 119; university and, 85, 88
The Church's Task in the World, 206
Cicognani, Amleto, 19
City Center (Oakland), 105
civil rights movement, 156
Claver, Francisco, 194, 247

Clemens, C. Herbert, 131, 157
Clink, John, 207
Clinton, William J., 237
Code of Canon Law, revision of, 116
Cody, John Patrick, 65
Coleman, John, 93
collegiality, 13, 14
Collignon, Fred, 91
Collins, Francis, 180
Collins, Thomas Mary, 143
Committee for Migration and Refugees, 225
Committee on Doctrine, 181, 184
Committee on Ecumenical and Interreligious Affairs, 184
Committee on International Justice and Peace, 237
Committee on Pro-Life Activities, 181, 184
Committee on Science and Human Values, 177, 180–181, 186, 189; demise of, 185
Committees on Mission, Family Life and Youth, 182
The Church: Community of Faith in Asia, 206
The Church's Task in the World, 206
Clark, Monica, 136
Condic, Maureen, 185
Conference of Latin American Bishops (CELAM), 197
Congar, Yves, 5, 9, 20, 119, 138, 166, 172, 176
Congregation for the Evangelization of Peoples, 246, 248
Congregation of Consecrated Life, 149
Congregation of Seminaries and Universities, 46, 62–63, 67, 79, 82, 117
Congregation of the Doctrine of the Faith, 18, 70
Conmy, Peter T., 129
Connell, Francis, 15
Connolly, James L., 9
Connolly, John F.X., 58, 64
Connolly, John P., 1, 2, 8, 153
Connolly, Nicholas, 2, 8, 131, 153, 157
Connors, Matt, 196
Constitution on the Church in the Modern World, 9, 11
Constitution on the Sacred Liturgy, 210

Cooke, Terence, 200
Coons, John E., 90, 105
Coppenrath, Hubert, 195
Corcoran, Harry, 58, 59, 65
co-responsibility, 111
Cosgrove, Henry, 16
Costa, Arquiminio R., 196
Council of Justice and Peace, 249
Council of Laity, 248
Council of Migrants and Refugees, 248
Council of Priests, 136, 157, 163
Council of Trent, 172
Courtney, Ron, 35
Crespin, George, 135, 155, 157, 163,
    212, 214, 223, 232, 239, 252
Cronin, Terence, 64
Cruz, Oscar, 219
culture, 120; development of, 119;
    Hindu, 202
Cunningham, Agnes, 118
Cursillo movement, 135, 137, 156
Curtis family, 127
CYO, 133

D'Souza, Henry, 219
D'Souza, Patrick, 203
Dabovich, Louis, 154
Daly, Edward, 195
Danielou, Jean, 119
Danielson, Dan, 155, 161, 209
Darmaatmadja, Julius, 234
Dawson, Barbara, 148
Day, Dorothy, 37
De Costas Lopez, Martin, 232
De Lastic, Alan, 212
De Lubac, Henri, 10, 119
Dean, Rita Eileen, 145
Dearden, John F., 9, 19
death and dying, law on, 167
Debreu, Gérard, 103
Decker, Raymond, 99, 103
Declaration on Christian Education, 168
Declaration on Religious Freedom, 11, 13
Decree on Ecumenism, 166
Dei Filius, 171
Delaney, Maureen, 147
Delaney, Rosemary, 147
Delbaere, Hugo, 199
Dennis, Bill, 131
Department of Human Values, 177

Department of Religious Studies,
    UC–Berkeley, 55
Derry, Joan, 152
Devereux, Ambrose, 65
dialogue, 121; as method of the
    apostolate, 123; Asian mode of op-
    eration and, 125; church and world,
    123; origin of, 123; responsibility of,
    116; universities and, 115; Vatican II
    and, 115; virtues of, 124
dialogue before decision, 113
Dickinson, Emily, 23
Diekmann, Godfrey, 15
Dignitatis Humanae, 11
dignity of the human person, 110
Diliberto, Steve, 88
Dillenberger, Jane, 72
Dillenberger, John, 46, 48, 56–58,
    63–64, 69, 76
DiLorenzo, Frank, 178, 227
Diocesan Council of Catholic Women,
    129
Diocesan Pastoral Council, 111, 113,
    136–137, 149, 255
diocesan priorities, 37
Diocesan Tribunal, 2
Diocese of Oakland, 18, 47, 54, 75, 85,
    138, 250, 251; benefactors of, 127;
    Catholic alumni and, 129; Catholic
    education in, 139–140; cultural di-
    versity of nationalities in, 146; estab-
    lishment of, 23; ethnic diversity in,
    135; goals of, 114; Lawrence Liver-
    more National Laboratory and, 122;
    lay involvement in, 127, 134; secular
    and religious priests in, 154. See also
    women religious
Diocese of Tagum, 18, 195
Discalced Carmelite Nuns of Berkeley,
    143
Dives in Misericordia, 197
Doherty, Edward, 99
Doherty, Katherine de Hueck, 196
Dolan, Hugh, 17
Dominican Sisters of Mission San Jose,
    148
Donahue, John R., 104
Dong, Bernadine Guangqing, 209, 247
Donner Laboratory (Berkeley), 98
Donohoe, Hugh A., 9, 131

Donovan, Mary Ann, 145
Donovan, Pearse P., 65
Dopfner, Julius, 6, 8
downtown church, importance given to, 34
Doyle, Ruth, 224
Drell, Sidney, 100
Duff, Frank, 128
Duggan (family), 128
Duignan, Maureen, 147
Dulles, Avery, 16
DuMaine, Pierre, 177, 180, 185
Dunleavy, Tom, 207
Dunne, John, 178

East Bay Area, higher education in, 85
East Bay Conference of Religion and Race, 131
East Bay Sanctuary Covenant, 147
East Timor, 232
Ecclesiam Suam, 111, 116, 121
economic justice, church and, 174
ecumenical associations, 5, 46
ecumenism, 9, 12, 75; Bishop Begin and, 42, 78; Mills College and, 44; Vatican II document on, 47
educational leadership, religious women and, 143
Egan, Edward, 178, 181
Egan, Jack, 10, 45
Eilers, Franz Joseph, 199
Ellis, John Tracy, 72
Emmanuel, S.J., 210
Encuentro, 224
episcopal conferences, 13
Escalante, Alonso, 18
Escaler, Federico, 194
Etchegary, Roger, 225
ethnic centers (Diocese of Oakland), 135
Eucharistic Congress (Seoul), 191
Eucharistic Theology, 166
Evangelii Nuntiandi, 188, 257
Evangelization of Peoples, 248
evolution, 181
Ex Corde Ecclesiae, 116, 118, 119, 125, 182
faculty dinners, church-university, 106
Fahey, Marietta, 148
Fallandy, Yvette, 149

Family Aid to Catholic Education, 137, 142
farmworkers' campaigns, 156
Farraher, Joseph, 65, 71
Farwell, Lyn, 103, 226
Fay, Bill, 218
Federation of Asian Bishops' Conferences, 14, 105, 125, 189, 239
Feeley, Patricia, 148
Fenton, Joseph, 4
Fernandes, Anita, 196
Fernandez, Anicetus, 60
Ferry, Jim, 194
The Fifth Bishops' Institute for Social Action, 193
Fike, Tom, 46, 131
Finau, Patelisio, 146, 224
Finau, Tenisha, 135
Finney, Clem, 33, 45, 156
Finney, Reggie, 156
Finnigan, Pat, 12
Fiorenza, Joseph, 225, 238
First Vatican Council. *See* Vatican I
Fischer, Eric, 178, 186
Fitzgerald, William J., 65
Fitzmyer, Joseph, 175
Flannery, Barbara, 138, 145, 160–64, 208
"Flatland Fathers," 156
Florentino, Pak, 234
Focolare, 213
Foster, Norman, 38
Foudy, John, 44
foundations, support from, 35
Franciscan Foundation, 99
Fransen, Piet, 16
Franz, Craig, 117
fraternal delegate, 189; benefits from being, 222
freedom–authority relationship, 109
Frideger, Marcia, 149
Friedman, Milton, 103
Friend, William, 178
A Friendly Place, 112, 147
Frings, Josef, 6, 14, 119
Fu Tieshan, Michael, 209, 242

Galbraith, John Kenneth, 103
Gallagher, Tom, 156
Garrone, Gabriel-Marie, 70, 72, 82

Gaskell, Mina, 148
Gaudium et Spes, 11, 12, 89, 116, 137,
    168–169, 177, 237
Gaviola, Mariano, 219
Gearhart, William, 185
genetic testing and screening, 179
Genome Project, 180
Gerarda Marie Sister, 153
Gibson, David, 225
Gilfether, Cyril, 128, 254
Gilson, Etienne, 89, 138
Gleason, Joseph M., 30, 128
Gleeson Foundation, 35
Gleeson, Walter, 35
Gold, Victor, 5, 43, 76
Gomis, Oswald, 219
Gorbachev, Mikhail, 101
Gotelli, Bernice, 145
Graduate Theological Union, 7, 12, 18,
    42, 46, 54, 56, 60–61, 75–76, 166,
    247, 256; Bishop Begin and, 53, 59,
    62, 79; Catholic participation in, 53,
    57; early days of, 74, 76; ecumenical
    dimensions of, 91; Roman authori-
    ties and, 68; UC–Berekley and, 82
Graung, Paul, 205, 223
Gray, John and Norma, 129
Greeley, Andrew, 104
Gregory, Wilton, 217
Gubbins, Susan, 239
Gudalefsky, Adam, 202
Guadalupe Missionaries, 18
Gumbleton, Thomas, 95, 122
Gusmão, Xanana, 240

Haas Business School, 104
Haasl, Ed, 36
Hackel, Charles, 131, 154
Hallinan, Paul, 19, 45
Hamao, Stephen, 191, 248
Hannon, Jim, 100
Hardisumarta, Francis Xavier, 247
Haring, Bernard, 14–15
Hartman, Craig, 38, 39, 160
Harvey, Phares, 198
Harvey, Will, 135
Hary, Mel, 32, 156
Hauck, Herman, 65
Hayes, Tom, 98, 182
Heafey, Ed, 35, 38

Healing Garden, 160
health care, role of religious women in,
    139
Hedley, George, 5, 44
Hegarty, James, 129
Hehir, J. Bryan, 95, 100, 197, 201, 225
Helfrich, Jerry, 156
Hellwig, Monika, 126
Helmsing, Charles, 12
Hendryx, Jeroom, 227
Hennessy, Rose Marie, 93, 140, 143, 208
Henrisusanto, Andreas, 194
Herkenrath, Norbert, 199
Hesburgh, Theodore, 117
Heschel, Abraham, 45
Hester, Maureen, 149
Hester, Michael, 128, 254
Heymann, Ira Michael, 35, 87, 105
Heyns, Roger, 55, 86
Hickey, James, 178
Higgins, George, 10, 15, 17, 19, 45, 93
Hill, Dick, 46, 71, 92
Hill, Robert, 46
Hill, Robert and Theresa, 230
Hoban, Edward, 19
Holland, Thomas, 15
Holy Family Center, 148
Holy Names Sisters, 31
Holy Names University, Performing
    Arts Center, 29
Holy Office, 16, 75
Hon, Tai-Fai, 246
Horsell, Kay, 130
Houlihan, John, 129
housing, women religious and, 148
Hout, Michael and Flo, 104
Howard, Clarence, 157
Hoye, Daniel, 197–198, 201, 225
Hoyos, Dario Castrillon, 210
Huang, Doreen, 242
Hubbard, Howard, 189, 193, 201, 210
Huesman, John, 59
Hughes, Bill, 225
human culture, autonomy of, 121
Humphrey, Zelda, 136
Hunt, George, 228
Hurlburt, William, 185
Hurley, Mark, 9–10, 15, 132, 178

The Idea of a Catholic University, 118

IDES, 130
Imbelli, Robert, 220
The Imitation of Christ, 23
Immortale Dei, 109
Inaestimabile Donum, 112
inner-city schools, women religious and, 141; revitalization of, 32
Institute for Social Action, 197
institutional ministries, reappraisal of, 140; women religious in, 144
Instruction concerning Worship of the Eucharist, 112
Inter-Friendship House Association, 112
International Auxiliaries, 4
International Commission of Theologians, 168
International Federation of Catholic Universities, 117
International Theological Commission, 172
Isaacson, Glenn, 35
Italian Catholic Federation, 129–130

Jackson, John H., 82
Jadot, Jean, 90, 92
Jarrett, Bede, 83
Jesu Caritas, 137
Jesuit School of Theology, 145
Jesu Caritas, 155
Jin Luxia, Aloysius, 241
JOBART, 46
John Paul II, 87, 110, 116, 118, 123, 125, 161, 168, 175, 177, 197, 210, 233
John XXIII, 1, 3, 5–7, 43, 45, 75, 87–88, 124, 168, 171
Johnson, Samuel, 258
Johnson, Sherman, 48, 76
Joseph (Father), 203
Joyce, Brian, 38, 114, 136, 138, 155, 163, 255
Jubilee West, 148
just war theory, 95
Justice in the World, 13

Kaback, Michael M., 179, 186
Kamm, John, 227
Kappler, Stefan, 161
Kaut, Bernd, 199

Keeler, William, 17, 181
Keeley, James, 23, 31–32, 89, 97–98, 158, 193
Kellum, Isabelle, 130
Kelly, Jack, 154
Kelly, Thomas, 193, 225
Kerr, Clark, 55, 86
Kim, Dae-jung, 197
Kim, Stephen, 207, 219
King Jr., Martin Luther, 45
King, Michael, 140
Kissinger, Henry, 232
Kitbunchu, Michael Michai, 214
Kleutgen, Joseph, 171
Knights of Columbus, 128–129
Knights of St. Peter Claver, 130
Kobach, Irene, 144
Koenig, Franz, 6, 56, 87, 106
Kohen, Arnold, 236, 239
Kolvenbach, Hans Peter, 245
Koo, Agnes, 135
Krol, John, 8, 19
Kung, Hans, 5, 9

La Salle Christian Brothers, 115
La Salle Educational Opportunity, 112
Ladies of St. Peter Claver, 130
LaFarge, John, 88, 131
Legorreta, Ricardo, 38
laity in the church, ministries and responsibilities of, 127
Lang, Elizabeth, 145
Lappé, Frances Moore, 103
Laubacher, James, 18
Laufenberg, Gesine, 136
Lawler, Thomas Josephine, 145
Lawrence Livermore National Laboratory, 97, 99, 122
lay ecclesial ministers, 133
lay leadership formation, 137
Lay People in the Church, 166
Leary, Mary Ellen, 129
Leary, Virginia, 4
Lebacz, Karen, 101
Lee, Jane, 160
Lee, T. Paul, 232
Legion of Mary, 32, 128
Leo XIII, 97, 109, 123, 171
Lercaro, Giacomo, 6, 8
Leven, Steven, 14

Lewers, Bill, 225
Li, Rupert, 192
Liang, Thomas T.S., 196, 216, 231
Light, Terrie, 160
liturgical changes, 3
Liturgy of the Hours, 137
liturgy, Council document on, 12, 23
Livermore group, 97, 102
Locatelli, Elisio, 235
Logan, Richard, 163
Loma Prieta earthquake, 24, 29, 33, 148
Loomer, Bernie, 73
Louisell, David, 57, 59, 65, 82, 129
Lu, Mathias, 223, 229
Lucey, Rose and Dan, 131
Lucid, Michael, 23, 31–32, 47, 151–152, 158
Lumen Gentium, 11, 38, 133, 169, 175
Luogang, Stanislaus, 208
Lutheran Seminary in Berkeley, 5
Lynch, Kevin, 55, 157
Lynch, Oliver, 113, 154, 156
Lynch, Robert, 225, 232
Lyons, Maureen, 147

Macchi, William, 133, 156, 163
MacGillivray, Lois, 208
MacKinnon, Donald, 135, 252
The Magi, gifts of, 251; poetic and catechetical interpretation of, 251; story of, 250
"The Magnificent Seven," 142
Maguire, Anthony, 214, 239
Maher, Leo T., 62, 70, 79, 153
Mahony, Roger, 172
Malone, Edward, 189, 194, 198, 218, 234
Malone, James, 95, 117
mandatum, 116, 182
Mangini, Richard, 134, 156
Manning, Bob, 230
Manuel, Wiley, 129
Marcos, Ferdinand, 200
Marmion, Columba, 166
Marriage Encounter, 137
Martens, Julio, 154
Martin, Hilary, 92
Martini, Carlo, 101
Martino, Renato, 207
Marty, Martin, 75

Mary Aloysius (Sister), 143
Mary Clotilde (Sister), 143
Mary Magdalene (Mother), 143
Mary Noreen (Sister), 143
Maryknoll, 189, 191–192, 194, 218
Maryknoll magazine, 191, 216, 245
Maryknoll Sisters, 248
Masatoshi, Izumi, 160
Matao, Cora, 247
Mater et Magistra, 5, 11
Maurovich, Frank, 89, 152, 156, 158, 193, 216, 227, 245
Maxwell, John, 36, 156
May, Michael, 101
McCabe, Nial, 154
McCarrick, Ted, 238
McCarthy, Edward, 200
McClendon, James, 67
McCool, Francis, 15
McCracken, John, 154, 254
McDevitt, Jerry, 14
McDonald, William, 71
McDonnell, John, 25, 32, 35, 38–40, 160
McGarry, Patrick, 117
McGee family, 127
McGhee, Cath, 134
McGowan, Thom, 131, 135, 157
McGrath, Mark, 174, 197
McGucken, Joseph, 6, 15, 35, 56–57, 70, 79
McGuire, Anthony, 201, 210, 225
McIntyre, James F., 13
McKenna, J. Fenton, 4, 132
McManus, Frederick, 15
McManus, Miriam Thomas, 143
McNear, George W., 128
McNicholas, Joseph, 4
Mealey, Margaret, 129, 133
Medeiros, Humberto, 9, 17
Mediator Dei, 3
Meier, Mary Jean, 41
Melka, Art, 131
Mercy Care and Retirement Center, 148
Mercy Housing, 148
Meyer, Albert, 6, 13, 45
Millea, Mary Clare, 149
Miller, Cap, 202
Miller, James, 179
Millet, Thomas, 57

Mills College, 5, 28, 43–44, 54, 85–86
Milosz, Czelaw, 95, 107
ministries, apostolic and liturgical, 26;
    religious women and, 145, 148
ministry to victims of sexual abuse, 163
Misereor, 199
Missio, 199
Mission Dolores, 44
Mission San Jose, 35
Mission San Jose Dominican Sisters,
    140
Models in the Church, 16
Moeller, Charles, 18, 70
Mondini, Battista, 169
Monjo, John, 234
Montali, Ralph, 131
Moore, Patrick, 204
Moore, Paul, 236
Moran, Bernard, 256
Moran, Ed, 128
Mori, Paul, 215
Morowitz, Harold J., 178, 187
Morrill, Barbara, 37, 142
Morris, John, 131
Morris, Olga, 128, 255
Mullin, Steve, 135
Murphy, Francis X., 6, 93
Murphy, Laurence T., 209
Murphy, Lillian, 148
Murphy, Michael, 195
Murray, John Courtney, 4, 10–11, 14,
    108, 174
music, liturgical forms of, 24, 32
The Mystery of the Church, 11

Nagler, Michael, 100
National Academy of Science, 178
National Catholic Welfare Conference,
    13
National Conference of Catholic Bish-
    ops (NCCB), 13, 70, 133, 161, 177,
    184, 199
National Conference on Religion and
    Race, 45
National Convention of Newman
    Clubs, 43
National Council of Catholic Women,
    133
National Office of Black Catholics, 224
National Organization for the Continu-

ing Education of Roman Catholic
    Clergy, 155
Native Sons of the Golden West, 129
The Nature of the Church, 11–12
Nebo, William, 97, 98
Nell-Breuning, Oswald von, 171
New Evangelization, 114, 138, 188, 220,
    257
Newman Center (Berkeley), 16, 86
Newman Club, 55
Newman Hall (Berkeley), 55
Newman, John Henry, 23, 127
Next Step Learning Center, 111, 147
Nguyen, Rosaline, 146, 216
Nicolas, Adolfo, 249
"No More Secrets," 163
Noe, Virgilio, 26
Nolesco, Rita (Ting), 248
Nomura, Augustine, 198
Noonan, John T., 89–90, 117
Norkett, Michael, 44
Norris, Frank, 2, 58, 88
nuclear arms, Catholic bishops and, 94,
    122
nuclear deterrence, 95
nuclear proliferation, symposia, 100
The Nun in the World, 5
Nuva, Terry, 224

O'Brien, Michael, 154
O'Connor, Joan, 145
O'Connor, John, 95, 122
O'Connor, Michaela, 135, 146, 252
O'Donnell, Bill, 131, 157
O'Donnell, Richard A. (Pinky), 27, 31
O'Hanlon, Daniel, 58, 94
O'Malley, John W., 6, 13, 119
O'Marie, Carol Anne, 147
O'Meara, Edward, 199, 200, 236
Oakeshott, Patricia, 137
Oakland Community Organizations,
    111, 137, 147, 156
Oakland Museum, 39
Oblates of Mary Immaculate, 4
Octave of Prayer for Christian Unity, 43
Office of Family Life, 134
Office of Human Development, 193
Office of the Propagation of the Faith,
    199
Office of Worship, 134

Oliveira, Albano, 30
Olowin, Ron, 182
On the Church in the Modern World, 116
Ondreyco, Mary, 147
Osborne, Bob, 129
Osborne, Kenan, 103, 226
Osuna, E. Donald, 23–25, 38, 158
Ottaviani, Alfredo, 14
Our Lady of Lourdes Church, 31
Our Lady of the Angels Cathedral, 40
Outler, Albert, 12, 108

Pacem in Terris, 5, 11, 123, 171
Pacific Lutheran Theological Seminary, 43
Pacific School of Religion, 48
Padilla, Wenceslao, 216, 229, 241
Parenti, Ivan, 16, 155
parish councils, resistance to, 113
Pastor Aeternus, 171
pastoral associates, 134, 144
Pastoral Care of Migrants and Refugees, 225
Pastoral Leadership Placement Board, 134
Patriotic Church, 209, 230
Paul VI, 7, 14, 17, 108, 111, 116, 119, 121, 123–124, 126–127, 168, 172, 188–189, 257
Paulist Living Room Conversations, 12
Pavan, Pietro, 11, 171
peace document (Catholic bishops), 95, 97
Pecklers, Keith, 240–246
people of God, 133
people on the margins, 147
Perez, Aurora, 145
Peter, George, 134
Petersen, James, 213
Petersen, Nora, 133
Philips, Gérard, 11
Phimphisan, George Yod, 205
Pike, James, 43, 44
Pilla, Anthony, 181, 225
Pironio, Eduardo, 191, 210, 248
Pister, Karl, 88, 93
Pius XI, 123, 171
Pius XII, 3, 4, 123, 132, 139
Pontifical Academy of Culture, 178
Pontifical Academy of Science, 106

Pontifical Council for Dialogue with Non-believers, 56
Powers, Joseph, 166
preaching, importance of, 24; prominence of, 23
priestly ministry, improvements in, 3; Vatican II influences on, 1
private sexual conduct of consenting adults, repeal of law governing, 167
Providence House, 147
Providenza, Luigi and Lady Augusta, 130
Puchacz, Mary Grace, 144
Purta, Paul, 65

Quadragesimo Anno, 171
Quevedo, Orlando, 213, 223
Quigley, Tom, 218, 225, 239
Quinan, Gus, 157
Quinlan, Karen, 167
Quinn, Bob, 16
Quinn, Edward, 192
Quinn, John R., 99, 149, 225, 247
Quinn, Joseph, 55
Quinn, Patrick, 29
Quinn, T. Michael, 65

Radcliffe, Timothy, 126
Radio Veritas, appraisal of, 198; fund-raising for, 200
Rahner, Hugo, 11
Rahner, Karl, 11, 120
Rambusch, Robert, 31
Ramm, Charles, 86
Ramos-Horta, Jose, 237
Ramousse, Yves, 135, 223
Ramsey, Michael, 124
Ranard, Donald, 198
Rayan, Samuel, 196
RCIA. *See* Rite of Christian Initiation of Adults
Regan, Joseph, 18, 195
Regas, George, 97
Reilly, William, 154
religious communities, strength of, 149
religious freedom, 13
religious liberty, issue of, 14; U.S. bishops and, 15
religious life, developments in, 4
RENEW, 257

Resh, Vincent, 246
Respect Life Office, 144, 253
Ricard, John, 238
Rinek, Judith, 145
Riordan, Patrick W., 31, 86
Rite of Christian Initiation of Adults, 97, 113, 207, 246
Ritter, Joseph, 9
Ritzius, John, 65
Robinson, Geoffrey, 239
Roche, Kevin, 38
Rohan, James, 153, 157
Roman Curia, reform of, 14
Roncalli, Angelo, 5
"Rosary Hour," 154
Rose Emmanuela (Sister), 143
Ruffini, Ernesto, 13
Rumford Act, 88, 158
Russell, Anne, 145
Russell, Robert, 188
Russett, Bruce, 104
Ryan, Mary Perkins, 140
Ryan, Phil, 154
Rynne, Xavier, 6

Sabatte, John, 34
Sacca, Raymond, 34
Sacred Heart Church, 33
Sacrosanctum Concilium, 133
Saigh, Maximos, 15
St. Albert's College, 59
St. Albert's Priory, 88
St. Anthony's Dining Room, 130
St. Francis de Sales Cathedral, 21, 33, 42, 127, 158, 252; closing of, 37; designation as cathedral, 30
St. John Chrysostom, 37
St. Joseph the Worker (Berkeley), 127
St. Mary's Cathedral, 28, 31, 35
St. Mary's Center, 147
St. Mary's College, 2, 40, 65, 100, 115, 122, 139
St. Mary's Parish Center, 112
St. Patrick's Seminary, 2, 18, 25, 57–58, 64, 65, 67, 77, 88, 166
St. Vincent de Paul Society, 111, 114, 128, 253
Saldanha, Virginia, 248
Salmon, James, 179
Samostra, Francis, 135

Sampson, Robert, 131
San Francisco Monitor, 152
San Francisco State University, 4, 44, 55
Sanchez, Elaine, 148
Sandburg, Carl, 23
Sanks, T. Howland, 171
Santa Clara University, 55
Santos, Rufino J., 199
Sapientia Christiana, 168
Sarati, Felicia, 135, 145, 163, 213–214, 223, 239, 252
Satis Cognitum, 109
Scahill, Thomas, 131, 153
Scalapino, Robert, 105
Schema XIII, 12
Scheut missioners, 199
Schillebeeckx, Edward, 5
Schmidt, Paul, 85, 156
Schneiders, Sandra, 95, 145, 166
Schubart, Henry, 28
science and the church, dialogue between, 188
Scotlan family, 136
Scotlan, George, 130, 135
Scotlan, Priscilla, 136
Sealantic, 80
Second Vatican Council, 11, 23, 38, 45, 76, 83, 87, 93, 152, 170, 189, 252, 253, 255; religious women and, 139. *See also* Vatican II
Secretariat for Promoting Christian Unity, 5, 45, 62, 67, 75
Selvanayagan, Antony, 211
seminary training, changes in, 56, 57; in Berkeley, 78
Serra Club, 130, 131
sexual abuse by clergy, 160; diocesan guidelines and, 163
Sharma, Anthony, 248
Sheerin, John, 15
Shehan, Lawrence J., 9, 18
Shen, Louie, 230
Shepherd, Massey, 48, 76
Sherry, Arthur, 65, 129
Shwe, Matthias U., 205
Siciliano, Jude, 148
Silva, John, 154
Sin, Jaime, 223
Singer, Maxine, 178, 187
Sister Formation Conference, 140

Sisters of Social Service, 148
Sisters of the Holy Names (Quebec), 140
The Sisters of the Sacred Names of Jesus and Mary, 143
Skidmore, Owings, & Merrill, 39
Skillin, Joseph, 154
Slakey, Bill, 131
Slavich, John F., 128
Slottman, William, 92
Society of St. Sulpice, 166
Solesmes, 3
Sontag, Raymond J., 56–57, 85, 88, 129, 131, 156–157, 254
Sontag, Raymond J., 85
Soublet, Morris, 130, 135
Souriha, Kan, 135
Spellman, Francis, 14, 119
Spohn, Bill, 98
Sprague, Sean, 216, 245
SPRED, 145
SPRSI, 130
Stanford Center for International Security and Arms Control, 100
Starrs, Paul, 59, 65
Stelmach, Harlan, 101
stem cell research, 185
Stern, Karen, 145
Stern, William, 49, 256
Still, Steve, 129
Stransky, Thomas, 5, 19
Stringfellow, William, 45
Strong, Edward, 55
Suenens, Leo Joseph, 5, 8, 111, 119, 153
Suhard, Emanuel, 166
Survivors Network of Abuse by Priests (SNAP), 164
Swimme, Brian, 188
Synod of America, 14, 227
Synod of Asia, 14, 214, 225, 227

table of the sacrament, 23
table of the Word, 23
Tagle, Luis, 213
Tang Yee-Ming, Dominic, 209, 229
Tappe, Walter J., 64
Tavard, George, 10
Taylor, Charles, 220
Teilhard de Chardin, 181
Telesco, Lee, 200

Temko, Allan, 38
Teskey, Nancy, 149, 188
Prayer: The Life of the Church in Asia, 206
theologians, role of today, 168
Thornton, James, 192
Tien, Chang-Lin, 105
Ti-Kang, Joseph, 224
To Teach as Jesus Did, 140
Tomko, Jozef, 125, 191, 234, 248
Tong, John, 227
Toppo, Telesphore, 213
Townes, Charles and Frances, 106
Tracey, Robert, 19
Tracy, David, 118
Traviss, Mary Peter, 141
Treinen, Sylvester, 18
Trisco, Robert, 15
Tu, Lucia, 224

UC–Berkeley. *See* University of California–Berkeley
United Farm Workers, 137
U.S. Bishops' Ad Hoc Committee on Ecumenism, 45
U.S. Bishops' Conference (NCCB), 79
U.S. Bishops' Office of Pastoral Care for Migrants and Refugees, 201
U.S. Catholic Conference (USCC), 79, 95
U.S. Conference of Catholic Bishops (NCCB), 95
U.S. economy, bishops' document on, 103
United States, international responsibilities of, 174
University of California–Berkeley, 5–6, 30, 55, 85, 117
University of California–Berkeley, Department of Religious Studies, 54, 82
University of California–Davis, 90
University of California–San Francisco, 5
University of San Francisco Law School, 4
University of Santa Clara, 4

Vadakin, Royale, 97
Valdivia, Antonio, 156

Valley, Gladys, 29
Valley, Gladys and Wayne, 37
Van Osdel, Boyce, 47
Van Thuan, Francis Xavier, 214, 223
Varanasi, interreligious importance of, 203
Varni, Edward, 154
Vatican I, 1
Vatican II, 1, 15, 76; critical issues, 11, 16; influences of, 1; Protestant observers at, 12
Vatican II Institute for Priestly Renewal, 156
Vaughn, John, 209, 247
Vidal, Ricardo, 223
Vigneron, Allen, 41, 160
Vinella, Carmen, 134
Vinsko, John, 197
Vohs, James, 35, 37

Wade, James, 154
Wagner, Alvin J., 154
Wall, Antoninus, 59
Wall, Kevin, 46, 58, 65
Walsh, Martin Eugene, 154
Ward, Hubert, 64
Warouw, R.S., 234
Wattson, Paul, 43
Wayne and Gladys Valley Foundation, 29, 35, 39–40
We Hold These Truths, 174
Weakland, Rembert, 103
Webb, Maureen, 144, 253
Week of Prayer for Christian Unity, 76
Weigand, William, 103
Weigel, Gustave, 15–16, 43
Weinandy, Thomas, 184
Weishaar (Father), 128
Wiesner, Mark, 161
Weltz, Ann, 147
Weston, Burns, 100
What Happened at Vatican II, 6
Wheeler, Benjamin Ide, 86
White, Robert J., 178, 186
Wiedner, Marie, 134, 137, 144, 163

Wilfred, Felix, 210
Williams, Thomas, 213
Winandy, Marcus, 234
Winston, David, 49
Woeger, William, 41
Wojtyla, Karol, 120
Wolff, Madaleva, 139
women in the church, 174
women religious, as change agents, 142; as theologians, 145; educational leadership and, 143; housing and, 148; inner-city schools and, 141; institutional ministries, 144–145, 148; new responsibilities of, 143; role in Catholic education, 139; role in health care, 139; Vatican II and, 149. *See* Diocese of Oakland
Wong, Danny, 135
Wong, Joseph, 191
Wood, William, 65
Woodruff, Roy R., 100
World Alliance of Presbyterian and Reformed Churches, 76
World Council of Churches, 75
World Synod of Bishops, 13
World Youth Day, 213
Wright, Marian, 135, 144
Wu, John Baptist, 234, 247
Wyszynski, Stefan, 8

Yelek, Antoinette, 145
Yik, John Chang, 214
Yinyun, Joseph Yi, 209
You Hung-sik, Lazzaro, 246
Youell, Frank, 129
Young Christian Workers, 4, 213
Young Ladies' Institute, 128
Young Men's Institute, 128

Zabala, Albert, 58, 65
Zagotta, William, 100
Zen, Joseph, 224
Zhang Hanmin, Damas, 216
Zucker, John, 46
Zuloaga, Ismael, 213, 226–227